To Murat
I hope
into t... ions
and id...
Colin

OUT OF TIME

The revolution underway in beliefs about being human

Colin Strong

First published in the United Kingdom in 2023 by Factaplus Press

Every effort has been made to attribute sources correctly and fairly but if any have been overlooked then the publisher will be pleased to include necessary credits in any subsequent reprint or edition.

ISBN: 978-1-7393574-0-5

Factaplus Press
7 Bell Yard
London
WC2A 2JR

For Olivia, Abigail, Imogen & Sylvie

CONTENTS

ACKNOWLEDGMENTS

Thank you to my friends and colleagues for their thinking and inspiration. In particular, I would like to thank Tamara Ansons for her constant inspiration and creativity, reflecting the way that what any of us ever produce is never our work alone. And my thanks to Peter Ayton and Magda Osman for their support on the way.

None of this is possible without the work of the thinkers, writers, organisers and publishers whose work is the basis the thinking on which this book is based.

I also thank my family and in particular Heather for their support through the long process of research and writing.

PROLOGUE

Victor Turner was a British anthropologist writing in the 1960s and 1970s, renowned for his work on liminality: the periods when people find themselves between more recognizable and unknown states. In his book, The Forest of Symbols, he talks of "rituals of affliction" which mark times of struggle. [1] The burden of affliction is both borne by the individual, such as at times of illness or sorrow, or by the collective community, as with periods of war or famine.

These are known as 'liminal periods' involving intense transition, "a process, a becoming" as Turner puts it. The individual or community that emerges from a liminal event may be quite different from those that entered. The unsettling process involves separating from what we have known, a fundamental dissolution of the previous mental and social mechanisms that guide and shape us as humans.

During these liminal periods—which can last from days to years—things we used to hold as true and unquestionable dissolve and become reinvented. Beliefs, norms, hierarchies, ways of living are rendered ambiguous and fluid. In a liminal state we are in a state of "neither here nor there".

This is a book about the liminal state we find ourselves in today. In part this could be attributed to living through the COVID pandemic. While this is certainly part of the story, there are also other roots that have created this current state of liminality. The first of these is digital technology, the second is climate change and at the time of writing, that of war with the Russian invasion of Ukraine creating shock waves. Borrowing a phrase from historian Lorraine Daston, together these mean we are living in a period of radical novelty and uncertainty so we are thrown into a state of 'ground-zero empiricism'. [2] As we struggle to make sense of a rapidly changing environment, we are much more reliant on "chance observations, apparent correlations, and anecdotes that would ordinarily barely merit mention".

This book of essays seeks to make sense of our current state of liminality. But more than that, this is a book of questions of what we wish humans to become from this state. It would be hubristic and arrogant to set out a confident and assertive account of what this process or becoming will result in. The book is not one of answers but of questions that feel right for us to be asking.

“Whoever is searching for the human being first must find the lantern," said the philosopher Friedrich Nietzsche. In this reference to the early Greek philosopher Diogenes, Nietzsche was asking something very pertinent to today’s debate. What does it mean to study the human-being? What are we becoming and what else could we be? [3]

The story that Nietzsche is referring to is the way in which, in 4th Century Rome, Diogenes would wander about the city in clear daylight with a lighted lantern, appearing to look as if he had lost something. When people asked him what he was trying to find, he responded, "Even with a lamp in broad daylight I cannot find a real human being”. Of course, his audience would point to themselves but instead he chased them with a stick, yelling "It is real human beings I want”.

As one might expect, just as if we tried this today, people found this demonstration hilarious. But Diogenes’ act was meant to unnerve those who settle for easy answers. In his view, a human being is not just something we automatically are, it is also something we must try to be. He was asserting that good examples of human beings are hard to find, and his lamp was his way of saying that he could not ‘see’ any human beings and that he needed to throw light on the issue.

Questions help us to crystallize what we hope for, a commitment to a future. The start of this begins in our questions as we gamble on a future that we cannot be certain will be shaped as we want. But without this starting point we have nothing, as lack of hope means lack of action.

1 When Things Come Apart

This is a book about beliefs and how they shape our lives. More specifically, it is a book about our beliefs about ourselves and the way they shape how see ourselves as human beings. We are living at a time when things feel as if they are coming apart, the way we have been living for decades or even centuries is being renegotiated. Our lives as humans are being upended by a combination of COVID, climate change and technology disruption, fundamentally challenging notions of who we are and how we see ourselves.

We often only start to examine the beliefs that underpin our daily lives when things start to fall apart. Only then can we see what the constituents are that have been holding together our notions about ourselves. Indeed, the ideas that are most powerful are the ones that we are not always aware are there. Isiah Berlin pointed out that the history of the way we think and how we act is a history of dominant ideas.[1]

We have no need to look at these dominant beliefs when things are working but when they are not, we are forced to examine them whether we want to or not. Writing at this time in human history, it feels that so much of what we took to be solid and true is now being questioned. With this, we can see more clearly what these beliefs are.

In contrast, beliefs that give us proficiency over our environment are quickly absorbed, we no longer reflect on them but take them as a given so we are freed up: why examine further if it works?

But when our environment changes then the practices, habits and routines that reflect these beliefs are suddenly set into sharp relief. These behaviours reflect a mastery of a world that no longer exists, and we are then thrown into a period of uncertainty. Psychologist Kurt Lewin talked about the way that change, when thrust on us, forces us to 'unfreeze' our minds, reconsider our lives, and work out a new set of beliefs and way of living. [5]

We are living in just such 'Liquid Times' where thinking, planning, and acting are not helping us the way they used to. [6] Our environment is in a constant state of change, we are operating without fixed, solid patterns. This means that we must learn to adapt our beliefs so that we are able to 'walk on quicksand,' adapting constantly to rapid change.

We can no longer rely on the beliefs that were a feature of our relatively stable and more certain past (compared to where we find ourselves today, at least for recent generations).

Of course, we could argue beliefs are not the same as reality: after all, what evidence is there that we are changing? Are we not the same people that we have always been? But it is not that simple. Belief is powerful, shaping events, not just thoughts. After all, people go to war on the basis of beliefs about nationhood, fairness and resentment: beliefs are not something peripheral to the course of our lives, they are at the very heart of shaping who we are and what we do.

Why does this matter?

We have always had a range of different beliefs about humans, who we are, how we operate, why we do what we do. These can come from a variety of traditions and perspectives which makes for a rich and vibrant community from science to the arts, material for both poets and physicists. While this is to be welcomed, there are warnings that deserve to be heard.

First, we need to understand the way in which our beliefs about ourselves do not exist in isolation. By ascribing to one set of beliefs, the jump to others is less dramatic. Sometimes it is as much about the trajectory of the adjacent issues that we need to be mindful. We can see the way in which people can become radicalised through gradual exposure of increasingly more extreme perspectives. This is not to say that everyone becomes radicalised and that a 'slippery slope' is inevitable, but that it is surely easier. We need to anticipate what might be waiting for us down whichever slope we are slipping. For example, we may consider that augmenting our bodies with technology can lead us to be superior beings, but history is littered terrible examples of the way beliefs about forms of superiority have led to atrocities. While one set of beliefs do not automatically lead to another, but we can slide into something that was once considered unacceptable and unthinkable.

Further, if we inhabit a monoculture of beliefs, then we narrow what is in scope of possibilities. Alternative perspectives become marginalised, slightly embarrassing siblings struggling for space in the places we normally look – mainstream publishers, newspapers, magazines, the first page of a web search result.

On this basis, the challenges we face offer us an opportunity to see more clearly what our beliefs about ourselves are. We can challenge these perspectives, rethink whether they make sense, giving us the opportunity to reconsider who we are, what we are about, what being human entails.

Beliefs about our future as humans

When looking at ourselves we all struggle to "jump the shadow" as Hannah Arendt put it; the task of looking at ourselves dispassionately is an endless and almost impossible job. [7] Nevertheless, given the importance of this, we need to try: Lewis Mumford talked about the importance of 'Intelligent Speculation': we cannot wait until things are obvious, as it is then too late to change the course of travel or at least understand the implications of it for the way we live. [8]

Science historian Lorraine Daston refers to the way in which COVID has meant we are in a period of radical novelty and uncertainty that, in her words, means we are "like a squid obscuring itself in ink". We cannot see what this new world means for us, but we are nevertheless renegotiating who we are and how to live as a result of it. [9]

This uncertain novelty from COVID, climate change and technology upheaval mean we have huge amounts of contested ground. For example, one theme we will be exploring is the competing views of the provenance of our behaviour and human agency. Are we mindlessly shaped by our drives and past experiences or are we consciously agentic, shaping our futures?

Another related theme is whether consciousness is 'within us' or distributed 'between us', embedded in the tools we use. Further, most Western societies are, for the large part, 'post religious' and yet it seems spiritual beliefs inhabit much of our way of being, despite the way in which science simultaneously offers a quite different view with which we also underpin our beliefs about the world.

And beliefs about what constitutes knowledge itself are being fought out with some convinced that we are suffering from the consequences of no longer agreeing on basic facts whilst others are challenging this positivist mindset, arguing for a pluralistic view of knowledge, that more than one way of looking at the world is valid.

Many see the world as a place of linear progress where the human lot is gradually yet consistently being improved, whilst others see a world of revolution and radical change ever waiting in the wings, due in no small part to the lived experience of many not seeing any improvement and feeling their lives and futures to be bleak.

These themes offer us grounds to speculate that we are at a point in our history where much of what we have understood about ourselves for centuries is now in question. Of course, the arguments are often being articulated in an inchoate way. We are understandably unsure of our position, unclear what, if anything, we ourselves might believe in this patchwork of beliefs about being human. This is playing out in the area of conspiracy theories and misinformation, with these representing a clash of belief systems of what represents knowledge as much as the specific content of the claims themselves.

About this book

Addressing these topics involves traversing a territory where we cannot collect evidence to give us the answers, for as HG Wells pointed out, the big questions in life are not be concluded empirically.

While this is not a Philosophy book (with a capital P), it is philosophical in its enquiry. Rather than trying to martial an argument by pulling together the necessary data for support, it aims to provoke, ask questions, and suggest linkages that may help join dots for the reader.

In this context it aims to continue the centuries old philosophical tradition of throwing light on the issue of what being human involves. The means by which this is done is through a series of essays because this is necessarily a set of explorations.

Humans have entered a new era and we may be in a period which could be as radical and transformative as any other we have lived through in human history. But while the events we are living through feel momentous and have huge meaning for the way we understand ourselves, we are all often too immersed in the currents of events to be able to have a clear understanding and narrative at this stage.

There is no overarching structure in mind. A grand theory of everything, would surely not only be arrogant but also a fool's errand. The point is to assemble perspectives on a range of topics that merit discussion and allow us all to pull-out themes. On that basis it is aiming to offer inspiration for readers who can then use the thinking as provocations, finding new associations and linkages whether tenuous and tentative or more certain and perhaps empirically supported.

The point is to surface the changing beliefs that seem to be shaping who we are, what we think about our planet and our fellow human beings. It is not to say the themes have not been discovered before. On the contrary, they are the subject of debate and reflection in many circles, but perhaps not always brought together with linkages drawn in the way that is done here.

To explore this, the book is a series of essays, the sequence of which broadly reflects the chronography of the writing. The first section reflects a long-term interest in the relationship between people and the tools they use, examining the way in which beliefs about technology influence beliefs about being human. Chapter 2 'Hacking Human Behaviour' sets out to challenge the narrative that, like machines, we can be 'hacked' and that others can understand us better than we can know ourselves. This sets the scene for Chapter 3 'Human Sense Making' examining the long history of a shared meaning we require of the human world, something that AI or other technology tools can offer us. Chapter 4 'Reading Minds' builds on this, looking at the way we understand each other and using the example of self-driving cars to demonstrate that as humans we share more than is immediately obvious. We see the way in which we are socially embedded creatures, dependant on a shared intentionality to be able to operate successfully in the world. Then in Chapter 5. Life in the Multiverse of Truths' we explore the process of gathering data about humans and suggest that we are living at a time where we must accept that there are multiple views of reality that we call on, rather than assuming there is one single truth or reality.

We then shift with a section that explores human change and transformation. Chapter 7 'On Changing' considers the complexities of changing, something that the themes of COVID, climate and tech have required us to do. We discuss the uncertain nature of this and how purposeful change to adapt to the future is gaining ground. Chapter 8 'Breaks in Time' draws on the work of philosopher Walter Benjamin, among others, to offer a sense of the spontaneous nature of humans challenging a long-held set of beliefs that they are determined by their pasts. Chapter 9 'To be a Cyborg' examines the beguiling opportunities that lie in changing from our mortal bodies using technology, transforming us into something that may be a fundamentally different type of human.

The next section is around the theme of our inner lives and our willingness or not to recognise it. Chapter 10 'Iceberg Minds' examines the way in which many have sought to deny the inner mind, or at least to diminish its importance. Within this we set out competing explanations of consciousness setting out the way in which distributed explanations of consciousness can be aligned with similar developments in psychology.

Chapter 11 'Denial wars' examines the way in which the notion of divinity has long inhabited our view of ourselves, setting up a divide between those that consider our human imperfections mean that our ability to make sense of the world is forever flawed versus those who consider our own individual perspectives are sacred. Chapter 12 'Creatures of Habit' shows the way our routinised behaviours are often part of a much bigger collective self. And Chapter 13, 'The Promise', examines the way in which primacy has been given to our personal perspectives and the extent to which this can be warranted or not.

We then move to a section on changing beliefs about different aspects of our emotional and spiritual lives. Chapter 14 'Not me but We' looks at the way in which our emotional lives might be far more connected than we might imagine and the way this is linked to a sense of common fate. Chapter 15, 'Living in the End Times' sets out the way that apocalyptic thinking is shaping narratives, linked to religious notions of original sin. 'The Everyday Alchemist', of Chapter 16 brings in the notion that COVID has allowed us to see more clearly and challenge the longstanding binary distinctions between objects and subjects. Chapter 17 'This Transcendent Life' examines how the way we have got closer to death has meant we have explored the importance of those who come after us for how we live in the present.

In the final section we explore the way as humans we are time travellers both from the past as well as into the future. And that our conception of the difference between these is not as distinct as we might always imagine. Chapter 18 'Whose Memory is it Anyway' looks at the way in which we are rethinking what memory is and the role it plays in our worlds. In Chapter 19 we look at 'Utopian Worlds' and the way we have the capacity to rethink different ways of living and being. Then in Chapter 20 we set out the way that 'Radical Thinking' is needed more than ever but in a way that relates to the world rather than in some kind of elegant but ultimately pointless vacuum.

The chapters can be read either sequentially or at random, the themes interweave and, just as it is for humans, each individual chapter is connected to another. At times, the references repeat across the individual chapters offering ways in which connections can be found between the quite different topics. The logic that does link these chapters is the way in which technology, COVID and climate change have in their different ways meant we can see more clearly the beliefs about being human that have dominated since the seventeenth century are now struggling to make sense of this changing world. This is not to say that people have not done this before, of course they have, but the debate is now being played out in a very salient way, right in front of our eyes, causing a much broader range of people to question and wonder.

SECTION 1: I, ROBOT?

Digital technology is entering an ever more intimate part of our lives, a constant watching and recording companion as well as offering us the ability to make our lives easier. Generative AI has created excitement and concern over the possibilities of the way our lives can be irrevocably changed.

Our tools provide useful metaphors for ourselves as humans but how far can this extend? Can we now be hacked, measured, understood and our behaviours efficiently shaped and smoothly predicted?

We sit on the cusp of revolutions in the way work, home, our culture is organised by the logic of technology. What are we starting to see emerge about the nature of being human?

This is a story that includes changing conceptions of consciousness both shared and individual, of the way distinctions between objects and subject are contested, of the politics of power pushing the labour out of sight and how racial and gender stereotypes still pervade but are left unspoken.

The many issues speak of the way technology has shifted sands, revealing new insights about the nature of being human that challenges our assumptions of there being a singular truth about us and the world.

2: Hacking Human Behaviour

We are in greater danger of a technological invasion of our minds than we are from a foreign army taking over our country, according to Yuval Noah Harari when he spoke at the World Economic Forum at Davos in Switzerland. The author of Sapiens: A Brief History of Humankind [10] went on to say:

"There is a lot of talk of hacking computers, smartphones, computers, emails, bank accounts, but the really big thing is hacking human beings, if you have enough data about me and enough computer power and biological knowledge, you can hack my body, my brain, my life. You can reach a point where you know me better than I know myself". [11]

Of course, hacking is not a new concept: we have long hacked down trees for example. But since the advent of digital technology, the term has become synonymous with the way someone uses technical know-how to break into computer systems and access information that would otherwise be unavailable to them. Using the term hacking in this context therefore not only means that people are typically doing this for nefarious purposes but, importantly, see the human mind as something akin to a computer system that can be broken into.

Hari is not alone in his dire predictions about the vulnerability of the human mind to 'disinformation' or 'fake news'. The World Health Organisation has coined the term 'infodemic', defined as "a tsunami of information—some accurate, some not — that spreads alongside an epidemic". [12] All the major tech companies have faced calls for more active management of the problem, not least Facebook (now called Meta) who supplied user profiling data to Cambridge Analytica which was used for personality profiling to serve personalised advertising. This technique was claimed to have been used to gain influence in US presidential elections and the UK's Brexit vote.[13]

In a recent paper by a leading psychologist in the area, Sander van der Linden, the rapid spread of online misinformation is considered a growing threat to democracy and to have serious consequences for a variety of societal issues, ranging from climate change and vaccinations to international relations.[14]

While the implications of disinformation have been well documented, the question that arises is that if we can be 'hacked', what does this tell us about humans?

Quite a lot according to Harari who suggests this has huge implications for how we see ourselves. He believes we should debunk the notion of 'free will', that humans make choices of their own volition and agency. His position is that this never was scientific reality, but a myth inherited from Christian theology. He suggests that Christians developed the idea of 'free will' to explain why God should punish or reward us: if choices are not freely made, then there would be no basis for this.

Can we really be confident that humans are at a point where we no longer have free will? And are we really at the point where our minds can be 'hacked' in this way? There is a lot to unpack here. This not only needs some philosophical thinking but also, we need to examine if there is evidence to support the claim. The sight of those that broke into the US Capitol building in January 2020 taking pictures of themselves to post on social media alongside the invocations to violence by Trump on social media can make it appear as if technology is manipulating behaviour. But is it really that simple? Philosophically do the claims for 'mind hacking' stand up to scrutiny but also does the evidence support it?

The philosophical limits to mind hacking

Before we breezily proclaim that minds can be hacked, it is worth noting that being able to understand the minds of others has long been one of the biggest challenges we face as humans. In a sense, we can never really be sure we know what another person feels or thinks. Philosopher John Locke posed a remarkably simple question to illustrate this point:

"How do I know if you see red the same way that I see red? What if you saw all red things the way I see green, but just call those items red?"

This simple thought experiment helps us to see that it is impossible to know if the experiences of one person are wholly shared by another. Of course, we cannot deny that understanding the thoughts and feelings of another is possible: indeed, it is highly valued in many fields such as medicine and education. In medicine, empathy for patients' experiences (symptoms, feelings) means that doctors can diagnose and treat patients not only more effectively but with greater compassion. Empathy means that teachers can understand the problems and needs of each student. Indeed, a lack of empathy for others means we could be considered an amoral sociopath.

But the boundaries of empathetic understanding are rarely clear: on the one hand our unique experience, thoughts and feelings are particular to us individually and it can be insulting to be told by another that they claim to know how we feel. On the other, for us to agree what red looks like then we must have some degree of empathy, ability to understand each other's thoughts.

Nevertheless, the way in which we can claim to 'know another' is not straightforward. There is a great deal of contested ground between, on the one hand being able to 'feel the pain' of another, and on the other hand to be able to engage effectively with a common ability to share concepts and respond in similar ways. If we did not have this then, as Ludwig Wittgenstein long ago pointed out, language and communication would simply not be possible.

We can see that philosophically there are reasons to be more than a little cautious about the notion of mind hacking; if we are not even sure that we see red in the same way, then more ambitious claims to mind reading should surely be treated with care. But philosophical considerations to one side, is there evidence to support the notion of mind hacking?

The technical limits to mind hacking

In 2012 an article by writer Charles Duhigg appeared in the New York Times outlining the way a team at US supermarket Target worked on a model intended to predict which of their shoppers were pregnant. [15] An anecdote illustrates the efficacy of their approach:

About a year after Pole created his pregnancy-prediction model, a man walked into a Target outside Minneapolis and demanded to see the manager. He was clutching coupons that had been sent to his daughter, and he was angry, according to an employee who participated in the conversation.

"My daughter got this in the mail!" he said."She's still in high school, and you're sending her coupons for baby clothes and cribs? Are you trying to encourage her to get pregnant?"

The manager didn't have any idea what the man was talking about. He looked at the mailer. Sure enough, it was addressed to the man's daughter and contained advertisements for maternity clothing, nursery furniture and pictures of smiling infants. The manager apologized and then called a few days later to apologize again.

On the phone, though, the father was somewhat abashed."I had a talk with my daughter," he said."It turns out there has been some activities in my house I haven't been completely aware of. She's due in August. I owe you an apology".

The story subsequently gained a huge amount of exposure in the press and created a great deal of currency for the power of data analytics to reveal things about us that, as is clear from the story, we ourselves or at least those close to us may not even be aware of. However, Colin Fraser, a data scientist at Facebook unpicked this story so that we can see it is not as revealing as it first appears.[16]

First, Fraser suggests that there is no way to in fact confirm that Target's algorithm predicted the girl was pregnant. Although the girl was sent a coupon book including maternity items, Target likely sent out a huge number of coupon books to large numbers of people. If Target simply sent out maternity related coupon books at random, then this very same incident could have still taken place; as Fraser points out, some of the coupon books would certainly find their way to pregnant women by chance, and some of those women might have had parents who didn't know that they were pregnant, one of whom might have gone to a store to complain.

But even if Target's algorithm did on this occasion predict that this girl was pregnant, the story tells us very little about the effectiveness of the algorithm at predicting pregnancy. It merely shows that the targeting worked at least once. We do not know how many pregnant Target customers didn't get these coupons – information that we would need to assess the accuracy or otherwise of the accuracy of the algorithm.

The error of logic in this story is to go from the specific to the general: simply because one person was correctly identified does not mean this is the case more broadly.

Fast forward to 2018 and The Guardian newspaper broke the story that voter-profiling company Cambridge Analytica had collected data for over 50 million Facebook users.[17] Cambridge Analytica claimed that they had gathered this data for 'psychographic' profiling tools, which meant they were able to customise political advertising to users' personality traits. Whistle-blower Christopher Wylie was quoted as saying:

"We exploited Facebook to harvest millions of people's profiles and built models to exploit what we knew about them and target their inner demons. That was the basis the entire company was built on".

The subsequent uproar means that Cambridge Analytica became a household name. However, just as with the Target example, evidence is elusive that the methods used to target political advertising had anything other than a negligible impact on voting behaviour. Indeed, the UK's Information Commissioner's Office concluded their investigation by saying Cambridge Analytica was not doing anything particularly unique: Information Commissioner, Elizabeth Denham, told the UK Parliament that "on examination, the methods that SCL [a company that is corporately interlinked with Cambridge Analytica] was using were, in the main, well-recognised processes using commonly available technology".[18]

As The New Statesmen's Laurie Clark put it, "...this assessment jarred with reporting at the time that had imbued CA with Derren Brown-like abilities to tinker with perceptions and sway the credulous". Clark goes onto say that while there is some evidence that psychographic marketing can work in the context of consumer goods, research by Brendan Nyhan has pointed towards this not being currently effective for political advertising. Further, personality profiling aside, research shows that political micro-targeting is simply not effective at persuasion.[19]

Writer Timothy Hwang, who formerly worked at Google, suggests that internet advertising generally is in danger of a "Subprime Attention Crisis," being overvalued due to the opaqueness of the market, and that very few of those involved are willing to point out that it has little impact on behaviour. [20]

The point here is not to evaluate the effectiveness or otherwise of data analytics and ability to micro-target and change behaviour but call attention to the way that the technological invasion of our minds is more of a moot point than might first appear.

Artificial Intelligence (AI) is the technology used for 'programmatic advertising', placing personalised marketing communications into websites that we are viewing; these are dynamically customised to reflect the wide range of data held about us individually.

Technology critic Jaron Lanier suggests we fall into logical traps in the way we evaluate the effectiveness of AI for these purposes. Of course, AI results look impressive but on the other hand, it is hard to know how well it performs versus other much more straightforward methods. We could, for example, show people the best-selling books in the category. Would this perform just as well as recommendations personalised by AI? The answer is that we don't know because there is no baseline for us to compare this to. They may be better but much of the time we simply do not know – which means it can be hard to evaluate just how good AI is versus other methods.[21]

It seems that the evidence that our minds can be 'hacked' by technology is not as robust as it first appears. How can we better understand the way in which the 'infodemic of fake news' is changing our behaviours? To do this we need to look at historical examples which predate the internet.

Disinformation is nothing new

There is a long list of ways in which minds appear to have been hacked that predate the technology which is often held responsible for misleading us. Going back 2,000 years, the Roman Republic was in danger of civil war between Octavian, the adopted son of Julius Caesar, and Mark Anthony, one of Caesar's trusted commanders.

To get public backing, Octavian claimed Anthony was unfit to hold office not only because he was always drunk but did not respect Roman values of faithfulness and respect due to his affair with Cleopatra. Octavian promoted his messages using poetry and slogans printed on coins and eventually became the first Emperor of Rome, ruling for over 40 years. [22]

In a quite different example, news media in several West African countries have periodically reported people being blamed of causing penises, breasts, and vaginas to shrink or vanish. The accused were often beaten, sometimes with fatal results. Vivian Dzokoto and Glenn Adams give the example of a 17-year-old male who "claimed that he had gone to fetch water for his father and was returning when [the perpetrator] came behind him, touched him and immediately he felt his penis shrink until it was no longer visible". [23]

In a more recent example from 1999, hundreds of people contacted the Belgium's National Poison Centre when they became ill after drinking Coca-Cola. However, laboratory analysis found the complaints were unsubstantiated although in some bottles there were very low, non-toxic but odorous, amounts of hydrogen sulphide. [24]

While the form and channels of 'disinformation' may be different from what we are used to today, in these cases people in communities have learnt information from others: what they have heard has influenced their response. This raises a challenge with the term 'mind hacking': it does not give us any means to examine *why* people are believing what they have heard from other people. At best it suggests humans are simply not to be trusted given they are prone to bouts of irrationality or even hysteria.

We receive a vast array of information every day: the question we need to understand is what are the mechanisms that mean certain sorts of information have a much more dramatic impact than others?

The wider context of our lives

To examine this, we can look at an area which is understandably of great deal of concern, the anti-vaxx movement. Journalist Arwa Mahdawi writing in The Guardian newspaper cited a range of surveys which indicated women were less likely to say they would seek a vaccination for COVID than men. This was despite global research suggesting that women were more likely than men to take the pandemic seriously and comply with public-health regulations. [25]

Is this due to the anti-vaxxer movement, which is dominated by women? Recent research from researchers at George Washington University found members of online communities previously 'undecided' on vaccines (such as pet lovers or yoga enthusiasts for example) are increasingly linking with anti-vaxxers. [26] Should we really ascribe the beliefs of these women to the mind-hacking skills of the anti-vaxxer? Mahdawi points to an alternative explanation:

"One reason women are disproportionately attracted to alternative medicine is because traditional medicine hasn't exactly done a brilliant job of earning their trust. Women's health concerns are often dismissed: one study found women with severe stomach pain had to wait 33% longer to be seen by a doctor than men with the same symptoms. Women's health problems are

also massively under-researched: there is five times more research into erectile dysfunction than premenstrual syndrome, for example, despite the former affecting 19% of men and the latter affecting 90% of women. In the US, medical research trials weren't required to include women until 1993 because women's bodies were considered too complex and hormonal".

And she goes on to make the same point that fewer than half of Black American adults said they intended to get a COVID vaccine, compared to 61% of white people.

"Black Americans have been experimented on (one word: Tuskegee) and forcibly sterilized. Black pain hasn't been taken seriously by the medical establishment because of enduring racist notions that Black people have thicker skin than white people. Minorities are also underrepresented in clinical trials, which can result in technology and treatments that don't meet their needs. Pulse oximeters, for example, which measure the oxygen levels in your blood and have been increasingly in use due to the pandemic, can give misleading readings in people with dark skin. A new study has found that misleading results happen three times more often for Black people. Probably because the colour of light used in the pulse oximeter can be absorbed by skin pigment. Which would have been something researchers would have caught straight away if they took diversity seriously".

We can see that anti-vaxx is not simply a problem about Russian disinformation bots; disinformation messages only have a receptive audience because there is fertile ground for them. As we saw from genital-shrinking panic, there is a strong link with the ideology and beliefs of a culture, in that case concerning fertility, procreation, and sexual performance. The outbreak of hysteria regarding Coca Cola has been attributed to a background anxiety at the time over wider concerns about the safety of food products. What might at first glance seem to be irrational behaviours, often in fact have their roots in a wider set of collective beliefs held in the population.

It is also all too easy to fall into the notion of a false dichotomy between digital social media and 'real life': it makes it easier to absolve ourselves of the responsibility that this is something for which the causes are at least partly of our making and as such are our responsibility.

For example, some reports of the attempted coup by the mob storming the Capitol building in the United States in January 2021 suggested the rioters were the unwitting victims of social media manipulation. This heralded many calls for greater controls on social media. However, even after this astonishing display, politicians still tried to overthrow election results with their own Congressional votes.

Sociologist Zeynep Tufekci writes:

"An overwhelming majority of the GOP representatives in the house spent the day in lock-down and came back and promptly voted to overturn the election. In a future scenario .... It's absolutely plausible to me that even more Republicans would have joined this blatant attempt to overturn the election and that their base would mostly have been fine with that".[27]

The *deus ex machina* event at once crystallised in a very salient way the potential threat to normalcy and order but at the same time drew attention away from so much of US politics. Technology researcher Nathan Jurgenson made a point about the shock many have expressed when they saw this happen in America:

"They apparently haven't paid any attention to Trump rallies before. This incident was hardly different, aside from the special access the participants were eventually granted to a government building". [28]

'Mind hacking' via social media is not quite so simple as it is often characterised: we cannot ignore the wider context in which it operates.

Addressing disinformation

It sems that much of the diagnosis of the problem of disinformation, and its solutions, is stuck in the notion of 'mind hacking'. Let us look at one solution that has had a lot of coverage, an online game developed by psychologists Jon Roozenbeek & Sander van der Linden. In the game, people play the role of propaganda producers: the aim of this is to help them to increase 'psychological resistance' to fake news. [29]

The game involves players fuelling anger and fear by appearing to manipulate news and social media: players can deploy twitter bots, photo-shopped evidence, and can incite conspiracy theories to attract followers. Players earn six 'badges' in the game, each reflecting a common strategy used by spreaders of fake news: impersonation; conspiracy; polarisation; discrediting sources; trolling; emotionally provocative content. van der Linden said:

"We wanted to see if we could pre-emptively debunk, or 'pre-bunk', fake news by exposing people to a weak dose of the methods used to create and spread disinformation, so they have a better understanding of how they might be deceived. This is a version of what psychologists call 'inoculation theory', with our game working like a psychological vaccination".

To gauge the impact of the game, players were asked to assess the 'reliability' of headlines and tweets both before and after playing the game. The study found that players' reliability ratings of the fake news had reduced by an average of 21% after completing it.

Clearly this approach has some elements of the solution but nevertheless has challenges, not least how to persuade people to play the game in the first place. The bigger problem, however, is that the game makes the mistake of positioning disinformation as a manipulation problem rather than a reflection of wider social and cultural factors determining what can seem plausible based on what is known and shared by our cultural reference points.

The issue is not merely one of how we go about processing information. How we critically process information will inevitably be a function of a much wider set of values, beliefs and attitudes that will be shared and shaped by the people we share our lives with. Without considering these wider points then we are endlessly addressing the symptoms rather than the broader causes.

Indeed, tech critic Evgeny Morozov suggests that news organisations are caught up fuelling a culture of misinformation, led by the need to drive attention, as shown in this example he gives about the Washington Post:

"...it has recently warned about damaging Russian cyberattacks on a power grid in Vermont (in a report followed in other media outlets, including the Observer). It seems that those attacks didn't happen and that the Washington Post didn't even bother to check with the grid operator. Apparently, an economy ruled by online advertising has produced its own theory of truth: truth is whatever produces most eyeballs". [30]

This is certainly consistent with research done by the US based Harvard Berkman Klein Center who have challenged the notion that social media is the primary vehicle for disinformation. They analysed allegations relating to voter mail-in fraud which was a huge controversy in the 2020 US presidential election. The researchers concluded that this issue was part of a systematic campaign amplified by a wide range of traditional media outlets.

They suggested that Fox News, a right-wing television network, was more influential in spreading beliefs about voter mail-in fraud than social media. They concluded:

"Our findings suggest that this highly effective disinformation campaign, with potentially profound effects for both participation in, and the legitimacy of, the 2020 election, was an elite-driven, mass-media led process. Social media played only a secondary role". [31]

On being human

The narrative that we are unwitting helpless individuals without free will begs the question of who then managed to develop the technology that meant our minds could be hacked? For if we truly thought that we lacked free will, how would we have the incentive to develop these sorts of tools? It feels as if there is a sleight of hand here – some people can have their minds hacked and lack free will, but the other people who are doing the hacking logically can only have free will do this task.

Indeed, the notion that we can be 'hacked' suggests that our beliefs come from a vacuum in which we are untouched by others. This narrow individualistic notion of humans is perpetuated by a Cartesian view of humans that our rationality requires the freeing of one's mind of any external authority. That view suggests that the essence of being human is the ability to separate oneself operating in an entirely individualised manner, honing the skills of rational living.

But, of course, this is not how we are. The mob that stormed the US Capitol building genuinely believed the facts that were laid before them from a range of news media, friends, colleagues, politicians and so on. There was a huge amount of information that means it is easy to believe democracy is at risk. To pin this on 'mind hacking', facilitated by digital tools, is to ignore the embedded and connected way in which we absorb and share information over time.

It is all too easy to adopt the false dichotomy between digital and 'real life' and makes it easier to absolve ourselves of responsibility. Indeed, the popular narrative that technology is revealing we are simple 'hunter-gatherers' whose minds can be hacked by smart devices is looking a little thin.

Examining these claims has helped us to better understand how we humans are in fact intelligent socially embedded creatures, rather than mechanistic, atomistic creatures that has long been the narrative of western philosophy for centuries.

3: Human Sense Making

Sense making is a more important challenge than ever for us to get right, given that the complex, interconnected nature of the world that technology has created means our lives often feel vast and complicated. A key driver of this is the way that AI is increasingly determining outcomes, with the logic behind the verdicts that have been arrived at is opaque. Writer Cathy O'Neil sets out how this pervades our everyday lives, from the well-respected teacher who is sacked due to a low score on an assessment test, or the student who unable to secure a job in a store due to their responses on a personality test, and those whose credit card spending limits are reduced simply because they had spent money at certain stores. [1]

Trying to unpick the sense of something that is complex and opaque is of course hard. We may fall back onto explanations that are easier to conceptualise, such as human agency, in just the same way we might use anthropomorphic terms to find ways of talking about the behaviour of a machine. And while it is tempting to think of AI as offering a straightforward 'truth' untainted by human subjectivity the reality according to many is that it is not just a technology. As the AI Now Institute tweeted, "AI isn't just tech; it's power, politics, and culture".[2]

This is no surprise to humanities researchers [3] who have long explored the culture of technology. One of the popular examples of the way in which technology choices reflect the dominant values in society is that of Robert Moses who was New York's 'master builder' between 1920 – 1970. He designed 200 overpasses on Long Island, but they were too low for the high public buses to get under them with the intent of making it difficult for 'lower classes' to get out to Jones Beach, a public park he had designed.

Expecting people to be able to understand and unpack the political mechanisms that have created this environment is ambitious. That is not to say that people are unable to do so but given the political, social, and technological complexities it is hardly surprising that people might struggle and find instead more ready explanations from those that we all as individuals have available.

So how do we as humans go about making sense of ourselves and each other? Can we be reliable witnesses, making sense of our own lives, asking and answering questions that offer understanding and clarity of who we are and why we have behaved as we did? Or are we destined to a life in which machines understand the world, us, and each other better than we know ourselves? If we pay heed to Google cofounder Sergey Brin then we might think the latter is likely, given he said: "you should presume that someday, we will be able to make machines that can reason, think and do things better than we can".[4]

Everybody lies

Of course, we can ask questions, ask people to narrate for themselves but a popular notion is that people are either not able or are unwilling to disclose the information requested of them. Indeed, 'Everybody lies', according to data scientist, Seth Stephens-Davidowitz. [5] The book of this title outlines the way in which new sources of insight can instead be captured because of the way in which technology is present in ever more intimate aspects of our lives, quietly recording our innermost thoughts (in this case, care of our Google searches.)

This is consistent with a huge body of work in psychology that sets out to capture implicit attitudes using a wide variety of techniques and measures in the belief that many of our attitudes are inaccessible through direct questioning approaches. This implies that our lack of awareness concerning implicit attitudes makes it impossible for us to properly share our preferences. Psychologist Anthony Greenwald and others claim that explicit self-report measures are problematic as they depend on this ability to report private knowledge.[6]

Alongside this, technology often seems able to give an account of us in a way that we may struggle to do for ourselves. In a study by researchers at Cornell University, over 1.5 million geotagged tweets were analysed from almost 10,000 people in the US. They wanted to understand if the content of the tweets themselves could predict the location of the user. In fact, they were able to create an algorithm that correctly predicted people's home cities 68% of the time, their home state 70% of the time and their time zone 80% of the time. [7] Similarly, a paper published in Nature found that the lifestyles of mobile phone users could be predicted from their patterns of movement. The analysis found it was possible to allocate to 95% of users a unique 'fingerprint' based on their movements so that it was possible to accurately predict at what time of the day individuals would be in a certain neighbourhood or town. When linking this information to mapping data, it was then possible to infer a great deal about that individual's lifestyle. [8]

What should we make of this? Clearly the information revealed by technology is impressive and interesting. But does it really tell us anything about peoples' inner lives? To do this we would surely want to understand their subjective, lived experience, how they interpret the world and account for their own behaviours. The evidence to support this does not seem convincing. There is a difference between revealing what people do and assuming this tells us how people think.

We can examine this further by returning to Stephens-Davidowitz. He compares the way in which spouses describe their husbands on social media posts with the words they use alongside 'husband' when doing searches (as shown below). This is offered as an example of the way in which we might say one thing (in a social media post) but really think another (as shown by searches).

Social media posts	**Searches**
The best	Gay
My best friend	A jerk
Amazing	Amazing
The greatest	Annoying
So cute	Mean

He considers that because we tend to see social media posts rather than Google searches, we may make the mistake of minimising how many women think their husbands are 'a jerk'. But while there is a certain logic that people may be less inclined to publicly call out their husband as a jerk (understandably), this surely does not mean technology is able to gain preferential status over asking people questions.

There may be a need to ask people about this in a sensitive way, but this is by no means a particularly new or challenging issue for skilled interviewers and survey designers.

We also know that people tend to be more polarised in their opinions on social media. We are also aware that we can hold two apparently contradictory views of an individual at the same time. It is entirely possible that someone's husband is both their best friend and considered to be a jerk. Indeed, is this not the basis of many relationships? It does not take all that much digging to arrive at a series of logical inconsistencies in the notion that 'Everybody Lies'.

Implicit measurement

This suspicion about asking people questions has encouraged the development of implicit measures that, it is suggested, can uncover attitudes or perceptions we would not otherwise be able to access. To qualify as 'implicit' it is assumed that participants aren't aware that the attitude or perception is being measured, don't have conscious access to the attitude or perception or have no control over the outcome.

But there is a great deal of evidence that implicit measures are not always as 'pure' a measure of attitude or perception as is sometimes thought. There is not a great deal of literature on this because, as researchers Russell Fazio and Michael Olson point out, it is rarely investigated. [9]

But from what evidence there is available, the case for a separate, implicit, dimension to behaviour is challenged as:

- participants can be aware of the study's purpose in terms of what is being measured which in turn affects the results;
- they are often aware that they hold certain attitudes or perceptions;
- despite the common assumption that the implicit method invariably yields honest answers, participants can fake certain attitudes and perceptions.

Indeed, there are often low correlations between self-reported and indirectly assessed attitudes. In these instances, it is often considered reasonable to assume that the indirectly assessed attitude is 'implicit' or unconscious and is the more valid response. This is even taken as evidence of the value of measuring implicit attitudes and an indication of the way in which we cannot trust what people tell us in surveys.

Of course, this is not necessarily the case. Low correlations between the two kinds of measures can arise for a multitude of reasons other than a lack of introspective access.[10] There is a large body of evidence showing that multiple factors determine whether 'implicit' attitudes, assessed with indirect measures, are related to self-reported 'explicit' attitudes. If these factors are controlled, then explicit and implicit attitude measures in fact often show substantial correlations.

The debate about this is huge and as such not one to explore fully here. But we can at least suggest there is a reasonable question mark about the degree to which we can access insights about people's inner lives without asking them questions. But to understand why this is the case, we need to step back from the vigorous epistemological debates concerning ways of collecting information, to ontological considerations – how we can properly understand the issues.

Making sense of species human

Just how we do we make sense of 'species human'? The tools we use have often become metaphors for the way we understand ourselves. Louise Barrett points to a range of historical examples in her book 'Beyond The Brain'. Socrates likened the mind to a wax tablet; John Locke considered it a blank slate; Sigmund Freud thought it a hydraulic system. [11] As Barrett points out:

"The mind/brain has also been compared to an abbey, cathedral, aviary, theatre, and warehouse, as well as a filing cabinet, clockwork mechanism, camera obscura, and phonograph, and also a railway network and telephone exchange,"

Digital technology, and AI in particular is arguably the latest wave of this, an inevitable next phase on our journey. To understand the way that this is shaping our understanding of ourselves, it is useful to explore the dual aims of AI. [12] One is technological: using computers to get useful things done, often by using methods that can be quite unlike those our minds use. The other is more pertinent to our current discussion: using AI concepts and models to inform questions about human minds. There has long been a close relationship between computer scientists, cognitive psychologists, and neuroscientists. We can see how we have moved from technology as a handy metaphor to help us think, to one that is assumed to have direct relevance to our conception of ourselves. On this basis, if the mind can be described in terms of a computer, then eventually it must be possible to build a computer that is like the mind.

But the difficulty of this comes from failing to recognise the degree to which our *shared meanings* as humans are critical in so much of our thinking. AI would need be able to 'understand' the way we live, and this is not how AI operates. AI works well in a very formally defined problem domain, what we might call a 'closed system'. This is where the situation is predictable, measurable, and importantly, no knowledge is needed from outside the very specific domain in question.

This is fine if we use computers to simply get useful things done in these closed systems. But it is not as simple as this because what is a 'closed system problem' can easily be open to dispute. How one person interprets a problem is different to the way another person does. For example, the challenge of wanting to understand how people make decisions at the supermarket shelf could mean investigating the store layout, different fixtures, placement of brands, packaging, pricing and so on. At one level this could be a very bounded problem which AI could conceivably map out and find some means of predicting the way someone would make a choice.

However, life is not this simple, as the decision taking place 'at the shelf' is not as contextless as it might first appear. People come to that shelf with a bunch of assumptions, associations, references, meaning the way they respond to the different information encountered will be very hard to anticipate. Indeed, the different features of that 'shelf environment' may have very little, if any influence on what they choose if they have already determined what they want to buy. In this way, we can see that exactly the same problem, of identifying what the shopper is likely to choose, can be seen as either a 'closed' or 'open' system issue.

Understandably, AI researchers tend to look at the world with a 'closed system' mindset, taking an engineering led, contextless view of problems. On this point Alison Adam's work on feminist technoscience suggests:

"Even ostensibly physical problems, such as the classic example used to teach AI, where a monkey must retrieve a bunch of bananas hanging from a hook on the ceiling by placing a chair correctly and then climbing onto it, are represented in AI in an abstract, mental way. This is despite the fact that this simple

task requires perception, common sense, grasping an object and movement. The monkey will know immediately as it moves through the task which bits of the environment change, and what stays the same. AI would have to recast it in a formal way, with rules and logic etc, to solve it which makes it highly complex despite it being trivial for our monkey". [13]

This is what is known as the frame problem, a particular issue for AI. When presented with an unfamiliar subject, a machine does not 'know' what information of that subject is important and what is irrelevant. A certain amount of knowledge about a subject is necessary to make that determination, and without that information in their database, a computer cannot make the distinction.

The knowledge that AI is dependent upon is never contextless. A nice illustration of this is offered by Terry Winograd on the apparently simple task of language comprehension, which requires a surprisingly large amount of knowledge. Consider the following two sentences: [14]

- The police refused to give the students a permit to demonstrate because they feared violence.

- The police refused to give the students a permit to demonstrate because they advocated revolution.

Untangling what the word "they" referred to in each of the two sentences comes easily to a human despite the identical grammatical structure of the two sentences. We can easily make sense of this as we know well if it is the police or the students who are more likely to fear violence or to advocate revolution. But AI on the other hand will struggle to differentiate between the sentences. The human context in which we operate is everything.

A very tangible example

While this debate may seem conceptual, there are nevertheless some very tangible implications. One example of this is in a paper published by Michal Kosinski and Yilun Wang. They reported that a machine-learning system they had designed was able to differentiate between photos of gay and straight people with an apparently high degree of accuracy. Over thirty-five thousand photographs from dating websites were used along with what was described as facial-recognition software. [15]

When given two pictures – one of a gay person, the other straight – the algorithm was able to successfully distinguish the two in 81% of cases involving photos of men and 74% of images of women. Human judges, by contrast, were only able to correctly classify the straight and gay people in 61% and 54% of cases, respectively. Following this, Kosinski, went on to make bold claims: that such AI will soon be able to measure the intelligence, political orientation, and criminal inclinations of people from the physiology of facial images alone.

Does this mean that AI can tell us things that we ourselves struggle with? As we saw earlier, are we now starting to understand that we are so hopelessly flawed that we will need to rely on AI to give us a clearer sense of ourselves? A vocal critic was found in the shape of Princeton professor Alexander Todorov, a leading authority on faces and psychology. Along with his collaborators he argued Kosinski's approach was in fact flawed: the algorithms could have been identifying patterns in cosmetics usage, facial hair, eye wear and even the angle they held the camera. Self-posted photos on dating websites, Todorov points out, contain a range of information not relating to the physiology of the face itself. [16]

Todorov, along with researchers from Google, tested this using a survey of 8,000 Americans. They asked a wide range of questions including "Do you wear eyeshadow?," "Do you wear glasses?," and "Do you have a beard?," as well as questions about gender and sexual orientation. The study showed that lesbians use eyeshadow less than straight women do, gay men and women wear glasses more, and young opposite-sex-attracted males are much more likely to have prominent facial hair than their gay peers.

Todorov and his colleagues convincingly showed how these obvious differences between lesbian or gay and straight faces in selfies relate to differences in culture, not in facial structure. Using a simple calculation and asking a small number of questions about appearance did almost as well in estimating orientation as the facial recognition AI. This is surely a good case in point of the way that AI offers a seemingly convincing explanation but based on a 'closed system' analysis of the problem. Only when we use what we know of humans and the culture we operate in (and in an 'open system' way) can we get a clearer understanding of the issues. It seems we are not as limited as we had thought but also that we need humans to help us to understand other humans.

The fact that AI pervades so much and appears to have compelling answers surely tells us something about who we are as humans and how our beliefs about ourselves operate.

Brainwashing

By looking back in history, we can see the way that certain beliefs can function as vehicles for our behaviours, shrouding the 'power, politics, and culture' that is in play. One such historical example, which may help us to see the mechanisms underpinning how we live today, is the phenomenon of 'brainwashing'.

The late 1960s saw a significant increase in Western societies in New Religious Movements (NRMs) and the conversion to these groups by young people. This triggered attempts, typically by parents, to rescue their children from these groups. These parents looked for explanations of why their child would join such a group, particularly when the ideologies often directly contradict their own. The answer was often provided by referencing brainwashing theory.

This suggests that conversion to an NRM was the result of forceful programming with a set of beliefs that are completely at odds with the beliefs the convert previously held. In a brilliant essay, writer Elizabeth Young sets out the way that the theory of brainwashing has its provenance in World War Two military studies. In the 1950s brainwashing was used as a convenient explanation for the apparent conversion to communism by American prisoners of war (POW) in China. [17]

Young describes how this theory was taken up by the Anti-Cult Movement (ACM) of the 1970s and continues to be used by these groups to describe what they consider to be the manipulative nature of NRMs, which are often considered to be 'cults'. The usage of the 'cult' word stereotyped NRMs as deviant, irrational and dangerous with belief systems that should not be taken seriously.

In the 1950s, 'brainwashing' was used to explain experiences of American POWs during the Korean War. It was a handy account of indoctrination by the enemy, who purportedly destabilized the prisoners' previous beliefs and replaced them with a total and unquestioning belief in a new set of ideology. Some

POWs were apparently sufficiently impacted by these techniques that they went on to state they believed in Communism, made critical statements against the US, and agreed with accusations that the US was using germ warfare. However, only eleven out of three thousand American POWs who appeared to have been converted to Communism maintained this position once they were free, with the others renouncing beliefs they had stated during imprisonment. CIA-supported research on the eleven prisoners concluded that, when taking into account the personal backgrounds of the former POWs, all had in fact been sympathetic to Communism and averse to American values *prior* to their imprisonment. The views expressed were not significantly at odds from those held before their alleged brainwashing.

Young suggests that brainwashing theory was circulated by the CIA as a propaganda tool aimed at assuring the US public that the allegations made by POWs were completely unsubstantiated and that the Communists must be using brainwashing, as no sane person would ever demonstrate Communist sympathies or germ warfare accusations.

While brainwashing became the core doctrine of the ACM the word 'cult' was appropriated to mean a religion that is maintained by devotion to a charismatic leader, above and beyond adherence to a set of beliefs. The ACM accused 'cults' of using techniques such as administering drugs, malnutrition, and hypnosis to explain why people allegedly professed beliefs seemingly contradictory to those they had previously held. The ACM picked up the term from the CIA disinformation campaign of the 1950s, using it to justify an extreme reaction to 'cults'. Hence just as the US government used brainwashing as a means of propaganda the ACM, also claimed that 'cult' members were victims. Brainwashing theory therefore gave the ACM a degree of scientific legitimacy which allowed for the 'rescue' of 'cult' members.

The CIA undertook two decades of extensive research on brainwashing to create more effectively deployable secret agents but concluded it was a failure. They considered there is no scientifically validated way to indoctrinate someone against their will. Despite this, the notion of 'cult' and of 'brainwashing' continues to be used widely.

This is not to suggest that AI is in anyway a term equivalent to 'cult' or 'brainwashing', but there are perhaps some learnings to draw on. There is always 'power, politics, and culture' wrapped up with deceptively simple terms. And these terms, far from helping us to make sense of the world are in danger of only offering at best a very shallow analysis of any situation and at worst something much more misleading.

The social facts of the chair

This discussion reinforces the way in which we are socially embedded creatures for whom making sense of the world necessarily requires making sense of each other. We cannot simply hand this over the technoscientific authorities that often assume humans can be understood through engineering-led, contextless concepts. As philosopher Mary Midgley points out, our world is social. We cannot make sense of money, parties, football and so on unless we unpick the 'social facts' of the situation:

"These are forms of practice shaped and engaged in by conscious, active subjects through acts performed in pursuit of their aims and intentions. They can therefore only be understood in terms framed to express those subjects' point of view". [18]

Of course, if our problem is purely in the physical world then we can see how this makes sense (although even here it is not without controversy as quantum physicists are finding). But so much of our human world is about 'context', on which basis we can borrow a popular phrase and suggest that shared meaning is a feature not a bug.

To better think this through, we can turn to artist Joseph Koseth. His famous 'One and Three' installations, involved assembling an object, a photograph of that object, and a dictionary definition of the object. His best-known work, 'One and Three Chairs,' seeks to ask what actually constitutes a chair in our minds: is it the solid object we see and use or is it the word "chair" that we use to identify it and communicate it to others?

John Dewey, American philosopher, psychologist and educational reformer also talked about the different way in which a human engages with a chair versus a dog:[19]

"A chair is a different object to a being to whom it consciously suggests an opportunity for sitting down, repose, or sociable converse, from what it is to one to whom it represents itself merely as a thing to be smelled , or gnawed, or jumped over....It is only by courtesy, indeed, that we can say that an unthinking animal experiences an object at all – so largely is anything that presents itself to us as an object made up of qualities it possesses as a sign of other things".

What both Dewey and Koseth are suggesting is that we are not necessarily aware of the meanings we bring to objects and the world in general. We may assume it is obvious what we do with a chair, but this is only because we live in a world of shared meanings. Dewey goes on to say:

"Just what is left of an object stripped of all such qualities of meaning, we cannot well say; but we can be sure that the object is then a very different sort of thing from the objects that we perceive".

We necessarily take for granted the huge range of knowledge, understanding and meaning that we bring to any situation. It is only when something significant changes that we can see the way in which we navigate a world using shared meanings. When we visit a foreign country, we can then see the way in which we have taken for granted the unspoken understandings of our culture as we stumble around with one faux pas after another.

To understand humans, we necessarily need to be part of the rich, complex, multi-faceted layers of meaning that make up human life. We can easily come unstuck by assuming that AI offers a way to make sense of this very human, complex world.

Indeed, this can be dangerous, as AI Now point out when they discuss the use of the technology to detect emotion, suggesting this:

"...raises troubling ethical questions about locating the arbiter of someone's "real" character and emotions outside of the individual, and the potential abuse of power that can be justified based on these faulty claims".[20]

There is much that AI is brilliant for. Proving theorems, playing chess, or even diagnosing medical scans but these typically do not require knowledge outside of the very specific domain in question. For human behaviour we need to remember Koseth's 'One and Three Chairs'. Because we are humans (studying humans) we can so easily forget how much there is of our embedded lives that we simply take for granted.

On being human

There is a curious way in which humans seem at times hell-bent on seeing ourselves as something that is only knowable via the tools that we use. It may be that these are through the way tools offer us models in which we can see and understand ourselves, but more disconcerting are the claims of the way in which technology and data can capture our 'real' inner lives that we ourselves are either unable or unwilling to share.

The degree to which we need to use technology to reveal our inner truths seems overstated. Perhaps it is less exciting to report that we can access our inner truths by asking each other questions and self-reporting. Or are we beguiled by the notion that there is a side to human life for which we have no access, that what we think we know just is not so? This susceptibility to notions that we cannot know ourselves surely means that claims of concepts such as cults and brainwashing have more power than they ought. Simply because we cannot always crystalise and articulate the factors that influence our behaviour does not then mean we are helpless victims of unseen forces.

'Social fact' is a useful term to help understand human behaviour, the way we intuitively operate within the shared knowledge of our friends, family, colleagues, and other inhabitants of this planet. Our behaviour only makes sense in this multidimensional, social, cultural context where we operate to an agreed set of understandings and meanings that are inevitably fluid, as well as being hard to identify at times.

The use of technological concepts to explain our 'inner' human life has surely intensified with the promotion of AI in ever more intimate parts of our lives. But in doing so, this has allowed us to see more clearly the gaps in the arguments, the incompleteness of the accounts and the need, more than ever, to understand the world through very human, social facts.

4: Reading Minds

We have established that we live in a world of shared meaning and social facts but what are the mechanisms that facilitate this? And how does the increased role that technology plays in our lives throw a spotlight on and enhance our understanding of what these mechanisms are?

That humans have endless capabilities for understanding each other in nuanced ways is well understood. We are all aware of the subtle eye roll or glance away that can communicate so much. The smallest of differences in our gestures carries a myriad of meanings that we can understand in a moment.

The ability we have to attribute mental states to others is called Theory of Mind (ToM). [1] Researcher Bertram Malle, asks us to imagine the following:

You observe two people's movements, one behind a large wooden object, the other reaching behind him and then holding a thin object in front of the other. [2]

We need ToM to understand that this simply describes a customer pulling out their credit card with the intention to pay the cashier. If we did not have ToM, we would not understand the sequence of movements or be able to predict either person's likely responses that we simply take for granted. But with the capacity to understand physical movements through mental states, we can interpret this complex scene into the intentional acts of offering and trading.

We understand how to navigate a wide range of situations and, in a way, 'read each other's minds' but how do we manage this when one of the participants is a robot? In a world where we may be cared for in our old age by a robot or drive on a road alongside robot-controlled cars, this is a question that is very much a live issue.

Reading the mind of a robot

Whether robots can be programmed to have a Theory of Mind about humans is addressed by AI researcher, Richard Sutton, in his essay titled "The Bitter Lesson". [3] He argues the history of AI suggests that attempts to build human understanding into computers have to date not worked as what progress there has been is purely through the ability to assert ever more brute computational force to problems.

The "bitter lesson" is that "the actual contents of [human] minds are tremendously, irredeemably complex...They are not what should be built in [to machines]". There will inevitably continue to be speculation about the possibilities of a more generalised intelligence form of AI, but for all intents and purposes we are not close currently and may well never be.

We should therefore turn to the corollary of this: what happens when we try to understand a robot as if it were another person? It is well understood that we use anthropomorphism, the human tendency to attribute human characteristics, either physical or psychological, to non-human agents. Many studies have shown that humans perceive robots as having human qualities, such as Roomba (a vacuum cleaner with a semi-autonomous system). [4] Others have found that we tend to assign greater mental abilities to robots that have a human appearance. It seems, at first glance at least, that ToM is active for humans not only in their relationships with other humans but also through our interactions with robots.

But surely, it's something of a surprise that we might apply ToM principles to technology: we do not do this for a range of other tools in quite the same way. But there are a number of reasons in which we might be forgiven for attempting this.

First, we could argue that the world of 'objects' (as computers clearly are) is not as entirely separate from us as we might think. The boundary between object and subject is in fact much more porous than we sometimes consider. We use tools to extend our capabilities: we can think of a shopping list we scribble out as a means of extending our memory, just as a hammer is a tool, we use to extend our physical capabilities. However, seeing tools as an extension of ourselves is not the same as attributing human-like qualities to them as we seem to do with digital technology.

But given the way in which the tech industry tends to imbue machines with human-like qualities, perhaps it is of little surprise that we do this ourselves. There is certainly a huge interest for technology companies to reduce the gulf between humans and machines, often achieved through appearance. SoftBank Robotics' Pepper, for example, is a "pleasant and likeable" robot built in a humanoid form and designed to serve as a human companion. [5] In addition to the appearance of robotics, is the human voice of digital assistants or indeed navigation aid on mobile phone.

The trouble is that many of these tasks are not actually powered by AI but humans operating behind the scenes. There can be a 'fake it until you make it' approach, with start-ups telling investors and users they have developed a scalable AI technology while quietly relying on human intelligence. [6]

Technology writer Astra Taylor calls this 'Fauxmation':

"AI pushes the human labour out of sight...: if we are in a restaurant, we are very aware of the activity 'behind the scenes', the clatter of the kitchen, the business of the waiting staff. Order food for home delivery via an online app and none of this is visible". [7]

Another example that has had a lot of coverage is the role of human moderators of content on social media, clearing it of upsetting and damaging content in a way that technology has yet to deliver the means to do automatically. [8]

It is therefore perhaps of little surprise that we assume technology has human like qualities; this is very much what we are encouraged to think even if the reality is less than appearance may suggest. But if we are imbuing technology with human characteristics, then what are the results of this in terms of what we can learn about ourselves? In what ways is our relationship with technology offering us a mirror to better understand ourselves? To explore this, we can turn to one of the topics that animates many, that of self-driving vehicles.

Thinking with others: driving

There has been huge excitement at the prospect of autonomous vehicles (AVs) with a great deal of investment pouring into the industry. This is of interest, as the very human nature of driving gives us a close-up view of how humans engage with technology in an especially dynamic manner. As most of us know from our own driving experience, an AV needs to make predictions about human behaviour in real time. For example, this is needed for us to pre-emptively change speed and direction to deal with another driver's decision to abruptly pull in front of our car on a motorway.

The Bitter Lesson seems to be in action here. Work using deep neural networks has shown how an autonomous vehicle can efficiently identify human actions in streaming videos as motion patterns, but they cannot take into account that humans can rapidly change their minds based upon their own thoughts, motivations, and things they see around them. [9] No predictive system functioning purely on past observed motion of the errant car could be accurate enough in such a complex environment as a high-speed busy motorway, without being able to take into account the context and nature of the other agents involved.

Human beings, on the other hand, can forecast others' future likely behaviour just by quickly assessing the 'type' of person involved (perhaps from subtle cues of the car driving behaviour as well as make and model of the car) and the scene around them (such as the forthcoming junction giving us an indication that the car maybe likely to change lane.)

There are many other examples where we can see the way that driving involves a wide array of needs to understand each other's minds. As Malle would point out, driving necessarily involves interpreting the intentions, beliefs, emotions and desires of other drivers. [10] We are constantly making rapid evaluation of other drivers based on their speed, position in the road, proximity to our vehicle, speed they are travelling, make and model of the car and so on. If someone is driving at speed and erratically in a beaten-up old high-performance car, then we can likely draw the conclusion that it is good to steer clear versus someone driving in a predictable manner within the speed limit in a family saloon. This is not to say these conclusions will always be right, but they may well also not be unreasonable.

It is no surprise therefore that accidents involving AVs do happen. For example, a Google car was driving in autonomous mode in the right-hand lane when it met sandbags blocking the street. [11] To navigate the sandbags, the car tried to move into the central lane. The self-driving car, along with the driver, assumed the bus would let them in; but the bus driver thought the car would wait."Unfortunately, all these assumptions led us to the same spot in the lane at the same time. This type of misunderstanding happens between human drivers on the road every day," Google explained.

What this report illustrates is the way that when we are driving, we are constantly working to correctly interpret each other's intentions. Subtle social interaction takes place such as eye contact with drivers being able to quickly confirm each other's actions and intentions with a mere glance. The lack of these social cues from AVs creates difficulties; we assume the usual rules apply but then find to our cost that they do not. Why is that?

Shared intentionality

When we are driving on a busy road, we are experiencing the same event with other drivers. We are all travelling with the shared intention (overall) of getting to our final destinations safely and in a timely fashion. Psychologists Philip Sloman and Steven Fernbach point out that when humans interact with others, we don't simply experience the same event, but we all *know* we are experiencing the same event. [12] This is a subtle but important point that changes much. The awareness of sharing our experience not only changes the nature of the experience but also what we do and what we are able to accomplish. When we are driving on a busy road this is exactly what is happening: we are interacting and to a large degree working together to make sure we do not crash. We work together to slow down at appropriate moments, know when to speed up and so on. Of course, this does not always work – crashes still happen – but these principles are at work.

Through this sharing of attention, we can share common ground as we know things that others also know. We all can sense what other people are doing and what they intend, so as Sloman and Fernbach write: "Once knowledge is shared in this way, we share intentionality – we can jointly pursue a common goal".

This chimes with philosopher Mary Midgely's account of human behaviour:

"When we want to understand a real person's action, we always start by looking for the motivational context. We try to spot the particular reason for the act and then to place it on our general map of motivation, a map that we must all use as we try to find our way through everyday life. We ask, was that

clumsy remark just a misplaced effort to be helpful? Did it express resentment? Was it even part of a spiteful scheme to make trouble? Or perhaps a bit of all three? .... It is the only way we can start to make sense of the life that goes on around us. Of course, it's fallible, but on the whole it works and its success is one of the things that science needs to investigate".[13]

We are socially embedded creatures that live in a world that only makes any sense if we locate 'social facts', the sets of information that we share about each other. Sloman and Fernbach point out that this means humans are capable of complex behaviour, as when multiple cognitive systems work together a shared intelligence can then emerge which goes well beyond what any one individual is capable of:

"Humans are the most complex and powerful species ever, not just because of what happens in individual brains, but because of how communities of brains work together".

ToM is an important means we have to navigate this network of shared understandings to make sense of the world. It is not only something that allows us to connect with other humans more easily, oiling the wheel of everyday relationships, but is an essential part of how the world works.

Computers are simply not part of this – there is a mass of meaning that we carry around with us that is not only subtle and nuanced but is also constantly evolving and changing in unpredictable and non-linear ways. The 'Bitter Lesson' tells us that a computer cannot keep up with this: the shared meaning, so necessary to the activity of driving (and indeed many human activities), is not possible when one of the parties is a machine.

The premium of ToM

This helps us to understand that there is a premium of ease that we receive because of the way ToM operates – we do not have to explain ourselves or seek explanations from others. Of course, we are taking a risk as we may be getting things wrong in the way we infer each other's intentions, beliefs, emotions, and desires. It is not a fool-proof exercise as we can all find out to our costs. But the more we can be confident in our ability to read each other's intentions then the more we can trust each other.[14]

A well-placed act of trust pays significant dividends: for businesses and governments, a level of trust with consumers means that contractual arrangements (to check the validity of the other's claims) can be reduced, thereby avoiding higher transaction costs. Economists Stephen Knack and Phillip Keefer even found a direct relationship between increases in trust (as measured in survey responses) and increases in national economic growth.[15] Therefore, it is in everyone's interests that trust flourishes – without it, society as we know it couldn't exist.

So how does this link to technology? On the one hand, there is a desire to encourage trust by making technology more humanlike, so we are tempted to apply our human-to-human style ToM mechanisms in this context. While it might be a good enough representation for some things, as we saw with autonomous vehicles it is a problem when there is an appearance of ToM not backed up by reality.

I remember vividly conducting a research project on human experiences of AI and watching as a young couple tried to use a Digital Assistant to set an alarm for them to cook some pasta. They kept attempting to set the alarm and adjusting themselves in tone of voice, choice of words and in the end gave up. They had assumed an easy human relationship and were surprised by the rigid way they had to deliver instructions – having to adapt themselves to the machine rather than, as might be the case in a human interaction, being able to find a middle ground.

If we stop trusting someone then we ask them to account for their actions. This links to the discussion around 'explainable AI' which acts as the alternative to Theory of Mind. Elizabeth Holm captured this well when she cited writer Douglas Adams who imagined Deep Thought, a computer programmed to answer the Great Question of Life, the Universe, and Everything. After 7.5 million years of processing, Deep Thought gave its answer: Forty-two. [16]

She suggested this encapsulates the issue we are facing with technology – she asks what good is knowing the answer when it is unclear why it is the answer? What good is a black box?" As she puts it:

Both an engineer and an AI system may learn to predict whether a bridge will collapse. But only the engineer can explain that decision in terms of physical models that can be communicated to and evaluated by others. Whose bridge would you rather cross?

This is all very well but we don't want to have to know the provenance of the bridge designer, we simply want to live in a world where we don't have to think about it. If we are seeking explanations from the technology that is being used then this is an endless task of seeking understanding and checking, an impossible job for any individual.

The UK exam fiasco

I am not targeted with advertising for payday lenders or stopped by the police who are patrolling neighbourhoods that an algorithm directed them to. There is little immediate downside of the way technology is applying ToM principles to me (as far as is visible in my day-to-day life).

But it is increasingly understood that this is not the case for many segments of the population, as set out by Cathy O'Neil in her book, Weapons of Math Destruction. [17] She chronicles the way that algorithms (the Weapons of Math Destruction as she calls them) that claim to quantify important traits such as teaching quality, reoffending risk, creditworthiness can often have problematic outcomes, reinforcing inequality, encoding racism, enabling predatory advertising to target vulnerable people, and even causing a global financial crisis (in the case she uses, sub-prime mortgage).

To some extent, their use to determine outcomes in marginalised segments of the population has meant that the impacts have not always been fully assimilated by others. To examine this, let's look at the way in which the results of the 2020 A-Levels (UK tertiary education exams) for students who never sat their exams due to the pandemic were allocated based on technology in the form of an algorithm. Almost 40% of students received grades lower than they had anticipated, [18] resulting in widespread protests by students across the UK who adopted the chant of "Fuck the algorithm". [19]

It is fair to say that these students felt their trust in the algorithms was misplaced: within days, their protests led officials to reverse course and throw out test scores that the algorithm had generated. [20] Many students were stunned by the way in which their individual results of this analysis were so out of line with what they had not unreasonably expected to achieve. It seems there was no 'sense checking' of the findings – schools were not able to review the results to see if they were appropriate for each student.

Part of the problem here is that machines will always operate in accordance with a set of rules and principles: the algorithm for the exams was operating at the population level not at the level of the individual. This meant that while the overall exam results were in line with the national results that might be expected, the results for any individual were not necessarily so. [1]

When a student receives a piece of paper with their exam grades on them, it is not accompanied by a detailed explanation of the process that were in place that facilitated the grading of their work. There is necessarily a trust in the overall system of how these are arrived at that does not require us to become an expert on education policy and practices.

The endowing of human like properties to an algorithm is not necessarily something that seems as irrational as it may first appear. We are not necessarily imbuing the algorithm with human capabilities; we are using ToM as a shorthand for the context of human values and considerations that we expect that the technology should be operating. And it is only when

---

[1] Another aspect was the way the algorithm placed more weight on the past grades' element of the equation if there were fewer than 15 students in a subject at a school. That meant students at schools (inevitably fee paying) schools were much more likely to benefit from grade inflation than those at larger schools. On this basis, inherent biases were made explicit, revealing to people what they already knew, that our education system is predicated on privileged monied segments of the population being able to afford private education.

they fail to do so that we then seek to dissect the way in which these are operating and demand explanation.

Our use of ToM can be seen as a type of shorthand operation, allowing us to suspend the need to analyse details about how or why we know something. If we had to operate in a manner where everything is explained, then it is more effortful but also simply not needed much of the time.

Context is everything

As science historian Lorraine Daston put it:

"…no universal ever fits the particulars. Never in the history of human rulemaking have we created a rule or a law that did not stub its toe against unanticipated particulars". [21]

She makes the point that the human labour involved in avoiding toe-stubbing is often erased from history despite the way that "effective functioning has been dependent on high-level judgment, often performed by those on the low end of the hierarchical division of labor".

In a way the work that is being done is making the equipment fit for purpose, manually buttressing them with the codes and cues needed to work with other equipment (e.g., road layouts, exam setting) but also all the assumed knowledge and shared intentionality that we have.

Matthew Crawford makes this point nicely when he writes:

... chopsticks are part of a practice of dining that includes, for example, the use of bowls rather than plates, and the preparation of sticky rice rather than, say, loose peas...Chopsticks belong to a different equipmental whole than forks and knives....Rather, in using things like chopsticks, or fork and knife, we involve ourselves in norms: it is just understood that one does things a certain way. These norms are for the most part inarticulate; they are tacit in social practices and in the equipment we use. This is one way in which other people condition the way the world presents itself to us, even when we do not interact with them.[22]

At one level, anthropomorphising technology looks as if we are framing our relationship with technology as a matter between the individual and a specific device or app and in doing so not considering the wider social, moral, and infrastructural relations. But in fact, what we are doing is using this as a shorthand for what we expect these wider relationships to be, what we think they should look like, what roles and norms they should adhere to.

Unpicking this allows us to understand the way that our thoughts and way of living do not exist on their own, in some sort of abstract space, waiting for individuals to see them by the light of pure reason. Instead, we can see the way that we make sense of the world and each other is through the context of our shared meanings.

As sociologist Zeynep Tufekci notes, [23] suppose we are standing on top of a high building and I say to someone: "They jumped". The *literal* meaning of this seems obvious: That someone has jumped. However, the context adds meaning so that it makes sense to construe the claim "they jumped" as, "Someone has jumped off the building". If then it becomes apparent that I am reporting my friend has simply jumped up and down once, there would be grounds to complain that I was being misleading, that someone had jumped off the building. [24]

In just the same way, the cues used by technology sets a context of shared meanings: if we are driving, we expect the shared intentionality of navigating our busy road alongside other drivers with all the norms, customs, and practices that this brings. Similarly, if we get exam results, we expect there to have been a backdrop of our individual performance to have been considered above other influences.

The way in which technology is described, the way it is designed, the applications it is put to are never neutral: instead, we can see the design features as 'social affordances', setting expectations for the way the technology in question works with our shared meanings, intentionality's, and our wider lives generally. But at the same time, what we have seen in this exploration is the way in which this wider setting is not something that is always crystallised and understood by people, that we use the shorthand of anthropomorphism to express the expectations that we have.

On being human

ToM means people are transformed from 'objects' into 'subjects' who can act intentionally and who have desires, beliefs, attitudes and so on that direct their actions. We need to understand other minds in order to engage in the complexity of the interactions that life in communities requires of us.

We explain *intentional* behaviours, by using a sophisticated framework of interpretation. Intentional behaviour must involve a desire for an outcome, beliefs about how a particular deed will result in that outcome, and the intention to carry out that deed; if the person then performs the deed, we understand it as an intentional action.

As such the proliferation of technology has shown us more clearly the way that as humans we operate in a teleological manner, in that we behave purposefully. That sets us on a very different trajectory than many accounts of human behaviour that suggest we are more 'reactive' to the world. Inherent in this explanation must be the importance of our inner selves, operating proactively in the world.

But even more than this, we can also see the way in which humans are extending the language and meaning of our active inner worlds to use as a means of explanations of the external world. Using this language as shorthand to explain the apparently non-human makes sense as, of course, the algorithms of the digital world in which we increasingly live are shaped by the human.

This leads us down a route where we are surely starting to see the way in which this shared language and meanings of intentionality references something deep and important. We are starting to get a sense that human consciousness is perhaps something that does not just reside in our heads. Instead, it is starting to dawn on us that this assumption that has been dominant in Western thinking for centuries, needs to be amended as it is becoming evident that our purposefulness, our intentionality, our self-awareness is something that very much sits between us and does not simply reside in our heads.

5: Life in the Multiverse of Truths

The importance of technology for measurement purposes has been increasingly apparent, given COVID and climate change are phenomena that we can only really measure and understand by using technology. Indeed, we live in a world where integration of digital technology means ever more of our behaviours are represented by data. Not only are we communicating by technology through social media or messaging but our behaviours are intimately tracked, for example, what we have chosen to buy, what we have searched for online or increasingly where we have been.

But at the heart of all this information that we have about ourselves, there is a subtle but critically important point. To what extent can the data that is chosen to represent us, reflect the reality of our many and varied lives? In a world of economic polarisation do statistics about national or global financial well-being reflect the life of many communities whose lives have hugely suffered due to COVID?

There is a tension between the way in which technology means that data is more available than ever before but at the same time this data risks not representing the very people whose lives it is intended to reflect. If there is no basis on which we can locate a shared understanding of how the world is, so that we are forever referencing different data sets with different interpretations, then we fail to navigate our collective lives and we risk falling into a position of polarisation and discord.

Our data centric world

Of course, humans have always attempted to represent the world through data – think mapping, scientific experiments, weather forecasting, censuses. But what has changed is the degree to which technology has today facilitated this process. Digital technology has fundamentally altered our ability to quantify the world both through the way in which phenomena are now effectively transformed into data but also via our ability to store and then make sense of that information.

The value of access to data is clear: whether we are a commercial organisation, government, or other public body, it is typically considered that we need a commonly agreed starting point. Some form of shared understanding about the world seems to be required if there is to be a possibility of progress and peaceful dispute resolution. Governments need data on the economy, health, wellness and so on. For brands, 'score-cards' will encompass a wide range of commercial metrics, employee measures, and consumer insights.

We take for granted that these numbers offer us straightforward and even irrefutable 'facts', and while we may disagree about policy or strategy, the data we use is expected to offer an objective description, that we can all agree on, of the world we inhabit.

Political sociologist William Davies describes this as the legacy of the Scientific Revolution that occurred in the seventeenth century. [1] The creation of modern government during that time not only required methodical record-keeping by a central professional administrative structure, but also depended on the emergence of people able to collect and make sense of this data. Davies sets out the way that the original premise of the disciplines that arose from this was to create the basis for a shared social understanding and therefore peace.

But we have challenges to this project. First, the way we are represented by data collected about us is being questioned in fundamental ways: when we look in the mirror of data collected about us, is it ourselves that we see? Second, our capability to make sense of the data collected about us is under scrutiny and many psychologists consider that we are to be found wanting. We deal with each of these in turn.

Our world as it was

It is tempting to think that we can collect data that offers a shared understanding of the world. Indeed, for us to avoid simply throwing 'alternative facts' at each other, then some form of agreement of the world as represented in data, is still as essential for peace as ever. But what are some of the challenges with this?

First, as media historian Lisa Gitelman points out, "'Raw Data' is an Oxymoron," [2] indicating that selection of data necessarily involves making decisions: about which data to look at, what variables to generate, what constitutes an outlier, and so on. These decisions involve human judgement, often well intentioned, but guided by assumptions or hypotheses concerning what is important and why. Indeed, we have seen the way in which COVID strained the relationship between policy and scientists use data. The notion that government policy was simply 'following the science' drew much criticism that this justified policy decisions that might otherwise have been more closely scrutinised. [3]

But alongside this there has been a hollowing out of the role of experts who collect and present data, suggesting that their 'objective' lens is a smokescreen for their own vested interests: Indeed, Michael Gove famously suggested that we have all had enough of experts. [4]

There has always been a balancing act on this issue. As Davies points out:

"The expert culture that was born in the late seventeenth century viewed society as just another physical object to be measured and observed, like human anatomy or the movement of the planets, and yet experts are also inhabitants of society, benefiting from its progress, potentially converting their own influence into money and power. This same problem afflicts expertise today".

Today we can see the way in which official numbers, whether from commercial organisations or government departments do not sit outside of politics. Many people consider that the data they see offers a version of reality that only reflects the world of a small and privileged proportion of society. As Angela Saini points out in her books ('Superior: The Return of Race Science', [5] and 'Inferior: How Science Got Women Wrong' [6]), expertise and the data that is collected can be used as a cover for fundamentally problematic views concerning gender and ethnicity.

The cause of this is, in no small part, self-inflicted: data can be collected and leveraged in a selective manner to justify commercial and policy activity rather than being sought a means of genuine insight. Too often the direction of travel can appear to start with the conclusion and *then* work back to find data to fit and validate the decision. This has led to a decline in confidence of data. Although 90% of people trust the

Office for National Statistics, it seems that only 26% trust the Government to represent the statistics in an honest fashion. [7]

The second point is whether we are collecting data that reflects what matters. There is a beguiling sense of authority to 'data' that can make it hard to disagree with. Often data that has been collected in an apparently neutral way via technology (such as data that passively tracks our behaviour, such as mobile phone records) which is considered superior and used to challenge other sources such as self-report survey data. Of course, this hides the wide variety of ways in which any data collection process comes with its own biases in the way it represents of the world.

On this, Davies suggests that "Numbers allow us to see the world objectively, but the flip side of that is that they eliminate feeling". He cites the way that, over time, numbers became a way of signalling that one was being objective and apolitical, focused on facts and immune to sentiment (see also Susan Herbst for more on this). [8] As such, personal accounts of lived experience can be relegated as being less important: numbers that have been collected may reflect what I am doing, how I am behaving in great detail. The data that is collected may offer a range of insights into the socioeconomic circumstances of the population. But they do not necessarily tell you what people are thinking or feeling.

Indeed, Matthew Salganik of Princeton University points out that some of the most important social outcomes and predictors are internal states, such as emotions, knowledge, expectations, and opinions. Internal states exist only inside people's heads, and sometimes the only way to learn about internal states is to ask. He goes on to say,

"Researchers who study dolphins can't ask them questions. So, dolphin researchers are forced to study behaviour. Researchers who study humans, on the other hand, should take advantage of the fact that our participants can talk". [9]

What we do matters but what is in our minds is equally important (if not more so). If we simply measure what people are doing rather than how they feel, or how they think about things, then we can fail to represent what really matters to us.

Davies points out that many of the classic economic indicators that are used to reflect societies are captured at the aggregate: GDP captures our economic well-being in the aggregate, and GDP per capita captures what this means for people on average. The challenge here is the degree to which taking an average really reflects anyone's life. The UK has the most extreme geographic polarisation of wealth and deprivation of any country in western Europe. The output per head in West London is eight times higher than it is in the Welsh Valleys; during the coalition government of 2010–15, median household wealth in London rose by 14%, while it fell by 8% in Yorkshire and on the Humber. The disproportionate wealth of London is the reason that Britain's economy is the fifth largest in the world: the majority of UK regions have a GDP per capita below the European average. [10]

Market and social researchers are acutely aware of the need to represent different groups, but granular data collection can be expensive. A national sample of interviews is much lower cost than a quota-based sample designed to properly reflect regional, social class and age differences. As power and resources have gradually become concentrated in specific cities and regions then relying on nationally representative numbers to represent all the population is, arguably, increasingly challenging.

The human deficit

Alongside questions about the adequacy of the way in which we are represented by the data collected about us, there are questions relating to our ability to make sense of this. It is to this we now turn.

One of the disciplines that emerged to make sense of the new sources of data was economics, which focuses on the behaviour and interactions of consumers and seeks to represent the way economies work. It is today broadly recognised that classical economics tended to assume that people have flawless data and can, therefore, make optimal, rational decisions. Of course, this was challenged by Herbert Simon [11] and continued by Daniel Kahneman who worked to develop 'a coherent alternative to the rational agent model'. [12]

Bounded rationality was the term that Simon developed to reflect the notion that optimal, rational decisions will always be limited by the complexity of the decision problem, the restrictions of the person trying to solve the problem, and the time available to make the decision. On this basis, people inevitably act as 'satisficers', aiming for a 'good enough' solution rather than always seeking to optimise.

This 'deficit' model of human behaviour is often applied to the way in which we go about navigating the wealth of data we have available today. It is claimed we live in an age of information overload, described as 'infobesity', with vivid descriptions of the problem:

"An uncontrollable flood of it overwhelms us, and we feel stressed. Our systems shut down, and our capacity to absorb additional information actually decreases. To cope with the flood, our brains develop tricks and habits. We rely more on information that is closer to home than on information from a distant source. We remember data presented in one format and forget data presented in another. ... All such reactions hamper our ability to make decisions based on the best available evidence, and performance suffers accordingly".[13]

It is also frequently argued that the public is simply poorly ill-informed when it comes to rudimentary facts and issues of scientific consensus. Part of this is laid at the door of the 'cognitive load' of acquiring knowledge. As academic researcher Daniel Williams puts it:

"For a typical citizen in a modern democracy with one vote among millions, the benefits of being informed are meagre. By contrast, the costs of becoming informed are significant, especially when compared to spending time and energy on things that are more enjoyable or impactful".[14]

Williams suggests we have rational motivated ignorance: that is, knowledge is just as frequently a liability as it is a source of power. If we do not know about something then it protects us from difficult truths, saves us from taking responsibility for our actions. [15]

Second, it is a not uncommon suggestion that our limited capabilities mean we are unable to process the sheer volume of data that claims to represent us, so we fall back into superstitious ways to pull stories from it. If we cannot deduce the rational reality sitting behind the data then we are irrational, using all manner of short cuts which leave us vulnerable to manipulation or simply poor interpretation.

A crippled epistemology?

Cass Sunstein was perhaps reflecting this perspective when he suggested conspiracy theorists suffer from a 'crippled epistemology', in the sense that they know very few things, and what they know is wrong. [16] But also, that they operate in informationally isolated social networks.

This 'deficit model' of how we intuitively understand the world follows the perspective that the human brain did not evolve to process complex information about politics, economics, or science. Rather, we evolved to survive on the savannah, where dealing with threats took our attention. According to New Scientist this means that we evolved to:

"...assume that unseen threats are lurking everywhere, that "outgroups" have malign intent, or that coincidental events are causally related. The cost of holding these assumptions was minimal, but the cost of not holding them was often death. Natural selection favoured the conspiratorial mindset". [17]

So why do may people seem to hold conspiratorial beliefs that seem at odds with the way the vast majority of the population look at an issue? The answer is surely multi-layered but one point relevant here is that we can all be persuaded to perspectives that may at first sight seem ridiculous. We can potentially succumb to a gradual 'slippery slope' of beliefs, where accepting one set of beliefs can then make another one more plausible. Psychologist Dan Ariely talks about this in relation to cheating:

"I have had lots of discussions with big cheaters – insider trading, accounting fraud, people who have sold games in the NBA, doping in sports. With one exception, all of them were stories of slippery slopes. You look at the sequence of the events – you look at the end – and you say, my goodness, what kind of monster would do this? But then you look at the first step they took and say, I can see myself under the right amount of pressure behaving badly. Then they took another step, another step, and another step".[18]

There is not a one step process of acquiring a set of beliefs, we are instead in a more dynamic process of belief acquisition and change. And of course, much has been said about the role of social media in "doing the heavy work of locating vulnerable people and guiding them through a series of ever-more-extreme ideas and communities". [19]

Does this mean that we are in a situation where confidence in data is undermined and, in its place, we are seeking our own explanations that sit outside a shared understanding of the world? Are we in danger of all slowly occupying our own separate worlds where we are increasingly out of touch with each other and even reality, pre-occupied by ever more unrealistic conspiracy theories? [20]

Our world transformed

There is a tension at the heart of conspiracy theories, as demonstrated by one of the leading theorists in this area, researcher Sander van der Linden who writes:

Clearly, people and governments have conspired against each other, throughout human history. Healthy skepticism lies at the very heart of the scientific endeavor. Yet there is something fundamentally dangerous and unscientific about the nature of conspiracy theorizing. [21]

In a sense, as philosopher Matthew R. X. Dentith points out, van der Linden is exposing the challenge at the heart of conspiracy theories: which is that we understand that conspiratorial activity is perfectly legitimate in a democracy. [22] At times governments need to be secretive to realise future benefit and commercial organisations need to deny some a claim of wrongdoing to be able to fully investigate it. But of course, governments and businesses *can* conspire and do wrong. Which means that the notion that there is something dangerous and unscientific about conspiracy theorizing is a problematic position.

There are also many examples of stories we think are incredible and must clearly be wrong and yet they turn out to be true. Denith flags the way that stories about the police and politicians protecting high profile sexual offenders from investigation might seem unthinkable, but also that if it had happened, it surely would have been exposed by the authorities. Yet as the Operation Yewtree investigation in the UK showed, well known men preyed on young men and women in the 1970s and 1980s. Attempts to expose this were ignored and even covered up by powerful members of British society. From Nixon to the Weapons of the Mass Destruction of Iraq, there are many examples of conspiracy theories that were found to be true.

Indeed, this is the same if we are on the other side of the fence: there are many instances where someone has claimed there to be a conspiracy, leading them to being accused of being a conspiracy theorist and then later being vindicated for having been right in the first place! The point is that what we know is not something static to be uncovered: the notion of what is reasonable or unreasonable to believe is not something that is fixed in time.

This leads us to an important point: it is a comfortable position to assume that there is one single, legitimate, and rational way of looking at the world which is there waiting for us to uncover. But in just the same way that we can be led through down a 'slippery slope' to more extreme views of the world, so it can be the case that what we understand to be true is something that changes over time as more information becomes available. It also depends on what we have come to know about the world both in terms of the past and present.

But if we find ourselves not represented in the data that we are seeing, if the data appears motivated by values that are antipathetical to our experience, or if it simply does not represent our concerns then we might be excused not paying attention to it.

It is surely less about 'irrationality', 'motivated ignorance' or 'crippled epistemologies' and more that there is more than one legitimate way of seeing the world. Just as what might at first sight appear to be a conspiracy theory can turn out to be true.

Implications

As pointed out earlier, in physical science it can be more easily argued that there is a single objective way of looking at the world. There is a huge temptation to assume that the logic and mechanisms of the physical world can be applied to human behaviours – it seems logical and 'scientific'.

If we believe the deficit model, then we implicitly accept the notion and possibility of a single, perfect, rational outcome. There is an implication that someone, somewhere can determine the best options and outcomes. But when it comes to human behaviour then what is rational is inevitably a function of the individual, how they interpret the world which is itself shaped by context of their lives. Even when our behaviour may look the same, the reasons for it can be entirely and utterly different.

Psychologist Teppo Felin talks about the way that as humans it seems natural to us that there is world that exists independently to how we think about it just waiting to be uncovered. [23] Of course, we can only ever seek to represent the world in our heads: this is the 'Bucket theory' of perception which suggests information we collect about the environment is passive and automatic. We assimilate a world that exists independent of ourselves, and our limitations means we can get this wrong.

Felin suggests an alternative approach of our beliefs reflecting the world in a similar way to a road map representing a landscape. Points on the map represent towns and cities, lines represent roads and motorways. We cannot externally verify and validate our beliefs: we cannot know the world independently from our own experience. This is the 'Searchlight theory' of perception: the way we make sense of the world is active, using guesses, theories, questions, and hypotheses, which means that the way we comprehend things is by directing perception and attention.

However, our representation of reality is necessarily based on a whole range of contexts, motivations, and backgrounds. Our perception is less about capturing a reality that is waiting for us through our limited abilities, and more that perception is always a function of the nature, abilities and aims of the people involved. This means that the closest we can get to any final agreed 'objective' truth is when we reach a consensus, and not when we are perfectly aligned. That simply will not happen. Indeed, we are suspicious of those that claim to be in possession of absolute truths.

The notion that there can only ever be one way of representing the world is looking problematic – we have different perspectives – which of course can become disconnected from the general consensus. [24] Which means there is a delicate balancing act to be had about the way we represent the multiverse of perspectives while at the same time facilitating a shared understanding of the world.

What we can do

The argument that Davies set up is that we need to have some reasonable degree of shared understanding of how the world works. Davies suggests this can also slide into assuming there is only one single legitimate view of the world. When we look closely at 'truth' then we can start to see that we all hold many different versions of it. But at the same time, we can all too easily dismiss alternative truths as problematic, as deficits in the way others see the world.

Indeed, one of the problems with tackling conspiracy theories is that each group (the conspiracy theorists and the critics or different sides of a political debate) tend to set out to disprove the other – rather than respectfully and open-mindedly looking into the claims and concerns. [25] Instead, it seems sensible to attempt to represent and respect the diversity of 'truths' that people have about the world. The motivation for this is pragmatic – government policy and commercial strategy have both long recognised this is needed to help ensure success in design and adoption of any initiative. Many has been the innovation that seems perfectly reasonable in theory and should be a resounding success but if people believe it is problematic then it will fail.

Sitting at the heart of asking people questions and ensuring a detailed representation of perspectives, values, attitudes, beliefs, and behaviours is an implied but not always recognised and articulated understanding. This is that there are multiple, perfectly valid truths held by different groups in the population that need to be identified, measured, shared, and understood. Of course, we do not need to agree with other people's truth, but we do need to recognise the legitimacy of them holding that perspective.

The actions of those that stormed the Capitol building were clearly problematic. But their actions do need to be understood and not purely dismissed as the irrational activities of a lunatic fringe. As one protestor put it, "I listen to my president, who told me to go to the Capitol". [26] Without this understanding we simply fall into delegitimizing the views of others by dismissing them as irrational and as such we fail to examine and understand them. This surely reduces meaningful discourse rather than enhances it. [27]

We sit in a world which has an abundance of data, all of which promises to tell us about people. While data may allow this, we are reliant on the skills of people who know and can navigate this landscape, who have a constant focus on ensuring representativeness but also to provide a way of weaving the data into a broad basis of understanding of the multiverse of minds.

Managing the multiverse

Reaching the conclusion that there is no singular 'rational' way to view the world and that we need to take care to represent, understand and respect the views of diversity of beliefs of the population chimes with psychologist Adam Grant. He challenges the way we favour the 'comfort of conviction over the discomfort of doubt, and prefer opinions that make us feel good, instead of ideas that make us think hard'.[28]

He talks about the way we can each carry with us the mindset of three different professions: preachers, prosecutors, and politicians. We become a preacher if believe our beliefs are threatened. We feel the need to deliver earnest speeches to protect and further our philosophies. And we become prosecutors when we identify errors in other people's thoughts and aim to show how they are wrong. When we want to be liked and look for approval, we become a politician.

We are too often preaching that we are in fact right, prosecuting those we consider are wrong, and engaging in politics to gain approval. The problem is that this does not leave us much time to reflect on our own beliefs and examine what we hold to be true. Instead, success requires us to adopt a fourth profession – that of the scientist."Treat your strategy as a hypothesis and your product as an experiment," he proposes. This approach values humility over pride, questioning over conviction and curiosity over closure. Instead of starting with the answers, we lead with questions, and see where the inquiry goes.

Research on the most important driver of any forecasters' success in prediction found it was less about intelligence and more to do with the extent to which they updated their beliefs. [29] Grant points out that "The best forecasters went through more rethinking cycles. They had the confident humility to doubt their judgements and the curiosity to discover new information that led them to revise their predictions".

In many ways we are already in a multiverse revolution: we have seen a decline in a single agreed understanding of the world as represented by a small group of experts. Instead, we are in active negotiation where we need to think like scientists, challenging our own narratives and interpretations and having the confidence to examine the hypotheses proposed by others. And this is the transformation – working out how to operate effectively in a multiverse and seek connection, overlaps and common ground while respecting difference and diversity in beliefs, attitudes, and behaviours.

On being human

That we can only really understand COVID and climate change as a function of the data we collect and through tools to make sense of it, has forced us to look more closely at the way these issues shape how we understand the world. The debates about how we use data, whose story it tells, the role of the analyst in shaping the narrative have emerged from the fringes to centre stage in our thinking. To what extent are the numbers we are seeing reflecting our own experiences? And if they do not, then why is that and to whose experience do they speak?

The political dimension of data analysis and science has long been a live debate in philosophical circles, but it is now becoming something that our recent experiences have brought centre stage. The apparent increase in conspiracy theorising and misinformation can be reconsidered – they are not always irrational and incoherent ramblings and instead we can start seeing them (although not all by any means) as legitimate challenges to received wisdom. They may seem at times to struggle to express things in a coherent manner, but this is understandable given the way in which dominant narratives that we live by means alternative perspectives can seem odd and at times hard to understand.

Against the backdrop of our monotheistic legacy, accepting that we live in a multiverse is in some way a radical position to take, challenging the way in which we have intuitively operated for centuries. Moving from a position where we assume that there is a consensus, a shared understanding of the world is not so hard for those who have not been represented in that narrative and have felt alienated and marginalised as a result. The work to be done is with what has been represented, to rethink the very nature of knowledge, respecting the plurality of perspectives and the validity of others' very different lived experiences.

SECTION 2: ESCAPING

Against the backdrop of climate change, COVID and technology disruption, it is understandable that much is written about change: how we live in changing times, the importance of personal transformation, the way in which powerful forces that may be hard to identify and control, are all driving change. In this section we will explore the different themes that are emerging, how the way in which the narratives about change that we have long held dear are now themselves fundamentally changing.

Much of what we will be exploring is the way in which we are now able to see more clearly the way in which our future is not inevitable – our past does not necessarily determine the way we will be moving forwards. This ties in with the way humans are purposive, proactive, creative and intelligent, able to see new opportunities and not simply be a prisoner of what has gone before.

Climate change, more than anything else, has imbued this discussion with a new urgency as in many ways this plays to the opposite point. The carbon released over the last few decades will have catastrophic effects for our collective futures that we will not be able to influence. However, this very fact has brought to front of mind that what we do now, how we organise ourselves and actively manage our futures is in our hands. We can choose that, or we can seek escape, from time, our bodies and even from ourselves.

6: On Changing

When COVID struck we more clearly understood how we can often successfully change and adapt to new conditions to protect populations. But of course, some of the changes made for COVID were devastating. For example, the impact on the world's mental health has been huge: disruption to schooling, home and working life led to a mental health epidemic with, in the UK alone, with 1.6 million waiting for specialised treatment and another 8 million who were unable to even get on the waiting list. [1]

Paradoxically this backdrop helps us examine more clearly the issue of human flourishing, how we go about exploring and enacting the best possible versions of ourselves and rearranging the environment to allow this.

This covers what can seem to be a forgotten part of being human: that of enacting desired outcomes so that we can flourish rather than simply survive. The business of change and transformation has long been recognised as difficult. The poet John Keats used the term Negative Capability to describe the skills and strength needed to manage this transformation, describing the state as being "…when a man is capable of being in uncertainties, mysteries, doubts, without any irritable reaching after fact and reason".[2]

We set out a number of complexities involved in thinking about change: how the desired behaviours are not always obvious, but also how the environment we are in can challenge our ability to enact those behaviours. Also, how our choices of behaviour are acts that occur in a human social, cultural context, as it is surely it is this which grants meaning beyond a simple hedonic experience. The case is made for a broader reading of the psychology literature, challenging a narrow 'rear-view mirror' perspective of humans. [3]

We are in a world in which we are now pushed into clear headed thinking about change. We can start to understand how this requires us to align the complex interactions between people and the environments we live in to reach outcomes that offer meaning and allow us to flourish.

Flourishing & behaviour change

Since Aristotle, there have been many ways in which we might think about what flourishing means. Philosopher Susan Wolf offers a 'Fitting-Fulfilment' view of flourishing suggesting, that indulging one's passions offers a particularly rewarding type of subjective experience, but this is not in itself what is valuable. [4] She considers the thing we love doing must also be 'objectively good'. And this is in part to do with a need that we can see one's life as valuable in a way that can be seen from a perspective other than our own.

Our drive for this is due in part to our need to see ourselves from an objective, external perspective. As philosopher Thomas Nagel would say, we are unique as a species as we are able to have a 'view from nowhere' upon ourselves. [5] In addition to this, we have a need for self-esteem. We want to be able to see ourselves as good and valuable.

We might add to this, considers Wolf, in this way:

"The thought that one's life is like a bubble that, upon bursting, will vanish without trace can lead some people to despair. The thought that one lives in an indifferent universe makes some people shudder".

If we can think of ourselves as being engaged in a behaviour of independent worth, then we may be able to put aside these feelings of despair. The feeling of being involved in a behaviour that has value, independent of our own narrow self-interests, means we become part of a community, sharing values and a common purpose. As Wolf puts it:

"By engaging in projects of independent value, by protecting, preserving, creating, and realizing value the source of which lies outside of ourselves, we can

satisfy these interests. Indeed, it is hard to see how we could satisfy them in any other way".

Our desire for a meaningful life is not about *feeling* a particular way but an interest that life *be* a certain way, one that can be admired by others and is connected in some way with independent value. Philosopher Lucas Scripter reminds us not to interpret this in too 'elitist' a manner – as he points out, not everyone is cut out to be a Steve Jobs or a Jane Austen. Rather, meaning is as much reflected in 'ordinary meaningful lives' involving personal relationships and aesthetic experiences. [6]

Nevertheless, the point we can take from Susan Wolf is the drive for meaningfulness which has an active component – behaviours need to take place. To flourish, it is not enough to dream, there needs to be action, as Goethe famously pointed out:

"Knowing is not enough; we must apply. Willing is not enough; we must do".

This is consistent with philosopher Agnes Callard's perspective when she points out in her book about change, 'Aspiration', that:

"Valuing involves more than caring: when we value something, we also evaluate it as in some way good or worth caring about". [7]

Dimensions of navigating change

The psychologist Kurt Lewin talked about the way in which change requires us to first 'unfreeze' our mental landscapes. [8] If we remain fixed in the ways we approach the world, then we leave no opportunity for change. But once unfrozen, do we always know what we want and how we want to flourish? What we are aiming for can often be unclear as writer Rebecca Solnit points out:

"The things we want are transformative, and we don't know or only think we know what is on the other side of that transformation. Love, wisdom, grace, inspiration – how do you go about finding these things that are in some ways about extending the boundaries of the self into unknown territory, about becoming someone else". [9]

Again, Agnes Callard also talks about this theme of uncertainty of transformation when she suggests:

"The aspirant's idea of the goodness of her end is characterized by a distinctive kind of vagueness, one she experiences as defective and in need of remedy".

This type of change is harder than a related theme, 'ambition,' which Callard describes as follows:

"An ambitious agent's behaviour is directed at a form of success whose value she is fully capable of grasping in advance of achieving it. Hence ambition is often

directed at those goods—wealth, power, fame—that can be well appreciated even by those who do not have them".

For a human to unfreeze and flourish then we may need to think of this in terms of 'aspiring' rather than 'ambition'. There is a period of intense uncertainty where we try and work out the direction we take. Indeed, when we embark on a venture of transformation that enables us to flourish, Callard would argue that people are usually aware that they will change in ways that are impossible to know and hard to understand. There is no one single point, rather a period of continuous change:

"When one makes a radical life change, one does not submit oneself to be changed by some transformative event or object; one's agency runs all the way through to the endpoint. The nature of that agency, as I shall argue, is one of learning: coming to acquire the value means learning to see the world in a new way".

This suggests that if we 'aspire' to flourishing, then we are continually reviewing, anticipating, changing not only as we learn and understand but as the external environment around us changes.

The external change-challenge

As we well know, our environment can sometimes change dramatically. COVID is an example of a dramatic change that was imposed on us. Suddenly we had a strict curtailing of a wide range of activity that we once considered normal. Many of the routines we had acquired to manage our world were suddenly no longer relevant, they had offered us mastery of a world that no longer existed. We were collectively and rapidly 'unfrozen,' to navigate a very fluid situation.

Sociologist Zygmunt Bauman suggests that we live in 'Liquid Times' where thinking, planning, and acting deteriorate over the long term. [10] This era of uncertainty is not a temporary stage but inevitable and permanent which means that people will have even more to worry about in the future. German sociologist Hartmut Rosa refers to 'social acceleration', or 'the shrinking of the present', making reliable expectations of the future increasingly problematic and fluid. [11]

This is against a backdrop of more liberalisation and privatisation that have increased the variety of products and services available in a wider range of areas from finance service and pensions to energy supply and telecoms. We are all now expected to make educated choices from of a wide range of options available. [12]

Linked to this, people no longer turn to the usual guides for behaviour whether it be the bank, doctors, media, teachers. These professions are all being disrupted as well and the extent to which consumer behaviour is now guided by these past gate keepers is, at best, debateable. In addition, when we were in environments with what philosopher Matthew

Crawford calls 'social affordances' in the form of close family, colleagues, and friends, these can lightly direct us into actions that we may well find rewarding and meaningful. But these societal structures are arguably giving way to more individualistic points of reference.[13]

The implication of this is that people must be increasingly self-reliant, working out how best to navigate increasingly complex environments and, within this, working out how to steer towards our own ends that may often be vague and unclear.

The social change challenge

As Wolf has pointed out, meaningful behaviours do not sit in a vacuum – they are only given meaning and purpose through understanding the interchange between the human inner life and the social context. As such, theories which seek to find explanations of human behaviour by leaning on notions of automaticity (such as the work of cognitive psychologists such as Daniel Kahneman [14]), will surely struggle to account for a full understanding of when, where, how and why humans seek meaning and a desire to flourish in their lives. Wolf points out that an understanding of the context in which the behaviour is embedded is critical – behaviour never takes place in a vacuum.

This is becoming increasingly clear as we see the increased popularity of more socially oriented explanations of behaviour. For example, Social Representation Theory (SRT) looks at the way behaviour can be understood based on the way sociocultural and cognitive processes impact the way new information is integrated with existing representations. From this perspective, two processes are key: anchoring and objectifying. Anchoring is how existing knowledge, based not only on individual ideas, but also shared language, and socio-historical beliefs, shapes how new information is understood.[15] Objectification is how the abstract connection with existing knowledge becomes more concrete and based on current experiences – through images, symbols, and metaphors. [16] With SRT we have a convincing explanation for the inter-dependency of behaviours between the individual and the social environment.

But with this we can see more clearly that change is not only a function of our own internal characteristics but also the physical environment we inhabit, as well as the social context of our lives.

If we are to help people change, as seems important given COVID, climate change and technology disruption then we need to properly understand what the mechanisms are that determine our behaviour. If we can identify these, we can then help make use of them to help facilitate better outcomes.

Rear view mirror psychology

If we are to understand the mechanisms that determine our behaviour, then we are naturally drawn to the discipline of psychology. But the discipline seems all too often to look at behaviour through a 'rear-view mirror', surely at odds with the challenge of flourishing. After first examining this focus of the discipline, we will examine an alternative perspective.

The apotheosis of this 'rear view' approach to understanding human behaviour is the popular notion that much of our behaviour is automatic, with some claims that as much as 95% of our behaviour is automatic and as such, non-conscious. While there is little evidence to support such as bold claim, [17] it is useful to consider the source of this perspective, which has its roots in the early twentieth century psychology of Behaviourism.

This assumed that human behaviour could be understood with animal experiments, and that our behaviour is largely automatic, the result of stimulus and responses that we have been exposed to in our pasts. The evidence for this came from animal studies where experimenters observed that rewards or punishments could be used to shape certain behaviours, such as rats choosing which direction to travel in a maze. Human behaviour was thought to be no different, even though the mechanisms underpinning behaviour may be more complex.

This approach started to unravel as it become clear that the tested animals' behaviour could not always be explained using simple 'stimulus-response' theory. There were novel behaviours (such as rats taking shortcuts or swimming in the right direction after their maze was flooded) which suggests that animal behaviour was, in fact, more prospective and adaptive than initial stimulus-response theorists, who expected the animals to flounder in unencountered circumstances, would have believed. The animals had demonstrated some capacity to mentally engage with the task and at some level consider future possibilities differently to the manner their associations have led them. [18]

Looking forwards not back

What the early Behaviourists failed to see was that when we adopt this perspective is that more automatic behaviours often started out as trial-and-error attempts to navigate the future. Just as when we learn to ride a bicycle, it takes us a while to master the basics and then become expert at it. In a way we can see these more automatic behaviours as less about the result of non-conscious forces in our environment and more a reflection of the way in which we have learnt to have proficiency in our environment.

This is what we might call the 'Obama effect', reflecting a comment about wore when President:

"You'll see I wear only grey or blue. I'm trying to pare down decisions. I don't want to make decisions about

what I'm eating or wearing. Because I have too many other decisions to make". [19]

This is very different to the notion that Obama is wearing only grey or blue because he has non-consciously learnt that these generate rewards and avoid punishment. Using this approach, we can think of automatic behaviours as being based on information that we have learned in the past as a way of mastering our environment. But if that environment changes, then the more automatic aspect of ourselves is less important – instead, we need to learn anew how to master the environment.

A compelling alternative account to the 'past oriented' tradition is 'teleological', meaning explanation of our behaviour can be understood through the values and goals that we are seeking. Our behaviour is enacted for a purpose, not because of historic causality. Martin Seligman is one of the leading proponents of a 'prospective' orientation to understanding human behaviour. [20] He considers that we construct an evaluative landscape of possible acts and outcomes which is used to guide our behaviour. The evaluation of the future clearly leverages our learning and memory of past experience but "an organism's ability to improve its chances for survival and reproduction lies in the future, not the past".

This is also reflected by psychologist Magda Osman when she points out:

"...humans aren't simply automata carrying out plans of actions in response to external stimuli, based on biological and neurological mechanisms. Humans are pro-active, not just reactive to the world around them". [21]

These sorts of teleological explanations of humans have long been marginalised, perhaps because of the origins of psychology in 16th and 17th-century philosophy and science. This was a time when the banishment of teleology seemed critical for scientific progress. Aristotelian explanations appealed to 'final causes'. Heavy items fell to earth because the earth was their natural resting place; the heavier they were, the greater their attraction and hence the faster they fell. This offered a clear explanation of our everyday observation. However, once Galileo and others were able to accurately measure nature, these sorts of teleological accounts were inconsistent with the laws that had been identified.

French mathematician Pierre Simon Laplace reflected this when he determined:

"We may regard the present state of the universe as the effect of its past and the cause of its future".

There is always a temptation to adopt a reductionist understanding of behaviour where we seek to understand cause and effect through a simple temporal relationship where one thing causes another to happen.

Of course, it is impossible to flatly deny the validity of any perspective about human behaviour. As philosopher Justin Smith put it:

"If you are committed on such a priori grounds …you will always be able to account for any complex behaviour … without having to revise your views". [22]

Meta theories of humans

While we can take to task the 'rear view mirror' reading of psychology, are we able to consider that prospective psychology works hard enough as a theoretical underpinning for understanding change? There is a clear resonance between the prospective orientation of Seligman and the notions of transformation that we explored earlier. But it does seem that the missing element when we think of behaviour change and flourishing is the way that this is also intricately tied in with the very social nature of humans.

A different axis is needed in addition to 'rear-view' versus 'prospective', which we shall describe as 'Fragile' versus 'Adaptive'. We can explore this by examining the debate about the degree that people could be relied on to 'do the right thing' regarding public health COVID-19 protective measures.

Fragile minds

At the outset of the pandemic there was concern that humans may suffer from 'behavioural fatigue' [23] : this is the notion that people are fragile and cannot be trusted to comply. However, as social psychologist Stephen Reicher has pointed out with respect to COVID rules, the evidence for psychological weakness is very thin. He suggests that implicit in this 'meta-theory' of humans is the assumption is that we do not start or maintain positive behaviours due to poor motivations on our part, or that we simply act as we want without regard for the consequences. [24]

It is easy to assume that humans are typically interested in immediate gratification and not up to the job of living effectively. We may *say* we want to behave in responsible ways, but this can often considered to be a smoke screen to cover up our less acceptable '*real*' preferences. This school of thought about humans as highly fallible and fragile (easily suffering from behavioural fatigue) would suggest that behaviour change comes about through things done *to us* such as regulation, defaults, and nudges.

Adaptive minds

If we take an alternative, 'adaptive minds' view of humans, this suggests that we are working on ways to 'construct' our lives, requiring careful navigation, negotiation and trade-offs. This approach suggests that we need to identify the barriers that get in the way of enacting positive behaviour and as such behaviour change programmes will lean more on barriers identification as well as educating, assisting, and facilitating. As Reicher suggests:

"It is an approach which starts from the question 'how can we help people adhere to policy' rather than 'how can we stop people violating policy'."

But is the 'adaptive minds' view of humans simply wishful thinking? The evidence relating to COVID would suggest not, as a wide range of measures to prevent the spread of the pandemic had very high levels of adherence, from mask wearing and social distancing, to minimising the number of people meeting and regular washing of hands. Despite media stories picking out individual stories to the contrary, polling has shown that these are all measures which the population was willing to adopt; for example, in October 2020 the number of Britons who claimed to be following the COVID rules was 73%, with infringements typically appearing to be minor. [25]

The high levels of compliance show us how humans are willing to put up with a great deal of hardship. Throughout our long history of adversity, past pandemics, wars, floods, and the like, we know that adherence is contingent on a collective spirit, that people feel everyone is in it together. We have seen the way that people volunteered in unprecedented numbers, have organised local support networks, clapped NHS, and frontline workers on a weekly basis.

Indeed, research firm Ipsos has found that the public have been consistently more concerned about the risk to the country as a whole than to themselves. [26]

Despite a range of challenges, adherence levels remained high, telling us something important and interesting about humans. What we have seen, however, are the huge fault lines in society where many people simply could not comply with the guidelines. People were in jobs that require them to be there in person, often working in non-physically distanced conditions, some were living in cramped multi-generational households, some had caring responsibilities outside of the home, others could not afford to take time off work when they started to show symptoms.

The point is that we are in danger of what Stephen Reicher calls 'psychologising' non-compliance as being about motivation or fatigue. Research on behaviour in emergencies and disasters shows that people are typically resilient: we are orderly and support each other, particularly if there is a sense of shared identity. [27] We need to think carefully about how we enable people to enact the right behaviour rather than assuming they won't because they are fragile or unwilling.

What we have learnt about human behaviour from the pandemic is the resilience of our social identity and the way we are willing to act as members of a group with mutual interests rather than work against each other as individuals. As Reicher puts it, "the public are not a problem that needs to be managed and controlled [rather], the public constitute the best resource available in a crisis".

Hence Reicher disputes the notion of 'fragile minds', making the point that there are many reasons why people may fail to act in accordance with the rules – we may not have the skills to do so; we all struggled at times to know what to do if someone does not respect social distancing when we see them, for example. We may not have had the resources to manage social distancing, not least as it's very hard to maintain if you live with others in a crowded space or have caring responsibilities. In other words, the assumption that humans, are purely shaped by a narrow, fixed set of self-interests does not necessarily hold.

On being human

COVID has led many people to rethinking their lives, wondering about how to live more fully, embracing radical possibilities for different ways of being. With this backdrop, the case is that changing our behaviour, not just our thinking, is key to flourishing.

Individuals, organisations, and institutions need help to facilitate change. People need to be able to find things which bring meaning to their lives, which they themselves enjoy. Furthermore, we need to recognise that behaviours are not 'stand-alone' but embedded in a range of personal, environmental, and social complexities. It is this very embeddedness which is used to help calibrate and assess the meaning we so look for in life but, at the same time, can make change hard.

Our choice of behaviour, our ability to adopt and maintain it, and the context in which it takes place are all inter-related. A 'rear-view' model of understanding behaviour is simply not going to help us find ways to facilitate flourishing. A human-flourishing perspective surely makes the case that the complex and interconnected manner of human behaviours means that we need to understand the systems in which we operate and then make choices proactively. We have been able to see more clearly that we are not prisoners of our pasts.

7: Breaks in Time

That we are on a linear path of progress and improvement, as many commentators suggest, seems under pressure with recent developments that have included Trump, Brexit, the storming of the Capitol building, the war in Ukraine and George Floyd to name a few. Some may consider these predictable bumps on the road of progress, while others may consider them symbolic of something more significant. Increasingly many would see the direction of travel we are on as leading to climate disaster and are looking for ways in which we can take an urgent change of direction.

From this perspective, the 'grown-ups' who know best' seem to be shrugging their shoulders at the wheel of the car which is heading along a straight road towards a dystopian future. The challenge we have is centuries of Western beliefs that mean the driver's eyes are fixed forwards, the hands are gripping the wheel and the foot is on the accelerator convinced of the rightness of the project.

We shall see how our beliefs about straight lines of the past determining the future are encouraged by the way the digital world we inhabit, which itself is built on centuries of Western thinking about progress and exceptionalism. But also, that the catastrophe of climate emergency we are now experiencing is in tension with this, causing the passengers to desperately try to wrest control of the steering wheel to veer sharply in another direction. [1]

German philosopher Walter Benjamin considered that significant change will not occur in the natural course of things, by dint of 'inevitable progress'. Left to itself, or 'brushed with the grain', as Benjamin puts it, history will continue as it always has. But this is not inevitable, and we can see how we are living in a period in which centuries of western belief of we engage with time are being challenged. [2]

Only grown-ups at the steering wheel

We start our journey with historian Rutger Bregman and his tour de force book, 'Humankind'. He sets out the reasons why many consider that only certain people can be at the steering wheel of the car as the passengers cannot be trusted. [3]

He cites Thomas Hobbes who argued that for humans to understand themselves, we need look at the way our ancestors lived. 'Read thyself,' he wrote by examining your own reaction you will "thereby read and know what are the thoughts and passions of all other men upon the like occasions". In the past

Hobbes considered we were free, were able to do what we wanted, but the consequences were "solitary, poor, nasty, brutish, and short". This was because we are driven by fear and as such seek safety which comes from "a perpetual and restless desire of power after power, that ceaseth only in death". This results in "a condition of war of all against all". Which requires taming for peace to be established – as long as we are all willing to relinquish our freedom.

His solution is to place ourselves into the arms of a sovereign which he named after a biblical monster: the Leviathan. It is argued that we can see this thinking today in the way that a technocracy of 'grown-ups' justify their authority: 'Give us power, or all is lost'.

There is a long history in the west of what Bregman calls the "veneer theory of civilisation": he cites a long list of influential thinkers and writers such as Thucydides, Augustine, Machiavelli, Hobbes, Luther, Calvin, Burke, Bentham, Nietzsche, Freud, and America's Founding Fathers who all took a very cynical view of human nature. From Saint Augustine, who popularised the idea that humans are born sinful, to Freud who considered "We are descended from an endless series of generations of murderers," our beliefs about ourselves are all too often shaped in a very pessimistic fashion. The argument runs that we must press forward ever-increasing degrees of civilisation by those that can be trusted, otherwise we are in danger of reverting to reliving our brutish pasts.

Evolution's linear hand

In the nineteenth century Charles Darwin published his work on the theory of evolution, which was also pressed into service for the veneer view of humans. For example, philosopher Herbert Spencer asserted that Darwin's theory meant "the whole effort of Nature is to get rid of [the poor] – to clear the world of them and make room for better". [4]

This helps us to see more clearly a set of beliefs that imbues much of our thinking, conflating the past with being uncivilised and the future as civilised. This means that we are very conscious of our 'animal' pasts, grateful for the way that DNA has evolved. Our ascent from the past is ever present with evolutionary explanations permeating our daily lives and used to explain a range of behaviour. Simple applications of concepts like 'nesting instinct', 'pecking order' and 'alpha male' have entered our lexicon as ways we make sense of our human nature.

Indeed, John Gray wrote "human life has not more meaning than the life of slime," asserting there is much less to separate us from other animals, however simple they may be. [5] Earlier, Desmond Morris' best-selling book The Naked Ape suggested humans are simply apes with much of our behaviour understandable by referencing animal behaviour and its evolution. [6] This all suggests the widespread nature of the Hobbesian notion we are wild animals that need taming.

Psychology professor Steven Pinker exemplifies this approach:

> *"...evolution has permanently saddled our species with many irrational and destructive psychological traits, including revenge, dominance, nepotism, tribalism, lust, and magical and anecdotal thinking. It's only institutions and norms that bring out the better angels of our nature that allow progress to be possible, and they face a Sisyphean struggle against our uglier instincts".* [7]

The linear path being taken as we speed ahead in our car is therefore not only for a 'better life', but it is to avoid the chaos and brutality of the life we have escaped, and that if we do not continue this path then horrors may await. [2]

But is the map really a set of preordained straight lines?

We can start to see the way in which the notion of a linear relationship between the past and present is so dominant that it can be hard for us to see. But the digital world we are increasingly inhabiting may be perpetuating this notion, not least in a discipline which very much has the relationship between past and present at its heart: that of history.

---

[2] We can plot a similar linear route from past to present in the beliefs that dominate much of the psychology literature, which as we say in Chapter 6, Martin Seligman refers to as being 'driven by the past'.

Peter Turchin, an ecologist from the University of Connecticut seemed to be strangely accurate in his prediction, from a decade previously, that 2020 would see a significant upturn in political volatility for Western societies. Turchin's work has involved using data to turn history into mathematics as opposed to narratives: this is a formal, explicit operationalisation of the way in which our pasts are seen to shape or even determine our present and future.

Turchin considered that we were reaching the peak of regular instability spikes that occur approximately every 50 years, while simultaneously the world economy was heading for a 'Kondratiev wave' dip, a steep downturn in growth. If nothing else, the combination of Brexit and the storming of the US Capitol building make Turchin's quantitative historical analysis seem highly farsighted.

Historian of science, Amanda Rees, sets out how there have long been ambitions for modelling scientific history, looking to the past to allow us to shape our futures. [8] 19th century historian Henry Thomas Buckle sought to identify 'natural laws' that governed society. His contemporary, Auguste Comte, had previously considered that the 'law of three stages' characterised human society as moving through 'theological' and 'metaphysical' stages, before coming to a scientific self-understanding which facilitated the building of a better society.

In some senses all of this is not all that dissimilar to what Thomas Piketty proposed in his 'Capital in the

Twenty-First Century' where he set out the way in which inequality and growth operate in opposition to each other, resulting in predictable periods of greater and less equality. [9] Cliodynamics is the term used for this discipline, supported by people such as Turchin who reject the notion that complexity makes human societies inaccessible for quantitative analysis, instead setting out that it is exactly this complexity that make mathematics essential.

Turchin gives the example of weather predictions that were at one time considered unreliable because of the difficulty and complexity of managing the necessary data. But improvements in technology to capture data and computing power to manage the analysis means it is now possible to mathematically model interactions between the system's various parts – and therefore to predict the weather. Turchin claims that cliodynamics does not predict the future, but nevertheless sets out the likely consequences of different policy choices.

Notably, Turchin positions cliodynamics within a broader evolutionary analysis, claiming that "nothing in human history makes sense except in the light of cultural evolution". Given Turchin's ecological background, this evolutionary approach to history is not unexpected.

In the same manner as Turchin, philosopher Steven Pinker considers that historians are unhappy at the attention "disciplinary carpetbaggers" like himself have received for applying scientific approaches to the humanities. [10] He considers that: "Given the noisiness of human behaviour and the prevalence of cognitive biases, it's easy to delude oneself about a historical period or trend by picking whichever event suits one's narrative". The only answer according to Pinker is using large data sets, for which he thanks 'traditional historians' for collating but he considers their role is that of assembling rather than making sense of the 'data'.

Pinker's global bestseller Enlightenment Now, sets out 75 graphs demonstrating humanity's apparently enormous progress over the last 200 years: increased longevity, better public health, reductions in crime and violence, declines in poverty, much greater access to education, and even enhanced environmental protection. [11]

Indeed, Roman Krznaric sets out in his book, The Good Ancestor, how Pinker is unashamedly optimistic and believes that "the cold, hard facts" point to a simple truth: "That what has already happened will continue to happen"., the path of progress is set to continue ever upward. [12]

Pinker appears unconcerned about climate change, biodiversity loss, wealth inequality, or technological risks such as bioweapons, and in its place puts his faith in geoengineering and economic growth to solve these challenges.

He quotes the nineteenth-century historian Thomas Macaulay to emphasize this faith in endless progress:

"On what principle is it that, when we see nothing but improvement behind us, we are to expect nothing but deterioration before us?"

Looking back

So, when we glance backwards from our driving seat, and look in the rear-view mirror, can we really see a clear line back into the past? It seems inviting to do so with computing power and available data meaning the disciplines such as cliodynamics seem to provide an inviting clarity, allowing patterns to appear as they did for weather forecasters.

But to show how 'historical facts' are more slippery than they first appear, we can look a little more closely at the evidence for this assumption of a straight line in history. This is the one that supports the rationale that the grown-ups in charge have rescued us from our brutish pasts, the belief that the current economic system has lifted billions of people out of poverty.

Economic anthropologist Jason Hickel [13] describes how Bill Gates tweeted an infographic to his millions of followers showing that the world has been getting better and better."This is one of my favourite infographics," he wrote."A lot of people underestimate just how much life has improved over the past two centuries". One of the graphs showed that the proportion of people living in poverty has declined from 94% in 1820 to only 10% today.

However, Hickel suggests the story is not as simple as it first appears. First, real data on poverty has only been collected since 1981 so anything before that, particularly going back to 1820 is meaningless. He suggests what the numbers in fact reveal is that the world went from a situation where people had no use for money to one where today most of the global population battles to survive on extremely small amounts of money. While the graph casts that as representing a decline in poverty, Hickel considered this could be seen as a process of dispossession that pushed people into a capitalist labour system, as demonstrated by the enclosure movements in Europe and the colonisation of the global south.

The second issue that Hickel notes is that the graph depicts a poverty line set as $1.90 per day. He points out there is a great deal of evidence that people living above this line still have very poor levels of malnutrition and mortality. He suggests that a more reasonable poverty line would be $7.40 per day to attain basic nutrition and normal human life expectancy. If we measure global poverty using this more realistic number then, he points out, the number of people living under this line has increased dramatically since measurements began in 1981, reaching some 4.2 billion people today.

The lesson from this is that we ignore at peril the social context in which data is generated: again, as Lisa Gitelman points out, 'Raw data is an oxymoron'.[14]

There are other ways in which our world, one which is increasingly ordered and organised through digital technology and the data it produces, can subtly reframe our beliefs in a way that can be ever harder to see. For example, genetics seem like a very straightforward way in which the past is shaping our present and future.

Many companies now sell testing kits with the implied promise of being able to trace our genealogy. Digital technology has made possible the interconnectivity of the test results, so we can reference a database of millions of people across the world to assess with which groups our genetic sequence is closest.

But just what are these results telling us? Our examples of cliodynamics, or analysis of poverty, show it is important to be clear about the provenance of the data, the limitations of these tools and the outcomes being implied. At first glance, it seems obvious our differences are discernible in our DNA, that it surely offers a clear-cut way to define who we are. The science seems straightforward: our genetic sequence appears to support the notion of 'Race', the idea that groups of individuals that we can recognize as biologically different from others. This seems believable: people are different from each other in many ways and these differences mean we can group together based on similarity. These variations are passed on biologically between generations and we can see the way these are distinct.

And while it has long been recognised that while there are people with physical similarities, such as those offered by conventional racial categories such as skin colour and hair texture, why do we single out these traits for classification?

Angela Saini points out, in her book 'Superior' that Race simply describes a group of individuals that we can consider as biologically different from others.[15] On this basis there could be thousands of 'social groups' all over the world, characterised by their gene frequencies, and as such therefore having biological distinctiveness. This is where the notion of Race becomes circular as people who are related to each other are clearly closer to each other genetically, and for any number of reasons we have historically tended to live in close proximity to our relatives. Saini points out that even neighbouring towns may be genetically different from one another in some slight but nevertheless statistically significant way.

She cites the work of geneticist Mark Jobling who points out that it is possible to group people any way we like. All that ancestry tests do is scan portions of people's genomes to find those who have genetically a little more in common, then cluster them together. In theory they can cluster them using any measure, such as those who live south of the equator and those who live north of it. But typically, as we know, companies most frequently use old-fashioned racial categories or nationalities.

Talk show host and entrepreneur Oprah Winfrey

famously took an ancestry DNA test and found she was linked to Liberia. While this might lead us to consider this is the location of Winfrey's 'black' ancestry, in fact it does nothing of the sort. It may well instead be a function of the appalling history of former slaves being 'repatriated' by white American leaders who could not countenance such people living freely among them. As Saini points out, ancestry testing does not show your past, as much as it discloses the people you are faintly related to in the present, and even then, only if they have also had similar tests done.

Having seen the nature of Oprah Winfrey's 'Black' ancestry, white supremacists in the United States began using the very same tests to prove how 'white' they were, to establish beyond doubt that their DNA consistent purely of European ancestry.

Simply by placing people into categories we strengthen the assumption that Race is biologically meaningful. Saini cites philosopher Lisa Gannett who warned this type of activity can be seized upon by people with racist agendas; an act of 'statistical racism' as she calls it.

Hence what might at first appear to be an issue as seemingly straightforward and incontestable as genetics, with simple linear relationships coming from the past shaping our present and future, the reality is so much more complex. Instead, we can see the way in which very small variations in socially constructed categories can be used to justify narrow conceptions of ‘how things are’. While DNA testing companies are well-meaning and we would not for a moment suggest they are racist, they operate in a world where the meaning of the result comes with an awful lot of belief baggage.

Voodoo correlations and dead salmon

The ease with which we can select data to tell a convincing story is illustrated by a paper written by neuroscientist Craig Bennett concerning the purchase of a whole but very dead Atlantic salmon. He put the dead fish into an fMRI machine used to study the brain. [16] Duplicating a typical neuroimaging experiment where instead of a fish under the FMRI machine there is a human, they showed it "a series of photographs depicting human individuals in social situations". This reflects a burgeoning area of research, in which is hoped to better understand the way material basis for behaviour by identifying which brain areas are activated while a person is exposed to social interactions that may for example, evoke happiness, jealousy or the sense of unfairness.

To maintain the rigor of the protocol the salmon "...was asked to determine what emotion the individual in the photo must have been experiencing". When they analysed the brain activity of the dead fish, they identified brain activity suggesting that the dead salmon was *actually thinking* about the pictures it had been shown.

The ease with which an entirely ridiculous conclusion could be made is a function of the statistical analysis of the data. While the probability of a false positive at any single group of brain cells was at the level one might consider appropriate for a freshly dead fish, the probability of a false positive within the brain as a whole, with its many brain cells, was not. As soon as Bennett and team applied a proper form of correction for multiple comparisons, the spurious activation in the brain disappeared.

This is not simply an intellectual exercise pointing to the dangers of not applying statistical techniques correctly. A study by Edward Vul and colleagues suggested that brain imaging studies were "the new phrenology" with "implausibly high correlations" reported between brain activation and particular forms of behaviour. Of 54 papers they examined, they considered that there was a 'red list' of 31 cases, often in high-profile journals including Nature and Science, where the authors made fundamental errors in data handling and statistics resulting in what Vul called 'Voodoo correlations'. [17]

In many senses these illustrate the importance of good scientific method not least because the lay person (as well as many researchers) simply does not have the resources, whether time or expertise, to forensically examine the veracity of the claims made from the data on which it was drawn. It is all too easy to martial facts in a way that supports a particular cause – this is nothing new. But what might be changing is that the debate about this is one where there is wider engagement and understanding.

Science is always a work in progress and that things are not fixed is well understood in the community. The combination of sensationalist media reporting with changing incentives structures of academia have tested this, failing to educate a wider audience on the often conditional and tentative nature of knowledge. How science proceeds is the subject of intense philosophical debate: Karl Popper proposed that science progresses by a process of falsification; theories for which predictions conflict with experimental outcomes are discarded, and science then progresses as a process of elimination. [18]

By contrast Thomas Kuhn considered this as an idealist view of science; he viewed science as entailing of periods of 'normal science' in which experiment and theory are conducted within a particular paradigm, with scientists steadfastly holding on to theories despite anomalies. Then very occasionally, the dominant paradigm is overturned. But even when this sort of paradigm shift occurs, it is not a function of reason alone but a shift in the dominant worldview that is held.[19] Given our entanglement with data, a Kuhnian explanation seems the more viable on.

On being human

Simply assuming that we can understand human activity from data is an activity that seems ripe with promise but runs the danger of ignoring the very human systems surrounding the way that data is produced. Historians have for good reason critiqued their sources, acutely aware of the importance and relevance of the social, economic, political, and technological power that shaped their account of the world.

It is a tough job for anyone working with data to 'jump the shadow' of their own worldview. There is an argument that we can never wholly avoid the subtle martialling the facts that reflect our own paradigm of understanding. We can see how we have come to notions of linear progression, predictability orchestrated by those in power who are able to 'manage these things'. But there are increasing challenges to the way in which this has led to a shaping of damaging narratives. Groups with vested interests or simply with unexamined views of the world can then crowbar their way into these narratives, using the very same principles to support their position.

We can see more clearly how centuries of human beliefs about ourselves are challenged. There is nothing inevitable about progress, indeed for many it is a mirage and not something that they have experienced. We have been able to see that the way we derive meaning from data, how we draw lessons from the past, is not something that is linear or inevitable but a function of the lens that we choose to bring. And all the while, there are demands to change direction as we head towards the cataclysm of climate crisis. Many feel they have no choice but to grab the steering wheel and veer in a different direction.

8: Subverting Time's Arrow

We were told, famously, that we are blessed to be living at the 'End of History', with Francis Fukuyama's book perhaps the most commonly linked to this concept, setting out how the current economic and social system should be considered as better than any other. And not only that but also it is "the only one possible, as the last horizon of history, the ultimate, definitive destination in the long march of humanity". [1]

Following this, we can see the way in which our understanding of ourselves, spanning centuries, is deeply embedded in theories of the natural sciences that have a positivist model of temporality between cause and effect. On this basis historical, political continuity can be understood as a single 'triumphal procession,' occasionally disrupted by uprisings on the part of the subaltern classes.

While the past may have been something that we are consistently improving on and leaving behind with a linear flow of inevitable improvement, something seems to have gone wrong with that narrative. The climate emergency may well be changing our perspective. We can now see more clearly the way in which past human activity is creating a series of effects that have sombre outcomes for our collective futures, in a very salient and visceral way. [2]

The impact of COVID on our lives has highlighted long historical injustices in the way marginalised groups have been treated, electrifying protest such as the mass Black Lives Matter movement. Statues celebrating a history dominated by slave trades are being contested, new relationships with the past are being negotiated.

Greta Thunberg has inspired millions to call for change in climate related behaviours, making the case that we are not simply the product of our past and that we can, with sufficient will, act to deliver a different future. Images from the past, showing how the world used to look versus how it is now, or how past environmental protests and campaigns have been crushed or ignored are now powerfully resonating in the present.

In this chapter we explore the ways in which, contrary to popular expectation, radical transformation can take place, how our notions of the past can be over-turned and the way in which this is happening right now.

Change does happen

The themes we have explored here come together in the work of Walter Benjamin who suggests that the job of humans is to activate the emergency brake of the train hurtling into the future. If the train were allowed to follow its course – which was already charted by the train tracks, then we will likely plunge into the abyss. History can then be less the inevitable "maturing of objective conditions" but instead allowing us to see that another world is possible if we interrupt this journey. [3]

To help understand this we can turn to French lyric poet Charles Baudelaire of whom Benjamin was an admirer. Baudelaire considered there was nothing more impressive than a good imagination for "disposing of an immense armoury of observed facts". For him, imagination "supplements" nature and "embraces also the critical spirit". We will explore the issue of imagination further in Chapter 19 but for now we turn to Harvard University political scientist Erica Chenoweth, who argues that you need just 3.5 percent of the population to actively participate in protests to secure political change. [4] This then opens the 'Overton window', a point in time when once radical and unacceptable policy shifts become viable.

We tend to think that change comes about with force, but as she sets out it is in fact sustained nonviolent civil disobedience that is the most effective way of achieving widespread social change. Her impressive research collected data from the 323 violent and nonviolent mass actions she and her collaborators could identify between 1900 to 2000 and analysed them in the context of 160 variables. Countries where resistance campaigns were nonviolent were 10 times more likely to shift to democracy compared to countries where resistance turned violent.

And the ways of mounting such civil resistance are often imaginative, using humour and creatively setting up ways in which those in authority might have their imposing veneer stripped from them. One example of this was an action carried out by a group of dissidents campaigning for an independent Western Sahara, a region occupied by Morocco. Under Moroccan law, it is illegal to fly the flag of Western Sahara. To challenge this, rather than participating in civil disobedience directly (which carried significant risks) protestors tied flags to the tails of as many feral cats as they could find. Chenoweth called this "a dilemma action," as the government forces had to "either chase cats around the alleyways or let the flag fly. It's a terrible set of choices for the opponent, and it's humiliating". [5]

These sorts of actions create dissonance, a way of creating disfluency in people's minds, challenging the presumed authority, and encouraging the notion that simply because something has been the case in the past, does not necessarily mean it will prevail moving forwards. Simply saying this is one thing but finding ways to articulate it in a way that causes people to engage and reflect is another matter altogether.

The spontaneity of humans that makes change happen

The wider point is that we are not trapped by our past, humans are capable of change, of grabbing the steering wheel to swerve the car. And yet this perspective competes with a huge body of work that set out how we are "borne back ceaselessly into the past". [6] Evolutionary psychologists, for example, suggest we are, among other things, fundamentally selfish and focused on the present: we have no choice, is the argument. Our past evolution has determined our behaviour, given we are the embodiment of thousands of selfish genes trying to self-perpetuate in the here and now.

So, what are we to make of this? Are we simply the result of our genetic evolutionary pasts that curtail our possibilities for real change? After all, this requires something radical, a notion of human agency, our ability to act in a way that is independent of what has gone before. Yet the evolutionary psychologist literature is immense and in a way part of our everyday language, reflecting how it is the way we see ourselves.

To tackle this, and see alternative perspectives, we can turn to medical physician and clinical neuroscientist, now writer and philosopher Raymond Tallis. As one of the most vocal critics of what he sees as an over-simplification of Darwin's body of work, he suggests:

"The truth of Darwinism is to see how we are natural in our origins; the error of Darwinitis is to imagine that

we are defined by our origins; in short to confuse our biological roots with our cultural roots". [7]

Tallis uses the examples of art, where the more enthusiastic advocates of evolutionary theory see the process of the creation of art as comparable to a peacock's tail – artists create their art to maximise their chances of mating. So even sponsorship of the arts could be seen as a 'reputation reflex' where the sponsor is advertising the health of their business, again in the same way as the peacock's tail. [8]

The problem, Tallis points out, is that artists are often relatively little concerned with the material benefits of their trade. Much less work could be undertaken to achieve the basics in life along with their success in mating:

'Artists have suffered – starvation, contempt, neglect – for their art. Hardly the biologically correct thing to do. Great artists are more often biological losers than they are alpha semen spreaders'.

Another example, and an area of behaviour which seems diametrically opposed to the notion of selfish genes is altruism, the act of selflessness for the good of others. This seems important to explore, as despite being the opposite of selfish, the topic is nevertheless often described in self-serving terms by, for example, 'warm-glow theory', a term economist James Andreoni used to suggest that motives for giving are inherently selfish. [9] We give money to feel the 'glow' that results.

A variety of studies report pro-social behaviour results in an increase in activity in reward-related brain areas (ventral striatum and the orbitofrontal cortex) which are correlated with feeling good. [10] So, the evolutionary argument would suggest that propagation of our genes, or at least an increase in personal 'reward' is why we perform altruistic acts, and that true altruism does not exist.

But can it really be this simple? An incident that left its mark on the collective memory of many was the tragic capsizing of the ferry, 'Herald of Free Enterprise'. On the night of 6 March 1987, the ferry had set off from the Dutch port of Zeebrugge for Dover with its bow doors left open. 193 people died, many of them drowning in the freezing waters. People struggled to save their lives but, notably also the lives of others. There were many examples of selfless human bravery such as a passenger on board called Andrew Parker who laid his body across a damaged walkway to form a human bridge. This action allowed 20 people to walk to safety, saving their lives. He was awarded the George Medal for his bravery.[11]

No matter how well an evolutionary psychologist claims to explain this type of behaviour is self-interested, I suspect most of us find this does not sit with us easily. Can it be possible to hold evolution as true while at the same time accepting that Andrew Parker's act of bravery is reflective of altruism rather than to generate a warm glow?

The answer perhaps lies in where we locate the operation of evolution. During the mid-twentieth century, evolution was considered to operate at the level of the individual, and this was soon to move to an even more reductionist position with people such as Richard Dawkins maintaining selection operates at the level of genes—the individual is merely the embodiment of thousands of selfish genes, each trying to self-perpetuate.

However, many philosophers such as Mary Midgely have argued that Darwin's work has been misrepresented and that he did not take such an individualist position. Instead, Darwin proposed we are not only a sociable species but are naturally more cooperative, affectionate, and interdependent than any of our animal relatives.

Darwin made the case that our social instincts are so crucial to our lives that they must have been developed through group selection: by the survival of coherent, sociable groups rather than fewer interactive ones. It is this social aspect which is where our motives are located, shaping the richness of our lives countering the idea of obtaining all our behaviours from the narrow notion of selfishness, or self-interest.

Philosopher Mary Midgely considers that Darwin himself saw things this way, with the immediate point of human behaviour being in its meaning for the people involved:

"This subjective aspect is its central function. These are things that are done for their own sake because they fulfil our nature. To understand them, we need to look at the distinctive part they each play in real life, not at speculations about how they might possibly have prevented some distant ancestor from dying".[12]

Of course, the reality is always an evolutionary function, but this does not mean that we are all 'objects' blindly obeying these laws while self-rationalising like crazy that they have some meaning. On this basis, the principle of altruism is entirely possible – we do not need to attribute the selfless acts of people such as Andrew Parker in terms which feel, at best, disingenuous. We can instead see how the subjective reality of human behaviour can comfortably sit alongside (or we might say 'within') evolutionary explanations.

This has more radical implications for our analysis: if our behaviour is not determined by the past then this offers us capacity to think for ourselves, to push the steering wheel to the left or right and radically change direction. To act altruistically and spontaneously. Behaviourism failed in its explanation of past conditioning determining behaviour for just as rats and pigeons would often fail to act according to behaviourist's predicted behaviour, so too human participants often failed to follow the behaviourists' expectations. We cannot explain our behaviour simply in terms of where we have come from.

Evidence for lack of a linear line

It is all too easy to get pulled into a narrative that we must keep pushing forward to achieve ever-increasing levels of civilisation by those that can be trusted, otherwise we are in danger of reverting to reliving our brutish pasts. Or we can take the Rousseau perspective, who argued that our "primitive and innocent" past was a time of pastoral equality and freedom, that could not survive the unavoidable necessity of structures and hierarchies. Either way, both Hobbes and Rousseau, so critical to the mindset of much of Western life, were theories of the inevitable evolution of society.

Anthropologists David Graeber and David Wengrow plotted the way that this notion of societal evolution was derived from unsupported assumptions. In contrast to the dominant worldview, they suggest there is a huge variety of social and political experimentation that earlier humans undertook over thousands of years. 'Primitive' peoples knew how to cultivate crops or build bigger settlements, yet sometimes chose to forage or fish instead as they wanted more time for leisure. They set out that every conceivable variation of organising human society and different ways of living has existed, in multiple places, for hundreds or thousands of years at a time. We are in danger, they argue, of mistaking the set of rules that we currently happen to live by today as the culmination of past experiments with social, economic and political organisation when in fact we can easily find equally as sophisticated societies from our pasts, putting into real question the evolutionary theory of human civilization. [13]

Who owns the facts?

Walter Benjamin, the German philosopher, cultural critic, and essayist also reflects this perspective, asking awkward questions about who owns the 'facts' and emphasising the ability to consider an alternative narrative as critical. We do not need to acquiesce to the view that humans are helplessly selfish, that our futures have already been written for us whether through our DNA, meta-cycles in history, or the non-conscious past conditioning of our responses. We are capable of unique and original acts that are driven by meaning they have for us in our lives now.

Who authors the story of our history is key, as suggested in 1891, by Senator George Graham Vest, a former congressperson for the Confederacy who was an advocate for the rights of states to secede:

"In all revolutions the vanquished are the ones who are guilty of treason, even by the historians, for history is written by the victors and framed according to the prejudices and bias existing on their side". [14]

This critique suggests that history is a writing of the past creating a narrative that aligns with its social and ideological dominance. There is a danger that the evolutionary or mathematical approach of considering history as consisting of datasets can be subject to Nietzsche's criticism that perhaps unwittingly those practising this are people who are "swimming and drowned in the flow of becoming," practising "naked admiration for success" and "the idolatry of the factual" – essentially describing the historian who always "nods his "yes," mechanically, … to any power".

Benjamin used the phrase, "brush history against the grain" meaning we need to see history from the standpoint of the "defeated, the excluded, the pariahs". It is their history that has been written out and it is only through accessing this and then "swimming against the historical waves" that different outcomes are possible.

Beautiful experiments

An example of the way that history marginalises some segments of the population comes from Saidiya Hartman's book 'Wayward Lives, Beautiful Experiments' which sets out a history of Black women in the US of 1890's through to the 1920's. This period of change in the aftermath of the abolition of slavery was also one of threat from white terrorism. [15] Hartman suggests that Black women escaped one racialized enclosure, the plantation, only to find themselves in another the Black city-within-the-city, or the ghetto.

The book sets out an account of the forms of refusal that were used to escape the enclosure, or to refuse to volunteer for servitude with Black domestic work considered a regular part of the social hierarchy. Industrialization and urbanization — were only possible due to the abuse and exploitation of Black women.

Beautiful Experiments challenges the notion that historical archives offer any kind of authoritative source of credible knowledge of Black women with the details of those she represents found on the periphery of archival refuse from which she then knits together a collective story for the majority of Black women in slavery's aftermath.

She also sets out how, in 1917 and 1918, Black females who were imprisoned for alleged transgressions protest the conditions of ritualistic violence in prison. Black women and girls led a multiracial rebellion of 'ungovernables' attempting to destroy the prison and creating a noise strike with their screams an act of resistance. Hartman suggests there is hope in the qualities of these women who were at the bottom of the social hierarchy through their desire to find freedom through 'beautiful experiments' in alternative modes of living.

On being human

Writer Thomas Frank suggests the presumption that we require a small elite of 'grown-ups in charge' and that popular democratic participation of the 'masses' needs to be limited, reflects a dismissiveness of ordinary people who are seen as "emotional and deluded". [16] On the contrary we can go back to the 1890's left-of-centre agrarian Populism movement (before the term took on a very different meaning). This was accused of a 'celebration of ignorance' [17] but in fact was a movement that historian Charles Postel called 'progress through education', with farmers readily listening to lectures, using the many lending libraries or indeed the universities that the movement set up.[18]

From the perspective of the 'grown-ups,' mass protest movements are simply out-breaks of irrationality and marginalized people are disregarded. The key, the 'grown-ups' maintain, is to ensure that the professional political class find agreement between themselves quietly, agreeably, and without too much interference from lower-ranking groups. This was arguably suggested by Barak Obama when he said that BLM activists should be willing to sit down and discuss their agenda with leaders in power rather than "yelling at them". Despite the appearance of a progressive, he has become seen by some as an exemplar of just this modus operandi, being the grown-up in charge.

It is noticeable that one of the most influential figures behind a change in direction has been Greta Thunberg. It is a teenager rather than a powerful politician who has inspired millions to call for change in climate related behaviours. Changing direction may well seem irrational and extreme because to question principles that have underpinned our lives for decades, even centuries, requires radical change.

It is hard to see how this will come from people that benefit from the way things are set up now; we can see that clearly with the rise of Black Lives Matter and Me Too. COVID and climate change mean we can see more clearly that change may well be driven by marginalised groups, and it is these groups that deserve more attention and respect.

9: To be a Cyborg

Elon Musk claims that the electronic brain-computer interfaces made by his company Neuralink will bring about a range of benefits including communicating with loved ones, searching the Internet, even replacing your television, streaming content straight into your brain.[1] This directly references Transhumanism, the loosely defined movement that promotes enhancing the human condition through the advancement of technology, originally inspired by the writer Julian Huxley.[2]

Transhumanists see humans as a work-in-progress that can be recast in any number of desirable ways. Many Transhumanists hope that through the responsible use of science and technology, we shall eventually become 'posthuman,' meaning we will have vastly more capacities than we currently have.

Enthusiasts consider that Genetics, Nanotechnology and Artificial Intelligence (Robotics) will converge, meaning that the distinction between biology, chemistry, and mechanics will become ever more blurred and then ultimately disappear entirely.

The movement proclaims that humans now have in their grasp the possibility to realize an evolutionary leap because of the rapid development in a wide range of biotechnologies. The goal then, is for human beings to get rid of their organic embodiment with all its associated precariousness allowing us to achieve a fuller, lengthier, and better-quality life in all senses.

So, with the new technologies that we are being offered, what does this tell us about our beliefs about being human?

Escape from the body

Humans have always been keen to explore any arrangement that offers escape from our mortal and fallible bodies. Some of the earliest 'religious' artefacts that have been found, such as Neanderthal ochre burials, indicate a belief in immortality. Modern religions suggest a degree of distrust of the body and the 'created' world. In addition to this, modern science can also be seen as incorporating an anti-materialist bias, what leading thinker Karl Davis considers the result of its tension against religion. He points out that:

"Science as knowledge of material reality paradoxically decomposes the materiality of the real". [3]

While not all will agree with Davis, we surely see the gist of this reflected in Elon Musk's more messianic claims. By getting rid of organic embodiment with all the precariousness that comes with it, the idea is that this opens the door to a better quality of life in all senses. Google employee and writer Ray Kurzweil predicts that that this convergence will culminate in what he titles the "Singularity," set to occur around 2045 when "the non-biological intelligence created in that year will be one billion times more powerful than all human intelligence today".[4]

As humanity continues towards "transcendent nano-consciousness," the physical world will be seen to be increasingly irrelevant. [5] Human activity is then gradually transformed, in Transhumanist researcher and enthusiast Hans Moravec's words:

"...from grossly physical homesteading of raw nature, to minimum-energy quantum transaction of computation. The final frontier will be urbanized, ultimately into an arena where every bit of activity is a meaningful computation: the inhabited portion of the universe will be transformed into cyberspace". [6]

This means that our living spaces in a Transhumanist future will not be built in a physical environment but on virtual estate. Struggles will no longer focus on land, but around the architecture of cyberspace, we will not engage with nature for our survival, but instead inhabit a never-ending sequence of computer games, a geek's wonderland as Davis puts it.

What does this tell us about being human? For if we are improving the human condition then surely, we need a way of defining what the human condition is to start with. We cannot improve on something if we have not got a benchmark. If, as Elon Musk is suggesting, we can improve on ourselves as humans, then implicit in this is an accepted understanding of what it means to be human.

This question has dogged us for eternity, but Transhumanists assumes that there are characteristics that define being human – that there is an 'essence' of humanness. Otherwise, there is nothing to improve on. So, let's look at this the notion of essences a little more closely.

Essence and appearance

The way we use the term 'essence' is to define what makes it what it is. By contrast, 'appearance' offers us an understanding of how things *seem* rather than what they are. There is a huge body of psychology literature showing that people have intuitions about essence and appearance. Douglas Medin and Andrew Ortony developed the term 'psychological essentialism' to reflect our tendency to essentialise *categories* of things. Since then, researchers have collected a large body of evidence that humans are eager 'essentialists'. We tend to think of the world as divided into categories, each of which have a real essence. [7]

Biological species are a prime example. We readily organise the animal kingdom into species, but we need to consider what gives an animal membership of their species. For example, why should a certain animal be a cat? It's not the fact it has fur, as a cat without fur is a still a cat. We tend to believe that what makes an animal a member of a species is less to do with its appearance but rather is some deep fact about it. In this case, it has a 'cat essence' even though we might not be able to articulate what that essence is.

With this in mind, we can be open to the idea that someone can be human even if they don't look human. Or perhaps they look human, and we refuse to accept they are human. This can be difficult for us to distinguish: philosopher Gary Gutting pointed out that the problem with vampires is that for much of the time it is hard to tell them apart from us mortals. [8] We may be talking in a perfectly normal fashion and be completely taken by surprise when we suddenly feel fangs on our neck. Despite our surprise, we are very well aware that whilst vampires may *look* human, they lack the essential qualities of *being* human.

But to return to the 'exam question', what is the essence of being-human? As robots get ever more life-like in appearance, they can seem to be human so if we do not have a clear sense of what is the essence of humans, then how will we tell apart a robot from a human? To return to Gutting, he makes the point that when we watch Shakespeare's play, A Midsummer Night's Dream, we have no problem knowing that although Bottom's head looks like that of a donkey, he is a human being 'on the inside'. His donkey appearance is in fact concealing his human essence. As robotics and digital technology occupy our lives in ever more intimate ways and companies seek to design machines that are as life-like as possible, will we always be able to understand that these robots are not 'human inside'?

Part of the challenge we face is that when we form emotional attachments then we 'essentialise' them. This means that we think there is a property which makes them hard or impossible to replace. Psychologist Bruce Hood makes the point that we don't form these attachments to polystyrene cups or anything which is clearly duplicated. [9] Hood undertook a series of studies where he convinced children he had a duplicating machine, telling them it was possible to duplicate any physical object. [10] They made scientific looking boxes using wires and lights, placed an object in one, and 'activated it'. After a few seconds, the other box would appear to start up by itself upon which he would open it up to give two identical objects. So once children were in the mindset their machine could copy, he then tested what he could get away with. He found they were happy to have their toys copied but when it came to a sentimental object like a blanket or a teddy bear, then they typically did not want to accept the duplicate.

In a similar although polar-opposite vein, Hood also asked people if they would be willing to wear a cardigan, offering a financial incentive. Most people agreed. But then he asked, 'Would you still wear it if you knew it belonged to Fred West?' (a notorious mass murderer.) Most people would then refuse saying it felt disgusting or dirty. We imbue an object with unseen qualities if we have an emotional relationship with it, whether that relationship is positive or negative.

The distinguishing essence of humans

There is a reasonable argument to be made that Transhumanism is closely related to the notion of essentialism even if this is not necessarily a link that is explicitly made. There is surely an implication that we have characteristics that can be enhanced, we can be better quality humans. [3] Why not have a robotic arm, life extending biotechnology or even memory implants? We do not live in a world of neat divisions between object and subject. Indeed, this is close to what philosopher Andy Clarke argues: we have always relied on our tools as an extension of our minds, whether wax tablets to extend our memories or computers to help us process vast amount of information. He would claim these tools mean we have always been cyborgs, at one with our technologies. [11]

But a challenge to the notion of Transhumanism is that we are in danger of making ourselves 'less human' somehow, that at some point quantitative change becomes qualitative and we no longer recognise

---

[3] The desire to 'essentialise' is a core premise of the western philosophical tradition which posits human beings as possessing an intangible 'rational soul' or 'mind'. This is considered to have an affinity with a divine dimension sitting outside of the bodily world and as such, setting us apart from all other life.

ourselves. [12] This is the central thesis of the most significant alternative to an essentialist view of humans, existentialism. The central posit of this philosophy is that we do not seek to only promulgate our species as animals do; instead, we look for meaning in our lives, and we do this by the taking of risks to overcome the limitations of ourselves and our situations. Interestingly, this sounds an awful lot like Transhumanism itself, the seeking to transcend our natural condition, towards self-chosen, concrete goals.

But there is a difference between Transhumanism and existentialism that is critical for our discussion. Because for an existentialist, as Skyẹ Cleary and Massimo Pigliucci point out:

"To be human is to live in ambiguity because we are forever caught in a tension between the facts of our lives and the will to overcome them".[13]

The very point of human life is to recognise the resistances we face, to accept our failures, but also to creatively rebel against them:

"This perspective matters because it emphasises that, while there are fixed elements to our being, we are not fixed beings since we are (or ought to be) free to choose our projects. An authentic life is about acknowledging these differences, and stretching ourselves into an open future. It does not follow that this openness is unlimited or unconstrained".

So, in many ways, being human involves a dance between individual freedom and submission. This is very similar to points made by Matthew Crawford in his book "The world Beyond your Head" where he writes about musicianship. The process of learning to play an instrument involves submitting ourselves not only to the direction (usually) of a teacher but:

"her obedience rather is to the mechanical realities of her instrument, which in turn answer to certain natural necessities of music that can be expressed mathematically". [14]

The important point for Crawford is that these limits are external to the self: he goes on to talk about how, with this example, "membership in a community is a prerequisite to creativity". There would be no 'Bluegrass' without a community of people who play Bluegrass music. They offer what Crawford calls a 'Cultural jig', a way of offering a scaffold for our creative lives, providing a structure for our creativity and thought.

In a sense then it is the human struggle with the fixed aspects of our lives that offer us the opportunity for advancement, growth, and creativity. This, according to people such as Crawford is where real freedom can be found and without these constraints and jigs, we would lead much more shallow lives.

Coming full circle

The French political scientist and polymath Alexis de Tocqueville famously commented that Americans are Cartesians without having read Descartes. [15] By this he meant that there is a widespread natural assumption in the West that the Cartesian view of rationality, that has long been the defining characteristic of being humans, requires the freeing of your mind of any kind of external authority.

The essence of being human then has the ability to separate oneself and operate in an entirely individualised manner, honing the skills of rational living. And in a sense, this is the notion that sits under much of the Transhumanist tradition – if only we can free ourselves from the shackles we live within and separate our core essence of rationality then we can achieve so much more.

This overlooks that, for many thinkers, being human is essentially about paradox. Spanish philosopher Jose Ortega y Gassel considered that a person is a "being which consists not so much in what it is as in what it is going to be: therefore, in what it has not yet become! This ... most profound paradox is our life".[16]

The desire of the Transhuman movement to resolve this, ironically flattens the notion of what being human is. As humans we aspire to change but we often do not know what we want; what we are aiming for can often be unclear as we saw in Chapter 6, 'On Changing'.

This suggests that we are continually reviewing and anticipating, changing not only as we learn and understand but as the external environment around us changes. The very thing that Transhumanists are striving for is the very thing that makes us less than human. On this theme, anthropologist Tim Ingold suggest that "where there is human life there is never anything but happening. Life *is* not; it *goes on*". He suggests that we are not in fact human beings fixed in time, rather that we are all always life-in-the-making and as such we could call ourselves 'human becomings'. [17]

Becoming more machine like

But are we, in a way, already living in a state of Transhumanism? Many argue that workers are transformed to behave like machines: humans are taken out of the equation as much as possible as the machinery itself generates the most value. And as such human employees are in service to that machinery as much as possible.

Authors Brett Frischmann and Evan Selinger argue that this is due to the digital technology's deployment drawing a line from Taylorism, the application of scientific principles to promote efficiency and productivity in the workplace. In this system, "Workers were, in fact, conceived as inputs, cogs, resources etc.; their work was broken down, analysed and programmed…At a fundamental level, Taylorism was a revolutionary system for engineering humans". Their thesis is that digital technology is simply an extension of what was already long in place.

James Bridle suggests this leads to hard-to-spot culture of automation bias, meaning that we value automated information more than our own experiences. [4] One such case is of pilots in high-tech aircraft cockpits that work with a wide variety of automation. A tragic example of this involved the Korean Air Lines flight from Anchorage, Alaska, on August 31, 1983. On take-off the crew programmed their autopilot with the information from air traffic control and, as usual, effectively then handed over control of the plane the computer systems. [18]

This is normal procedure, and the autopilot was pre-programmed with a series of waymarks designed to take it through over the Pacific to Seoul, but due either to an error in the settings, or a flawed understanding of the system operation, the autopilot did not maintain its preassigned route. Instead, it remained fixed on its initial heading, taking it ever more north of its envisioned route.

By the time it left Alaskan airspace it was already twelve miles north of its expected position. Over time this increased to hundreds of miles from its intended course. Investigators concluded that there must have been several cues which should have alerted the crew to what was happening. It appears they noticed but disregarded the increasing travel time between beacons while complaining about the poor radio reception, a symptom of drifting from the normal air routes.

---

[4] Writer James Bridle notes that *"Computation does not merely augment, frame, and shape culture; by operating beneath our everyday, casual awareness of it, it actually becomes culture. That which computation sets out to map and model it eventually takes over".*

The problem was that no cues triggered the pilots to query the system, or to check their position. They maintained their trust in the autopilot even when they entered Soviet military airspace. Fighter jets were scrambled to intercept them, but they flew on. Three hours later, still totally unaware of the state of affairs, they were fired upon, wrecking their hydraulic systems. The cockpit transcript of the last few minutes of flight found multiple failed attempts to restart the autopilot.

As Bridle points out, we inhabit an environment where if there is an unambiguous set of directions from a computer that by its nature exhibits no such ambiguity or uncertainty, then it is only natural that we follow it:

"Computation replaces conscious thought. We think more and more like the machine, or we do not think at all".

On being human

In a way we can see how this ladders up to a more encompassing world view where human activity is gradually transformed and transplanted by computation. This leads us to entangle with another of our disruptive forces, climate change. If our minds can be digitised, then they can be loaded onto digital platforms. It is a beguiling notion that we can simply evade the existential challenge of climate change – in many ways the ultimate form of climate denial.

Technology is frequently called on to offer ways to transform our lives as humans but in this case, it is used to transform not just our lives but our very way of being. In this sense, Transhumanism tells us something about what it means to be human although not in the way that might be expected.

It is less about how we can optimise ourselves to overcome our obstacles but more about how we can recognise that it is the tension between our limitation and desires that is a significant part of being human in the first place.

SECTION 3: LOSING OUR MINDS

In an eerie way, as humans there is a continuity to our experience, which is the knowledge and understanding that we have an inner subjective experience of the world. While many might consider that our inner lives are what shape us as humans, we often have an uneasy relationship with that part of ourselves. We could say that our inner life is often in danger of being refused or rejected on the grounds that it simply does not exist.

But at the same time, we can see the way that human beliefs are often underpinned by a belief in the sacred, that there is a reality that sits beyond the immediate, tangible reality of our day-to-day lives. We make no assertion concerning the veracity or otherwise of the beliefs, simply that they play a bigger role in shaping the way we engage with the world than is always obvious.

10: Iceberg Minds

If you do an online image search 'iceberg', then one of the first photos that comes up is by Ralph Clevenger.[1] The significance of this is that it is commonly used as a metaphor for the life of humans. The iceberg is designed to illustrate the notion that the vast majority of our behaviours (typically 95% is the percent quoted) are determined by mechanisms of which we are simply not aware, being 'below the water'. The small part we can see, in our consciousness, accounts for only a tiny proportion of our behaviours, suggesting they are of little or no real consequence.

It is no coincidence that the iceberg is often used as a metaphor for consciousness, given the way climate change is leading us to rethink ourselves and our place on the planet. We will explore the way that climate change and technology disruption are causing us to question and rethink our relationship with our beliefs about consciousness and with this, our notions of what it means to be human.

The specialness of humans?

Réné Descartes, writing in the Seventeenth Century is often credited with first formally invoking the idea of consciousness, considering it to be the contents of a person's mind to which only they are privy. But from this simple beginning it has been tied up with defining who we are, how we live and what it means to be human.

While it is considered by many as one of the most defining characteristics of humans, it is a topic that sits uneasily alongside science, defying properly satisfying explanations for this phenomenon. Icebergs are one of many metaphors that have been used come to our aid in describing consciousness – with the tools we use often acting as explanatory devices including wax tablets, telephone exchanges, hydraulic systems, clockwork and of course the computer.

While conversations about consciousness take place more often among philosophers than the public at large we can nevertheless see the way in which these have shaped so much of how we operate. If we see consciousness as something uniquely human, then we will see ourselves as having a special place in the universe meaning we can use the natural world around us in a manner of our choosing. If we do not consider that we have any inner life shaping our behaviour, then this has implications for how we seek to exert agency in the world and design systems for humans to operate effectively. And if we believe consciousness is something that is not uniquely human, then we open ourselves up to a very different conception of how to operate alongside not only the natural world but also our life which is entangled in objects.

It is important to note that this chapter is not about examining in depth the arguments for different conceptions of consciousness. Instead, we are looking at how these shape beliefs about being human and in turn, what the implication is of this for our lives. It is through this that we can say something about which explanations about consciousness have the most relevance for the world we are finding ourselves living in but also, as we shall see, how previously marginalised notions on this topic are starting to take centre stage.

Dualism

Writer Philip Goff sets out in his book 'Galileo's Error' [2] how, even before Descartes, it has been a core premise of the western philosophical tradition to posit that human beings possess an intangible 'rational soul' or 'mind'. This is considered to have a divine dimension outside the physical world, separating us from the other forms of life on the planet. Indeed, Aristotle considered that plants have vegetal souls (which enable nourishment, growth, and reproduction) while animals also possess an 'animal soul' which provides sensation and locomotion. But importantly, neither plants nor animals can be disconnected from the world of birth and death. Humans, however, possess a soul or intellect which grants admittance to the 'less corruptible sphere' and has affinity with the divine 'unmoved mover'.

Two thousand years later, Descartes continued this hierarchical continuum of living beings with the 'Great chain of being' – which offered a distinction between mechanical, unthinking matter (minerals, plants, animals, human body) and the pure thinking mind (available only to humans and God). On this basis, it is humans alone that are a mixture of both matter and a thinking mind. Only humans can feel and experience their bodies and mechanical sensations; all other living things are simply automata, unable to have actual experience and as such unable to feel pleasure or suffering.

Similarly, Galileo held a very dualistic perspective with division of nature into two categories: one of physical objects which have mathematical properties and the other of disembodied minds with consciousness. Galileo held that immaterial minds are beyond scientific understanding. This has been challenged by more recent philosophers who consider that the conscious mind is not something mysterious but can be understood through the application of psycho-physical laws: basic principles of nature, as fundamental as the laws of gravity or electromagnetism, which govern the interactions between the nonphysical mind and the physical world. Philosopher David Chalmers considers this as the 'hard problem of consciousness,' the challenge of clarifying why brain activity gives rise to experience: our feelings, thoughts, emotions, in other words the inner world we all possess. [3]

The separation of our mental world from physical surroundings seems to offer humans a sense of exceptionalism: the world we inhabit is one of mechanistic biological systems with human consciousness a phenomenon over and above these systems. Goff suggests that this worldview, not often explicitly articulated but nonetheless ever-present, leads to an unhealthy relationship with nature in at least two ways.

Firstly, it creates a notion of separation, implying that as holders of immaterial minds, humans are a qualitatively different class from the mechanistic world we inhabit. If we do not see ourselves as in anyway consistent with a tree, then we have nothing in common with one. There is, says Goff, no true kinship with nature if we consider dualism to be true.

Secondly, Goff suggests dualism implies nature has no value in and of itself. If it is entirely mechanistic, then the only value nature has is to either maintain our survival or to create pleasurable experiences for us. In other words, dualist thinking encourages the notion that nature is not respected as something that has value in its own right. This reflects why Arctic ecosystems are now reaching the threshold beyond which the Greenland ice sheet will plummet into irreparable melting, raising sea levels by six meters.

There may therefore be more of a linkage between our minds and icebergs than simply serving as a convenient metaphor. Writer and campaigner Naomi Klein considers that dualism represents a "corrosive separation between mind and body—and between body and earth—from which both the Scientific Revolution and the Industrial Revolution sprang". It very much set out the way in which the natural world lacks the consciousness that was synonymous with making human existence sacred. [4]

Dehumanizing

Not only do some commentators consider that dualistic notions of consciousness risk creating environmental damage, but this is also inextricably linked to ways in which we dehumanize our fellow humans. Ecologist Andreas Malm and the Zetkin Collective look at the relationship between fossil fuels, climate change and racism. [5] Malm points out the way that every time a European far-right party denies or downplays the climate crisis, it makes a statement about immigration. He also suggests that when such a party rails against immigration, it is de facto commenting on global heating.

His book is a careful unpicking of the way huge amounts of political energy has been thrown into the war on the fictional problem of an 'immigrant invasion' rather than on climate. It is in this way that climate change has led to a demonisation and dehumanisation of some peoples – indeed it is common for these groups to be considered by others as 'less than human'. And to be less than human means that we are stripped of the attribute which is deemed to separate us from the wider world – that of consciousness.

This is consistent with the way in which dualistic notions of consciousness have long offered those that are sufficiently motivated the means to access a set of beliefs which dehumanises others. We can track this back to Aristotle and his claims that the ability to reason is what makes us human. Which meant anyone unable or less able to reason must therefore be less than human. As such, he believed that some people, who he called "barbarians" only had limited ability to reason which meant they were natural slaves. Unlike cattle, barbarians could understand and react to rational thinking, but they lacked the ability to actively pursue it. The notion that some people are naturally suited to slavery had terrible consequences for humanity long after Aristotle's death.

Consistent with this, Malm highlights the way that extraction of fossil fuels requires "sacrifice zones" that are typically inhabited by non-white populations such as Native Americans, the Ogoni people in the Niger Delta, Arabs in Iraq who have to be pushed aside. This cannot work unless their humanity is weakened. If they counted as full humans, then the act of seizing their territory would be indefensible. Malm calls this 'frontier racism': "When there is a commodity to be appropriated on the other side of some line in space, the lives of the population present there might have to be seriously disrupted, which demands and calls forth their 'inferiorisation'."

This dualistic perspective of human consciousness is one that many would consider has at least contributed to those with power being able to navigate the world in an exploitative and divisive manner. Strangely, however, while dualistic notions of consciousness have dominated, pointing to the specialness of humans, the last century has seen the rise of the almost polar opposite. There has broad discussion on how humans *lack* an inner life. It is to this we now turn as, of course, this also has huge implications for the beliefs we have of what it means to be human.

Disappearing minds

Rory Sutherland, vice chair of advertising agency Ogilvy UK and regular commentator on human behaviour, gave his particular flavour of how the mind works:

"I think the way we think we decide and the way we actually decide don't have that much in common. The conscious rational brain isn't the Oval Office; it isn't there making executive decisions in our minds. It's actually the press office issuing explanations for actions we've already taken". [6]

Of course, the notion of our inner thoughts being only a small part of who we are has a long history, albeit not one that we can trace back to Aristotle. We can perhaps start with writer and philosopher Aldous Huxley who proclaimed in 1874 that mental events could be likened to a steam whistle that contributes nothing to the work of a locomotive. [7] William James, also writing at this time, characterized our inner life as not influencing the brain activity that generates them "any more than a shadow reacts upon the steps of the traveller whom it accompanies". [8]

From then on and for much of the twentieth century consciousness was a taboo topic, seen as a somewhat mystical notion not suitable for 'proper' scientific study. The high point of this consciousness-phobia was the Behaviourism of the 1920s and 1930s, pioneered by the psychologists John B. Watson and B. F. Skinner. Psychologists in the nineteenth century had investigated the mind by introspecting their own conscious experience. Watson and Skinner objected to this method as non-scientific: people's private experiences cannot be rigorously examined in the lab. The Behaviourist creed was that the only proper subject matter for scientific psychology was observable behaviour.

Consistent with this, scientist Frances Crick suggested that "You, your joys and your sorrows, your memories and your ambitions, your sense of personal identity and free will, are in fact no more than the behaviours of a vast number of nerve cells and their associated molecules". [9] A recent example of this tradition is perhaps Nick Chater's book, 'The Mind is Flat: The Illusion of Mental Depth and the Improvised Mind'. In his view 'mental depth' or the notion that we have an inner life is simply an illusion for which we have fallen 'hook, line, and sinker'. His notion of the mind is that it is entirely 'in-the-moment' and "almost everything we know about our minds is a hoax, played on us by our brains".

This means that we have no real inner life and are unable to give any sensible account of ourselves:

"If you ask me what I did, I will give you a reason, and a reason for that reason, and so on; and I can do this so fluently I have the illusion the chain of reasons was pre-formed inside me. But the reasons are mere rationalisations, invented only when they are required, and not a moment before. In fact, if you ask me the same question in a slightly different way, I will probably give you a different answer".[10]

So how has this view of the mind gained ground? The case can be made that this is a function of the way we have always used tools as metaphors to help us understand who we are. Indeed, our relationship with technology is one which can be hard to see as it is just so much part of our everyday life.

Technology and consciousness

That technology changes how we think and make decisions is nothing new; many writers have made this observation. The metaphors we use surely influence the narrative we have of ourselves. And the dominant technology narrative that we currently use today is that of Artificial Intelligence (AI). So how does that influence the narratives we have of ourselves? [11]

The key aspect of AI that should concern us here is the way in which it assumes that the mind works as an abstract mode of logic. This is very much rooted in the Cartesian method of deduction where our reality is determined by a process of deduction. The tradition of analytical philosophy has dominated AI assuming that true knowledge is purely a mental process that can be separable from other aspects of human experience. The dominant model in AI, connectionism, is based on the idea that the human brain can be modelled through 'artificial neurons'. The connections between them are measured in weights and each node has a threshold, which along with the sum of input weights and the activations value (calculated via the activation function) determines whether the node gets activated.

Behaviourism is very much entwined with this approach to AI. These models are based on the idea that associations are limited to what can be directly observed by the investigator: specifically, stimuli, reinforcement, and the observed behaviour of the organism. The aim of this was to make psychology more objective and scientific, as only measurable inputs and outputs were to be accounted for, whilst the hard to pin down inner states could be ignored. The notion of consciousness, our inner minds accessible only by introspection is therefore at best marginalised as something that is not of sufficient interest or value to understand human behaviour.

The inner mind that will not go away

In a way then, it seems that the dominance of technology in shaping our belief systems suggests that a materialist view of who we are might lead us to buy into the belief that there is no inner life. And yet, we seem to struggle to give up the notion of a world where we lack this. Philosopher David Papineau asks why the dominant explanation for our consciousness is a materialist one but that humans find it almost psychologically impossible to believe that conscious experiences are physical processes in the brain. [12]

Is this a shortcoming in humans or a reflection of their everyday lived experience? A small number of philosophers, including Gary Gutting, Mary Midgely, and Thomas Nagle, have explored how our daily lived subjective experience means we cannot help but 'know' there is an inner mind. In this vein, Nagle famously asks, 'What is it like to be a bat?' He argues that mechanistic theories of mind miss out the essential factor of consciousness, that is, there is something that it is (or feels) like to be a particular being.

Mary Midgley also skewered this perspective in her inimitable fashion:

"...if we really believed that our conscious efforts in thinking did not affect our actions then we would no longer have any confidence in those conscious efforts at all. And people who, for some reason, actually do lose that kind of confidence stop making those efforts, including the effort to go on reasoning. They are the people who are now described as depressives". [13]

And Gutting also points out, we have a problem:

"We know that our experiences depend on material systems like the brain that science can, in principle, exhaustively explain. But we find it hard to make sense of the idea that experiences themselves – seeing red, feeling pain, falling in love – could be purely physical....What science can observe is public and objective, what I feel is private and subjective." [14]

And not all experiences seem to be the steam whistle after-effects of neurons going about their business. 'Mary's room' is a thought experiment about a neuroscientist who is an expert in colour perception. Mary lives in the future, at a point in time where there are no further facts to learn about colours and their perceptions. [5] However, Mary has been colour-blind

[5] An interesting side note is an observation the example of the Kogi, an indigenous group who reside in northern Colombia. Selected children are taken from birth and put in a dark cave for the first nine years of their lives to begin the training as Mamos (which means sun in Kogi), for guidance, healing, and leadership. They avoid light as much as possible to be attuned to the natural world as their emergence into it after being raised in darkness gives them a lifetime of deep appreciation.

from birth and has never seen anything other than black and white all her life. Fortunately, because of Mary's research, an operation has been undertaken that gives her normal vision. After the operation and the bandages are removed, Mary for the first time looks around her room and sees a bouquet of red roses sent by her husband. At that very moment, for the first time, Mary experiences the colour red and knows what it looks like. The central question of this thought experiment is, despite Mary knowing all the physical facts about colour, there is a singular and strangely important fact she did not know. What the colour looks like. It is hard to conclude other than that physical science cannot therefore express all the facts about colour.[15]

So, we can understand from this simple thought experiment that there are different types of experience. There is a way in which experience is physical, so if someone enters a room, we can see them in the same way that a surveillance camera 'sees' someone. Gutting calls this 'psychological consciousness (an objective reality observable from the outside). But the camera has not got subjective experience, what Gutting calls 'phenomenal consciousness' (a subjective reality observable only by introspection).

The difficulty with subjective experience and our inner lives generally is that it is hard to measure and impossible to directly observe. But then again this is not limited to the topic in hand. Many of the natural sciences are engaged in researching topics that cannot be directly empirically observed. So, science cannot directly observe quarks, black holes, dinosaurs or the big bang. But what natural science does is use the limited evidence that it has available and then use this in conjunction with reasoning and conceptual models to build a theoretical understanding of how these phenomena work (or worked).

In just the same way, the inner lives of humans cannot be directly inspected – despite the claims of the more ambitious neuroscientists. But again, this does not mean that motivations, beliefs, attitudes and so on do not influence our behaviour. It just means that they are hard to study.

This leaves us in a difficult position as at once we can see the way that dualistic theories of consciousness seem to be implicated in placing humans in a position of primacy in the world which is arguably part of the reason for the climate emergency we find ourselves in. On the other hand, dualistic theories do not seem to quite hold up to scrutiny in terms of our everyday lived experience and similarly seem to lead to beliefs that have dehumanizing ways in which people are treated (and that we treat ourselves). [6]

We turn now to a quite different set of beliefs relating to consciousness that is starting to emerge which is

---

[6] How we make a distinction between ourselves and other 'things' that occupy the world seems a critical topic to explore if we are to understand how our conception of being human is changing. A classic 'Descartes' model of humans suggests a stark distinction between humans and inanimate objects. A materialist model suggest that there is nothing exceptional about humans and that we are mechanistic systems alongside the world around us.

entirely at odds with both materialistic and dualist notions. This is the revolutionary notion that consciousness is not in our individual heads but is in fact distributed between us.

Panpsychism

Panpsychism is the belief that consciousness is a fundamental and ubiquitous feature of the physical world. Philip Goff is a leading advocate of this perspective, and he sets out the way in which panpsychists do not consider consciousness a sacred mystery which must have arrived at by magic. Rather, animal, and human consciousness is not explained in terms of anything more fundamental: the basic consciousness of basic physical entities is a fundamental claim of the theory.

This is not to suggest that *everything* is conscious. While fundamental constituents of the physical world are conscious, it does not mean every random arrangement of conscious particles will result in something that is conscious in its own right. Goff points out that most panpsychists will deny that socks are conscious but assert that they are ultimately composed of things that are conscious. Perhaps more importantly, he points out that this also does not mean consciousness like ours is everywhere. The complex nature of human consciousness is the result of millions of years of evolution, and it is clear that nothing of this kind is held by individual particles.

The main attraction of panpsychism according to Goff, is its:

"ability to account for the reality of consciousness. We know that consciousness is real and so we have to account for it somehow. If a general theory of reality has no place for consciousness, then that theory cannot be true. What panpsychism offers us is a way of integrating consciousness into our scientific picture of the world, a way that avoids the deep problems associated with dualism on the one hand and materialism on the other".[16]

We are seeing this reflected in emerging themes from psychology with accounts how the intellectual capability of a group goes beyond what any one individual is capable of.

As psychologists Steven Sloman and Philip Fernbach put it:

"Humans are the most complex and powerful species ever, not just because of what happens in individual brains, but because of how communities of brains work together".[17]

We do this by dividing up 'cognitive labour'. If a work colleague, neighbour, or friend is the expert then why not rely on them? Operating like this is hugely efficient and effective but the boundary between one person's ideas and knowledge and that of the team can be hard to distinguish. We all supply different things and do not really know where they came from. Explanations for behaviour look increasingly as something that reflects a consciousness that sits between us rather than located firmly in our own individual heads.

If we carry this logic through, then should we look more carefully at the natural world? A popular book, 'The Hidden Life of Trees: What They Feel, How They Communicate,' suggests that trees have the means to communicate and help each other. [18] The author argues that trees of the same species are communal, often forming alliances with trees of other species. The book's author Peter Wohlleben, a German forester, suggests that trees have evolved to live in interdependent relationships, facilitated by communication and a shared intelligence not unlike that of an insect colony.

Similarly with animals, then anyone living with a pet will inevitably imbue them with an inner life suggests Erica Fudge, Professor of English Studies at the University of Strathclyde:

"If we cannot access an animal's mind then pet ownership becomes potentially meaningless, for without a mind for us to access (or for us to believe we can access) we cannot really say that a pet loves, as such a claim would be simply anthropomorphic, and we need pets to be able to love if we are to be able to claim that dog love really is a kind of love. We need pets to have minds in order for them to be pets".[19]

Many of us tend to have a dissonance about our relationship with pets and animals in general. On the one hand, living with animals we understand their behaviour using the same terms as we describe each other such as being happy or wanting things. On the other hand, many people will readily state that animals are simply a set of neurons and that our tendency to imbue them with human attributes does not offer any evidence to the contrary.

What then about robots? Technology has advanced somewhat since Descartes time, it is easier for us to imagine objects as autonomous actors in a world where cyborgs, virtual reality, virtual assistants, sex robots, and self-driving cars populating the every-day and near future.

Indeed, there is much discussion about the way in which equipping robots with an 'inner mind' can make them more effective. [20] Researchers programmed their Pepper robot, made by SoftBank Robotics, with the ability to vocalise its own "thought processes". In a series of experiments, the researchers explored how this inner speech influenced the robot's actions. In an experiment, Pepper was helping a human set a dinner table. When the human asked Pepper to ignore etiquette by placing a napkin in the wrong place, the robot started 'talking to itself', deciding that the human may be confused and questioning whether it should proceed with the action. Once the user verified their request, the Pepper robot reportedly said 'to itself': "This situation upsets me. I would never break the rules, but I can't upset him, so I'm doing what he wants," and placed the napkin in the spot requested. The extent to which this mechanistic representation really reflects a human's inner life is of course dubious at best. But we can see the way in which we can easily believe that if we choose to believe robots can have an inner life, then why not many other things?

In fact, writer Timothy Morton believes all beings are interdependent and that everything in the universe has some kind of consciousness, from "algae and boulders to knives and forks". [21] For Morton, with an awareness of this interconnection we achieve 'ecological thought': that all forms of life are connected in a vast, entangling mesh. This interconnectedness penetrates all dimensions of life.

On this basis no life, construct, or object exists independently from our ecological entanglement. This implicit knowledge we have brings with it huge uncertainty from the proliferation of unpredictable themes such as global warming, capitalism, and mass extinction. Morton calls these sorts of themes 'hyper-objects', objects that are so massively distributed in time and space that they are not only hard for us to see but knowing how to respond is complicated. However, hyper-objects do become more visible during an age of ecological crisis, and alert humans to the ecological dilemmas, defining the age in which we live.

On being human

There is a battle of narratives taking place between different conceptions of consciousness, with the dualistic notions of our inner lives rapidly being contested by alternative explanations. Technology and climate change are the protagonists for a fundamental re-evaluation of who we are and what we might become or indeed for our demise. The notion that there may be another organism in the shape of the COVID virus, which can dominate our lives across the globe, may have shaken the notions that we can feel comfortable in the idea that we are 'top of the tree', in charge and in control of the world.

In this environment it is no wonder that there are challenges to each other's narratives of our views of the world. Arguably much of this is taking place in the form that may not always be intellectually coherent, carefully crystalised and framed with models of consciousness explicitly underpinning them. But nevertheless, we can look at the ways in which debates about human life will always inevitably be shaped by implied models of consciousness.

Returning to Ralph Clevenger's photo of an iceberg, it is fitting that the image used is not quite what it seems, being composed of four separate pictures. As Clevinger was reported to have said:

"The shot of the clouds was taken here in Santa Barbara. So was the underwater. I took the picture of the top part of the iceberg in Antarctica when I was

there on assignment. I took the picture of the bottom part of the iceberg in Alaska, above water. I just cut out a section of an iceberg and then flipped it and put it underwater. It was really that blue, though. We didn't colour it or anything. The digital guys put it together".

Clevenger happily pointed out that the image proved to be highly successful at helping brands make their marketing points, netting him sufficient revenues to put his children through college. This tells us that ideas sit between us as metaphors, images and stories; what we believe is not purely in our hands, reflecting the notion of consciousness as something not entirely in our heads but distributed across our world.

11: Denial Wars

We found ourselves in a situation at the height of a pandemic, with people protesting that COVID was a cover for governments exerting ever greater control of the population and denying that the disease was sufficiently serious to warrant the measures being taken. In a different but related case, despite fires raging across North America and in Southern European countries amidst record temperatures, a US poll found attitudes to the topic of climate change barely altering. [1]

At times it can seem as if no matter how much evidence is given to people about the existential dangers we face, there is a refusal to shift from their beliefs. It seems as if this is the precise opposite of a rational and scientific outlook to the world. There is no shortage of facts about the world that seem not make any impression on those who are participating in protests against lockdowns, threatening doctors treating COVID patients. Or those who insist that the human causes of climate change are simply an irrational narrative dreamt up by scientists with a political axe to grind. And even if we argue that people understand that human climate change is a given, there seems a lack of 'follow-though' in terms of changing behaviour.

COVID and climate change illustrate very vividly the way in which it seems humans engage in a 'wilful ignorance' on the implications of 'inconvenient truths'. We shall see through this chapter that perhaps the reality is less straightforward but by examining it we can also better understand the changing nature of the beliefs we hold of ourselves as humans.

Motivated reasoning

There is no shortage of explanation of the mechanisms that underpin this apparently irrational behaviour – the main type one being known as Motivated Reasoning. For example, Dan Kahan, Professor at Yale Law School outlines the way in which the cultural values we hold define our social identities which in turn shape our beliefs about disputed matters of fact (e.g., whether humans are responsible for climate change; whether the death penalty prevents murder).

He shows how this explains why groups with different cultural outlooks (such as left or right of centre political orientation) disagree about important societal issues. On this basis disagreement is not due to people failing to understand the science or even that they lack relevant information. Instead, according to

Kahan, disagreement is generated from the way "people endorse whichever position reinforces their connection to others with whom they share important ties". [2]

The form of motivated reasoning at play here is that advocating beliefs that are not consistent with the sentiment in one's group could threaten one's position within the group, in which case people may be motivated to 'protect' their cultural identities.

In another example political scientists Brendan Nyhan and Jason Reifler found was that when people on one side of a political argument were shown evidence that one of their 'politically advantageous' beliefs was wrong, they would refuse the findings and 'double down' on their mistaken conviction. [3] In a study they undertook, participants were given fake newspaper reports that seemed to corroborate a number of widely held fallacies. In one, it backed the notion that Iraq had weapons of mass destruction (WMDs) prior to the Iraq War taking place. In another, it set out that President Bush had enforced a ban on stem cell research. Both claims are factually false. But when presented with counteractive information—such as a quote from the President in which he conceded that there had been no WMDs in Iraq— then the participants' responses fell along political lines. Liberals and centrists (perhaps as expected) accepted the counteractive information. Conservatives, on the other hand, did not.

Indeed, some Conservatives become more committed to the false claim about WMDs after the correct information had been given: the correction therefore 'backfired'— Conservatives who received a correction setting out that Iraq did not have WMD were in fact more likely to report that Iraq had WMD than those who were in the control condition.

Perhaps we use motivated reasoning to reduce the discomfort we feel when presented with information that we are wrong. This is related to confirmation bias: that we are motivated to defend the idea that one of our beliefs is right, so we look for evidence to confirm it. On this basis, philosopher Lee McIntyre suggests:

"Motivated reasoning is a state of mind in which we find ourselves willing (perhaps at an unconscious level) to shade our beliefs in light of our opinions; confirmation bias is the mechanism by which we may try to accomplish this, by interpreting information so that it confirms our pre-existing beliefs". [4]

The irrational elephant

This is not all that different from the conclusions that Jonathan Haidt reaches when he argues people are fundamentally intuitive, not rational. He supports his case by research which asks people about bizarre scenarios that require people to make and then defend ethical decisions. These include questions about whether it wrong to have sex with a dead chicken or with your sister. And whether it is O.K. to defecate in a urinal or whether if your dog dies, you can defend eating it. His studies found while most people would consider these things are wrong, most cannot explain why. [5]

He explains this by using the metaphor of an irrational elephant ridden, but barely controlled, by a rational rider. Haidt considers that the central mistake of psychologists and philosophers is that we try to explain the rider rather than the more important elephant. The trouble is, in his mind, that the rider does little more than offer post hoc rationalisation of the actions of the elephant. [6]

In a different way, Andreas Malm, author of 'White Skin Black Oil', argues that denial is a palliative; it allows us to manage the anxiety of climate change as the threat grows. And it is in this context that we are vulnerable to authoritarian leaders that offer an escape from our insecurities and paranoias away from 'their objective reasons'. [7] This suggests that the more objective the reasons to be afraid, then the more tempting the offer will be.

There seems a convincing body of knowledge that motivated beliefs explain our apparent denial of climate change. But can we really understand human behaviour on the basis that we are fundamentally flawed and self-interested? Are we destined to be creatures that simply rely on their own intuition at the expense of facts? This explanation suggests that people seem unable to disentangle reality from fiction, illusion from reality.

While there is inevitably some truth to this, we find a different conclusion when we need to take a journey through Western philosophy and the scientific tradition. This takes us to the issue of human perception, challenging the notion that we are destined to live in a way that is helpless in the ebbs and flows of irrationality.

Divine perfection of classical economics

To unpick this, we start our journey with classical economics: this discipline tends to assume that people in markets have perfect information and given this, can make rational decisions. The logic is that given perfect information and no other constraints, such as our time or other resources, then we should never have to make sub-optimal decisions.

The notion of the possibility of perfect rational choice has remained a dominant narrative for centuries, carrying with it religious undertones of omniscience. We return to Teppo Felin (who will shape the start of our journey here) when he points out:

"The very idea of rationality implies that someone—the agents themselves, the system as a whole or the scientist modeling the behavior—perceives and knows the optimal or best option and thus can define whether, and how, rationality is achieved. Rationality, then, is defined as correctly perceiving different options and choosing those that are objectively the best". [8]

It is such a widely held belief that is tempting to assume that individual rationality and choice simply is reality. Indeed, as theologian Timothy Stacey suggests, it is the notion of independent rationality that 'rises above mere beliefs'. This idea is what he calls 'the myth of the absence of myth'. [9] He is attuned to philosopher Mary Midgely who points out:

We are accustomed to think of myths as the opposite of science. But in fact they are a central part of it: the part that decides its significance in our lives. So we very much need to understand them. Myths are not lies. Nor are they detached stories. They are imaginative patterns, networks of powerful symbols that suggest particular ways of interpreting the world. They shape its meaning'.[10]

On this basis, Timothy Stacey suggests, the notion of the self-independent rational actor itself can be seen as a myth, given this is a story that people are living by. Given science and mathematics are considered to operate in a sphere of rationality that somehow transcends our day to day then it is perhaps of little surprise that one of the precursors of economics was an early eighteenth-century English minister called Thomas Bayes. [11]

His life is not well documented, and his most famous work 'An essay toward solving a problem in the doctrine of chances' was published posthumously, after his friend Richard Price brought it to the attention of the Royal Society. The essay was about the way we derive probabilistic beliefs about our world as we come across new information. Price set out the example of a human who emerges from a cave and, for the first time in his life, sees the sun rise. On that first morning, he does not know if this happens every day or if it is an unusual occurrence. But every single day he comes out of the cave, he sees the sun rises, and is therefore increasingly confident that this is a permanent phenomenon. On this basis he can assign a probability to his prediction that the sun will rise the next morning which is almost but never exactly 100%. With every day that passes, the probability rises as he accumulates ever more evidence.

Bayes and his friend Price did not see the world as intrinsically probabilistic or uncertain. On the contrary, Bayes was a believer in divine perfection. Indeed, his first publication was titled 'Divine Benevolence' which sought to answer the question of how there could be suffering in the world if God was truly compassionate. He considered we should not mistake our own human imperfections for the imperfections of God, whose designs for us we may never fully understand. It is of little surprise that he was a supporter of Isaac Newton whose work considered nature was a perfect symmetry directed by predictable laws.

Bayes proposed that we gain knowledge about the universe through approximation; – as we gather more evidence, we get ever closer to the truth. This perspective was developed by French mathematician Pierre-Simon Laplace. In 1814 he published a set of principles known as 'Laplace's Demon'. [12] It set out a philosophy that if we hold perfect knowledge of present conditions and perfect knowledge of the laws that govern the universe, then we can make perfect predictions. On this basis, famously, the movement of every single particle that exists in the universe should be as predictable as balls on a billiard table. The divide between the perfection of nature and our human imperfections in our ability to measure and understand meant Laplace saw the value in relying on probabilistic inferences.

But it was an English biologist and statistician called Ronald Fisher who arguably had a more significant impact on today's statistics than Bayes. Fisher disliked a key element of Bayes theory, the notion of the Bayesian prior which posits a starting point for prediction from which subsequent observations are used to amend. This, considered Fisher, was subjective and incompatible with the concept of objectivity so he set out to create a type of statistics that was free of this contamination.

In its place Fisher proposed frequentism, which conceives of uncertainty in statistics as an issue relating to the collection of data from a sample of the population. In this way, Fisher views uncertainty as something inherent to the experiment, not as intrinsic to our ability to understand the real world – thus avoiding the subjective human input that he considered Bayes had introduced through the use of a prior estimate.

Uncertainty in frequentist statistics is represented by sampling error. This does not rule out subjective inputs: for example, there are assumptions relating to the distribution of the underlying population or in the definition of the sample population. Arguably the subjective element is more hidden whereas Bayes specially catered for it albeit the notion was that this was then amended.

In many senses the value of the Bayesian method is that the researcher needs to explicitly identify the relevant context through the prior probability: without this there is a danger of statistically significant, but ultimately spurious relationships, as lampooned by Tyler Viglen on his website, 'Spurious Correlations'. [13]

However, both approaches have at their heart the implication that as you collect more data we will eventually get to the point of perfect measurement. Our imperfect tools, in the eyes of both approaches, suggest that the zero figure will never be reached in reality, the notion of perfect accuracy is nevertheless a theoretical possibility.

Divine humans

Bayesian thinking, as psychologist Teppo Felin points out, influences many psychologists' views of humans. For example, Nick Chater suggests that the "problem of perception is that of inferring the structure of the world from sensory input". [14] These inferences operate in a Bayesian manner based on repeated encounters with an objective environment, the reality of which can be increasingly well understood by repeated exposure over time.

The central argument is that perception is a process where we interact with our environments and over time learn its true nature. The social sciences are built based on object perception as Bayesian inference. Indeed, Daniel Kahneman argues, "we know...that the human perceptual system is more reliably Bayesian".[15]

With that in mind, we can understand why Kahneman's work suggests "the behaviour of agents is not guided by what they are able to compute but by what they happen to see at any given moment". Sight is given centre-stage as the means by which Bayesian observations are made, with visual analogies or illusions frequently being used to make his point about the limits of perception and rationality. Indeed, much of Kahneman's early work was concerned with vision – so perhaps it was of little surprise that his perspective may be that humans capture their environment based on the physical characteristics of that environment. This reflects the notion that perception is a 'true representation' of the environment in a camera like fashion.

The divine perfection of AI

Beliefs in technology, and more specifically AI, have reflected this perspective. Tech critic Kate Crawford and tech historian Alex Campolo consider AI systems are seen as enchanted, beyond the known world, yet deterministic in that they discover patterns that can be applied to everyday life. [16] This is very much rooted in the Cartesian method of deduction where our reality is determined through an abstract mode of logic. This tradition of analytical philosophy has dominated AI and indeed continues to do so. We can see centuries of Western philosophy underpinning the popular beliefs around AI.

And with this, it can be hard to see an alternative to the myth of divine perfection that surrounds AI. The notion of disembodied super intelligence has highly transcendent undertones. In response, those casting a more critical eye over the tech landscape suggest this surely ignores the way in which the AI is 'trained'. As Alison Adam puts it:

...in training the system to respond in the 'correct' way, the developers are supplying all the interpretation in a propositional form outside the system. The operator supplies all the meaning to the input and output...in order that the system may be trained....The machine is not somehow taking over, organizing itself and freeing itself from its master. For all that it might be difficult to establish what is happening due to the complexity of the operations [17]

An example of the difficulty that ensues lies in the following, although there is some dispute about the actual authenticity of the case it has passed into legend as an example of the limitations of AI:

Once upon a time, the US Army wanted to use neural networks to automatically detect camouflaged enemy tanks. The researchers trained a neural net on 50 photos of camouflaged tanks in trees, and 50 photos of trees without tanks. Using standard techniques for supervised learning, the researchers trained the neural network to a weighting that correctly loaded the training set—output "yes" for the 50 photos of camouflaged tanks, and output "no" for the 50 photos of forest. This did not ensure, or even imply, that new examples would be classified correctly. The neural network might have "learned" 100 special cases that would not generalize to any new problem. Wisely, the researchers had originally taken 200 photos, 100 photos of tanks and 100 photos of trees. They had used only 50 of each for the training set. The researchers ran the neural network on the remaining 100 photos, and without further training the neural network classified all remaining photos correctly. Success confirmed! The researchers handed the finished work to the Pentagon, which soon handed it back, complaining that in their own tests the neural network did no better than chance at discriminating photos.

It turned out that in the researchers' dataset, photos of camouflaged tanks had been taken on cloudy days, while photos of plain forest had been taken on sunny days. The neural network had learned to distinguish cloudy days from sunny days, instead of distinguishing camouflaged tanks from empty forest. [18]

Within this example we can see the perception debate being played out: on the one side echoes of Thomas Bayes' Divine Perfection as the heart of AI, seeing humans as the poor relations. On the other hand, we can see the way in which AI has feet of clay: the power is derived from human inputs and understanding.

The multi-stable

Visual illusions are considered examples of the disconnect at times between what is seen and what is in fact there. This is often used as a key example of decision-making frailty – our perceptions, as evidenced by visual illusions, lead us astray. Felin points out we can see how an equivalence is made from perception to rationality and thinking. The imperfect tools we are born with mean we cannot access the world *as it really is*.

But visual illusions do not necessarily provide a good illustration of our fallibilities, instead they simply demonstrate how our visual system works. A two-dimensional picture will always struggle to represent a three-dimensional environment, in the Ponzo illusion, the white lines that are in the distance are seen as bigger by humans despite being the same size on the two-dimensional surface. While Kahneman considers this "illusion is caused by the differential accessibility of competing interpretations of the image," [19] Felin argues:

'Visual illusions based on perspective are inappropriately exploiting and interpreting a more general problem, which is that two dimensional images cannot fully represent three-dimensional reality'.

The point that Felin makes is that illusions are not necessarily symptomatic of our faulty decision making but a mechanism that allows us to operate effectively in our environment, necessarily translating the flaws of representation from a 2D environment.

There is no independent, objective means of measuring what we see and assessing this versus an objective standard. For example, a range of studies that show colour and brightness are always determined by the context that the object appears in - objective measurement is simply not possible.

This means we necessarily need to think of judgement being 'multi-stable' in that any stimulus can result in different perceptions because even something as seemingly simple as colour or brightness always has some ambiguity and is open to different interpretations.

This contrasts with the approach of those working in the heuristics and biases school who underscore the 'actual' properties of the stimulus and infer there is only one, fixed interpretation possible. Instead, the nature of the perceiver does matter. This is nicely illustrated by Matthew Crawford: [20]

"Take a moment to look at the walls in whatever room you are in. I am at a library, and the walls are a slightly yellowish beige. If asked their color, that is what I would say, and not give it another thought. If I look more closely and get analytical about it, I notice that in the particular lighting conditions in this room at a

certain time of day—and today is a bright day in April rather than a hazy day in August—different parts of the wall are "really" (that is, empirically) different shades of beige, some darker and some lighter, some with a glare from the window, some illuminated by an overhead fluorescent lamp, some closer to the warmer-colored reading lamp, and others in shadow.

There is a disconnect between what we actually see and how we think about it:

"To begin with, my previous experience enters into my current experience. I have experience with how the appearance of things varies in reflected light from various sources, one of which (the sun) moves in certain characteristic ways according to the season…As an acculturated member of society, I happen to know how painters proceed when painting a wall. They don't carefully draw geometric shapes with slightly different shades here and there; they show up with five-gallon buckets and knock it out. … I have this stock of social knowledge, and it seems to condition my immediate perception of the wall as uniformly beige. … The uniformity of the wall's color is a social fact, and what I perceive, in everyday life, seems to be such social facts, rather than the facts of optics. The facts of optics are not being challenged here, but their role in understanding human perception is limited….To perceive the wall as variously colored, I have to suspend my normal socially informed mode of perception.

Philosopher Maurice Merleau-Ponty writes that empiricism "is not concerned with what we see, but with what we ought to see, according to the retinal image". [21] And again, as Nagle pointed out, a bat sees the world very differently from humans: perception originates from a perspective, or point of view. [22]

The focus on the limits, errors, and boundedness or bias in perception underplays a fundamental point about perception, namely that perception is organism, context and species-specific.

Alternative approaches to perception

Work by psychologists such as Gerd Gigerenzer shows that people can do very well when applying simple heuristics. These heuristics are not necessarily dumb, they are simply imperfect, which is very easy to show. [23] A lot of psychology experiments that show dubious behaviours have been designed deliberately to do that. It is easy to show that people make mistakes – there are thousands of visual illusions, for example – but that does not automatically make us visually impaired.

When we understand how and why these illusions come about, we discover the 'mistake' was made because of an inference, which, in this particular case, is not valid, but may very well be valid in a broad range of other contexts. These inferences can in fact be clever because we are using information to go beyond what we can see. This can sometimes be literal, to make physical judgments, such as how far away things are, which is not evident in the data that comes into our visual systems. We can do all of that because we go beyond the information given when we use inferences.

An example of this is inattentional blindness. In their classic experiment, Daniel Simon and Christopher Chabris show the way in which a person in a gorilla suit walking in a film sequence can be missed because the participants in the study were 'primed' to count the number of basketballs passes. [24] Kahneman uses this as an example of how we can be 'blind to the obvious'. But on the other hand, if participants were 'primed' to watch for the gorilla, and then report on the number of correct basketball passes, they would likely not get the correct answer. [25]

Here we can take a different perspective on primes; we can think of them as the equivalent to questions or theories that direct our awareness to certain features of our environment among the huge array of things that we could choose to look at. In that experiment we could be asked to look at all manner of things from the hair colour of the actors to the gender and ethnic composition. Any of these are clear but only if you are looking for them and not something else. The fact that we miss some is not a function of blindness or bias, but an entirely rational and successful process given what we set out to do. These offer evidence of the way we naturally direct our perception and awareness: primes are an example of how this is done in everyday life.

Linkage to denial

If we are not the imperfect, flawed and irrational beings that is commonly assumed, what explains the way in which we seem to so determinedly ignore what seems to be staring us in the face? Climate change and COVID being two prime examples.

Philosopher Neil Levy suggests that 'bad belief' formation does not inevitably correlate with identity. For example, there has been little evidence (at least historically) that anti-vaxx sentiment, or indeed opposition to genetically modified organisms are predicted by group identity. [26]

He suggests that there are, of course, some beliefs that are predicated on our identities, particularly when those beliefs are core to the nature of the identity. Evolution, for example is a case in point: while some theological views are consistent with evolution, others are passionately committed to a story of creation where God created the world in seven days. For this group of believers, evolution is clearly inherently threatening to this 'identity-constitutive commitment'.

But, as Levy suggests, other cases such as climate change are less clear. As he points out, the notion of climate change can be threatening to those who support free markets, as any adequate response would involve heavy regulation of the market. However, when we dig into it, we can see that there is not necessarily an inherent requirement for those to the political right to object to climate change.

There is always a gap between our ideological stance and any policy position. For instance, most people who call themselves fiscal conservatives express as much support for government spending as those who do not think of themselves as fiscally conservative. And on the topic of climate change, Levy describes how only recently there was no partisan divide on the environment, either between politicians or among the general public in the United States.

This would suggest the opposite of Kahan – that we rarely reject something due to conflict between ideology and policy. Levy goes onto point out that the same right-of-centre that frets about market interference strongly supports subsidies to fossil fuel interests. While the rhetoric might be that climate change is threatening because it interferes with the market, those who engage in the rhetoric seem willing to interfere with the market to see off the threat. In other words, if we were to accept motivated reasoning as the central plank of why people adopt the extreme beliefs we are seeing, then surely, we would expect there to be much more broad consistency between tribal ideologies and the policy positions: the evidence does appear to call this into question.

This is not to say that a motivated reasoning explanation is wrong but simply that it is not the full explanation of why we find people adopting positions which seem so much at odds with what we might expect. At the very least, through our discussion about the nature of rationality, we can see that an alternative case can be made for the way in which we approach these most difficult topics of our time. From our own perspective then there may be good reason why we appear to act with 'wilful ignorance'. As we saw in Chapter 2, there may well be very good reasons for people to doubt official explanations.

On being human

We are at the centre of a storm where denial of certain 'inconvenient truths' about the world are taken as evidence of the human fallibility in decision making. This makes most sense if we support the notion that there is a single unwavering truth that requires unearthing – a reference to the search for divinity that was explicitly present in the early work of people such as Bayes and Fisher but is also frequently implied in the dialogue around AI.

The 'world-to-mind' model of perception that has dominated since Descartes does not consider the way in which we as humans direct or originate perception. As we enter a period where we face critical existential decisions, then we are starting to see more clearly that other ways of looking at issues exist. As we seek to find ways forward, to act in a way that is necessarily collective, then it is becoming more obvious that a 'mind-to-world' perception' is a helpful way for us to better understand human behaviour. This is requiring a fundamental shift in our thinking about rationality, seeing it as a function of our active engagement with the world. As such this is reorienting the way we think of ourselves as humans.

12: Creatures of habit

We are, so the saying goes, creatures of habit. These are often characterised as routines that we do not need to think about but nevertheless many consider account for a broad range of our behaviours. And not only do we not have to think about them, but new ones can form often without our active engagement. Indeed, at the outbreak of COVID there was much discussion about the possibility of new habits being formed and to what extent these will remain once the pandemic subsides. This was of course of interest to retailers and brands but also policy makers who saw a range of new, more sustainable behaviours being adopted as people spent more time at home and were able to recycle more effectively and use their car less.

As climate change requires us to form new behaviours, often changing deep seated activities we have adapted to over many years, then the difficulty of forming new habits is discussed. How can we best do this, what does it require? And in this context technology is often brought to the fore, as an aid to help us develop new habits.

Climate change, COVID and technology have therefore pushed us to examine more closely the way in which we think about habits, what these actually are and what their adoption by us to engage with the world means. But also, the conceptualisation of routinised behaviours as habits tells us something about our beliefs about ourselves that is now being challenged. Are habits something that the world does to us or that we do to the world? Are they purely the stuff of our everyday behaviours or is there something bigger about them, connecting us with a broader shared set of meanings with the culture we inhabit? We will see the way in which habits we had for a world that no longer exists means we look more closely at this phenomenon, in the process reshaping some of the most important beliefs we have about ourselves.

The creation of habits

A famous experiment tested the hypothesis that cinemagoers' habit of eating popcorn while watching a film was so deeply embedded that they would not pay attention to the quality. Participants were placed into two groups with one being given fresh and other stale popcorn whilst at the cinema; the control groups who met in a generic meeting room (where the practice of eating popcorn is not so engrained), were also divided on the same basis. The key finding was that there was little difference between the amount of stale or fresh popcorn eaten by those in the cinema but those in the meeting room ate significantly less stale popcorn. Psychologist Wendy Wood suggested:

"People believe their eating behaviour is largely activated by how food tastes. Nobody likes cold, spongy, week-old popcorn. But once we've formed an eating habit, we no longer care whether the food tastes good. We'll eat exactly the same amount, whether it's fresh or stale". [1]

This notion that we form habits that are very predictable and stable has led to brands spending millions on marketing communications, with the intention that new habits will be spawned. At least this is if we reference operant conditioning, the typical body of theory that is used to understand habitual behaviour, drawn from studies on animal learning.

This is also referred to as incentive sensitization, where particular cues, once we have experienced them, themselves seem to acquire incentive-type properties, meaning they are infused with emotional properties that the customer may find positive. With repeat usage of the product, the potency of this emotion appears to grow continuously, further solidifying the habitual behaviour. [2]

Much of this sort of discussion about habit is congruent with a long tradition in psychology which considers the behaviour to be the result of innate or learned experiences. William James argued that our mental plasticity, the ability of the brain to rework its connections, means we can readily adapt to stimulus-response pairings. The philosophy that influenced James was Associationism, as set out by John Stuart Mill who considered that laws of order governed mental phenomena: according to Mills, habits, once established, will remain fixed and be performed automatically.

This is the scene set for the notion that our digital tools are influencing our lives in ways we are simply not aware of: behavioural scientist Schlomo Benartzi suggests that as the online world is so visual then we easily fall into an instinctual way of thinking, as this allows our minds to more easily act on superficial first impressions. [3] There is a significant body of work by people such as B.J. Fogg who devised the term 'persuasive technology', as a means of using digital technology to modify and build habits. [4]

The start-up Dopamine Labs boasted about its use of persuasive techniques to increase profits: they were reported as saying "Connect your app to our Persuasive AI and lift your engagement and revenue up to 30% by giving your users our perfect bursts of dopamine," and "A burst of Dopamine doesn't *just* feel good: it's proven to re-wire user behavior and habits". [5] It is also commonly considered that social networks and video games work on the basis that users never know when they will get the next "like" or game reward, but when it is delivered, it is done so at the ideal moment to foster the 'dopamine dose' and keep them on the site. Increasingly AI is used to develop a *persuasion profile* of users' unique susceptibilities which are developed in real time and then leveraged to encourage users to stay on the site and make them return again and again for longer periods of time.

Clearly given the amount of investment in the use of technology to develop habits, we might be expect them to be effective. [6] However, the evidence does not always suggest this is the case. For example, around one third [7] of people who buy fitness trackers cease using them within six months, and over half eventually stop them altogether. [8] Most studies looking at effectiveness of fitness trackers have produced, at best, weak findings. One well designed study found that after 12 months of use, an activity tracker had no overall impact on the 800 participants' overall health and fitness. [9] Another study examined whether integrating a weight loss program with a fitness tracker could help participants either lose more weight or enhance their health. The results in fact showed that those *without* trackers lost more weight than their counterparts and those with trackers were in fact no more active or fit than those without. [10]

These results surely suggest that the notion of habit may be a little more complex than training animals. Part of the difficulty is that we are often reasoning from effect to cause, as Steve Sloman and Philip Fernbach point out in their book, 'The Knowledge Illusion'. [11] We are called upon to diagnose the behaviours we are observing which might be the result of any number of causes. In contrast, going from cause to effect is a much more straightforward activity: if someone is reported as angry then we can predict they may well have had an argument. If someone is reported to have had an argument, then it is a much harder task to determine if it is this that might have led to their anger.

When we look at routinised behaviour (avoiding the term habit for now) then can we really be confident that it is behaviour that has been enacted due to a set of reinforcements and punishments? In other words, how can we unpick whether this is something that had been done to us or if the behaviour is something that we are doing to the world? If it is something done to us, then we might expect this to be independent of goals that we might have. We could point to the behaviour of an OCD patient who cannot help but to repeatedly wash their hands. There is no simple way we can unpick whether this is a behaviour that is automatically triggered by a stimulus (or cue) or if it is the activation of a goal instead. In other words, does the behaviour we are doing have meaning for us? If we are choosing to look at it with a dispassionate eye then it is easy to assume it does not, not least as other people's behaviour may often seem a little odd to others.

While this may seem a little pedantic, this surely has significant implications that might be explained by considering the difference between a habit and a ritual. As psychologist Nick Hobson points out, these might appear identical in structure, but the ritual is imbued with a sense of meaning, whereas the habit is not. Hobson suggests many of our most important rituals would simply appear arbitrary and trivial if the meaning were removed: the 21-gun salute of a military funeral then would become nothing more than a group of soldiers firing into the air rather than the mark of bestowing the highest honour to a fallen comrade.[12]

Surely, particularly if we are looking from afar, it is hard to identify when something has meaning for the people involved which means that the distinction between a habit and a ritual becomes one which reflects the degree of meaning that accompanies it (rather than assuming one has meaning while the other does not). Given the 'baggage' of these terms we will assume that habits and rituals can be used interchangeably: we will reference these collectively as 'routines'.

Routines as mastery

Australian philosopher Elizabeth Grosz suggests that all living things form routines as these enable us to manage external forces and effects through the minimal application of energy and conscious awareness. In a sense, therefore, routines are a matter of expertise over the environment, allowing us to tame it effectively.[13]

If we look at how we learn a skill – such as riding a bicycle – then we can see that we have to pay close attention to the mechanics of what we are doing. We must carefully think through how we manage our balance, pushing the pedals, keeping the handlebars straight and so on.

By contrast, the expert's performance deteriorates if they focus on the mechanics of the task. Expertise allows for and in fact requires, that attention is placed elsewhere. They are freed up to think about the pothole that is in front of them for example. Paying too much attention to the mechanics of the task will interrupt the flow and cause the expert to stumble on the basic task. In fact, a classic dirty trick of sports people is to ask their opponent to explain how they managed to conduct their expert behaviour.

In this way, habit systematises the world for us, which then allows our expertise to express itself. As Alva Noe puts it:

"Habits are basic and foundational aspects of our mental lives. Without habit, there is no calculation, no speech, no thought, no recognition, no game playing. Only a creature with habits like ours could have anything like a mind like ours" [14]

Elizabeth Grosz suggests:

"In this sense, habit is not that which reduces the human to the mechanical but rather is a fundamentally creative capacity that produces the possibility of stability in a universe in which change is fundamental. Habits change the disposition to action; they entail a change, a new virtuality, a new tendency to act, a new potentiality."

In this context, routines are less about the way the environment creates certain outcomes in the individual and is instead more reflective of the way in which we have become skilled in navigating our environments. It is because of routines that we can take certain things for granted which is hugely liberating. Instead of seeing them as inevitable forces that will shape our passive minds, we can see them as ways in which we learn about and master the environment. If certain choices lead to more positive outcomes and we avoid more unpleasant outcomes, then it makes absolute sense to adopt these routines. They enable us to obtain positive outcomes with the least amount of effort involved.

This is not to say that these routines operate at a conscious level, As Elizabeth Grosz points out:

"Habit produces an 'obscure intelligence' that operates below the level of will, consciousness, intentionality or reflection, an intelligence in which all forms of life participate...Thus habit does not arrest or mechanize, or reduce consciousness to unconsciousness or automatism...It is as close to instinct as possible, yet with the possibility of invention, newness, transformation and learning, an intuition acted rather than known".

But if we see routines as a form of expertise rather than the non-conscious passive accumulation of learned responses, then we can start to understand why persuasive technology is less effective than the designers may hope for. A mechanistic view of routines looks at the individual as an object – the mechanisms, it can be argued, do indeed necessarily reflect the way habits operate. They fail to see the wider perspective of the individual as a subject embedded in a context. If we are to harness routines, then we need to see it as a means of embedding the expert navigation of the world in which we live.

Looking at routines in this contextualised way makes a lot of sense, particularly if the behaviour in question is complex – such as exercise. In this instance, there are many more reasons to participate in exercise – maybe enjoying collaborating with others, a desire for competition, wanting to be outdoors, wanting to feel better about ourselves and so on. There are also many reasons why we might not get involved in sport. We may fear failure, looking silly, be concerned we will see just how out of shape we are, be concerned about the costs of participation (e.g., time and money) and so on.

If we were taking a mechanistic view of routines, we can argue all we need is to get a fitness device and this will set us on the road to fitness and wellbeing. If we take the view of ourselves as objects then surely if we are in an environment where the different attributes of routines are optimised, then we will be in good shape in no time.

Understanding

So, we can see that routines help us to understand that what we *do*, not just what we *think* is a fundamental part of what it means to be human. As philosopher of religion Kevin Schilbrack points out, the traditional Descartesian model of humans suggests that our engagement with the world is to 'represent' it in our minds and that our bodies cannot do this. Descartes would consider that our routines are the expressions of us 'going through the motions' in an automatic, non-conscious manner, rather than thinking. [15]

This view is challenged by philosophers, such as John Dewey, who, in line with Alva Noe and Elizabeth Grosz, considers that we can understand knowledge from the perspective of practical action. Dewey observed that what we know is less a purely static body of knowledge but instead is the result of an ongoing interaction between ourselves and our environment. [16] On this basis we can see there are different schools of thought with rationalists such as Descartes looking to reason as a source of knowledge, behaviourists (or empiricists) looking to our senses, while the pragmatists consider action is also a source of trustworthy knowledge.

Schilbrack suggests that the pragmatist's perspective of our routinised behaviours, means we can understand them as a means by which we "seek to move the participants from disquiet to resolution, they involve the testing of hypotheses, and hence they are a form of inquiry". In other words, people use them as a means of enquiring about problems and to overcome difficulties, and as such, they are a source of learning.

This means that as humans we are embodied and social, actively 'being-in-the-world' with the routines we deploy indicating a way of engagement with our environment. This process then involves things being revealed. To explain, if we can see routines as the means for achieving practical outcomes, then they clearly involve practical knowledge. This is not purely knowledge of how to perform the routine itself, but importantly, knowledge of how to relate not only to the physical but also to the social world.

The routines we deploy unavoidably require knowledge of social rules and roles: for example, rituals of deference involve an understanding of authority in a given context. Of course, this is why they can have a key role in maintaining social norms and cultural values but the flip side of this is they can also be used to access possible alternatives for being in the world. In other words, they offer us the means by which we have freedom to transform our individual or collective selves.

Freedom

The notion that routines can offer us freedom is fundamentally different from the prevailing notions for autonomy, considers cultural theorist Michael Crawford. The traditional notion of what it is to be free means satisfying our own personal preferences. These preferences are considered as beyond rational scrutiny as they reflect the 'authentic self'. [17] In this model, our ability to reason or think is the means to determine the optimal way to satisfy our ends. Crawford suggests the ends themselves are subject to 'a principled silence', out of respect for the autonomy of the individual's choices: if we comment on other peoples' choices then we would lapse into paternalism and as such we need not do so. This agnosticism about the human ends we strive for is, Crawford argues, aligned with the market ideal of 'choice'. This highly individualistic notion of what constitutes freedom and rationality

"disarms the critical faculties we need most in order to grapple with the large-scale societal pressures we now face... [and seems]...ill-suited to our current circumstances, if what we want is to preserve human possibilities from going extinct".

Crawford helps us to continue a radical reinterpretation of routines: he considers they have the effect of structuring our attention which relieves us of the burden of choice. He goes further in suggesting that genuine agency is not a matter of choices freely made (as in shopping) but paradoxically, is the result of submission to the world around us that has its own intractable ways. He makes the case that we only become competent when we are disciplined by a practice; we become subtly attuned to the key features of a situation that are invisible to a layperson.

As theologian Theodore Jennings puts it, "ritual action is not only the product but is also the means of a noetic quest, an exploration which seeks to discover the right action or sequence of actions". [18] Ritual knowledge is for Jennings a means of garnering practical wisdom which is not gained by disconnected observation or reflection but through action itself.

This is fundamentally different from the idea that we all create meaning for ourselves: if we are all independently seeking to discover our 'true preferences' then we are compelled to maximize the choices we make, thus dissipating our energies. We are used to the notion of autonomy meaning the liberation from the constraints imposed by our surroundings, but Crawford makes a compelling case that

"independence is won through disciplined attention, in the kind of action that joins us to the world. And—this is important—it is precisely those constraining circumstances that provide the discipline".

He gives the example of musical improvisation in a band:

The improvisation is possible because all parties are attending to one another. It is fruitful only because they are also steeped in forms; the history of their art has become the genetic material, the constitutive fiber, of their own creativity. A master jazz musician quotes from The Real Book with the same ease that a master preacher does from the gospels, and the allusion is gotten. It may be taken up and commented upon by the other players; it may be pushed forward toward possibilities that hadn't existed moments before, as they come into being only through the improvisation itself. One must be alert, opportunistic.... membership in a community is a prerequisite to creativity.

This reflects Jennings's theory: where a repeated action, such as chopping wood with an axe, is an *exploratory* or knowledge-*producing* act, in that trial and error we discover what to do and how to do it. In the act of using an axe, the axe itself teaches us through our hands, arms, and shoulders how it should be used. As such, routines involve discovery because they involve altering our environment. Especially in the initial phase, Jennings suggests, a routine provides a structured way to be open to and approach new situations or objects, offering the possibility of exploration and discovery.

Once a community has learned something through its routinised inquiries, the repetition of these acts means that knowledge can be used and shared for future inquiries:

"This relatively stable repertoire provides the necessary framework for exploration in much the same way as a mastery of relevant data and theoretical construction".

Metaphysics

There is yet another way in which we can examine the issue of routines which is by reference to theology which of course involves huge amounts of routinised behaviours (commonly referred to as rituals in this context).

Writer Catherine Bell suggests that routinised activities aim to socialise us with a 'ritualized body'; in other words, our participation in ritual structures our senses, including our "sense of reality". [19]

The routine facilitates this by bringing the individual body, the community, and "the largest image of reality" into a "felt continuity". The "ritual informed body" is then a microcosm of the world we inhabit, reflecting not only the structure of society but also the structure of reality itself. On this basis, ritual metaphysics is not simply a matter of giving us a mental *representation* of a larger world, but of giving us the experience of *participating* in the patterns and forces of the cosmos.

Drawing on Bell's writing, the routines create a ritualized body as we engage with the structured *and structuring* environment of the ritual. Through the deployment of certain oppositional structures—such as the opposition between what is masculine and what is feminine, what is above and what is below —the ritual shapes the understanding and the experience of those involved. As we come to master the ritual and internalize these schemes, our bodies come to appropriate this ritual world in our "habits, dispositions, and gestures". As such, participation in these rituals serve to "impress these schemes upon the bodies of participants".

This is consistent with the thinking of philosopher Byung-Chul Han who considers that rituals generate a community in which resonances occur. By this he means a sense of 'accord', or 'common rhythm':

"Rituals produce sociocultural axes of resonance along which may be experienced three different kinds of resonant relationship: vertical (e.g., to the gods, the cosmos, time, or eternity), horizontal (within one's social community), and diagonal (with respect to things)"[20]

He makes the case that without this resonance we are thrown back on to atomised, isolated selves. Again, echoing Crawford, he sets out how a drive for authenticity and narcissism work against the experience of resonance. But for him, resonance is "not an echo of the self," rather the "other" is inherent in it. The danger we have is that "Where resonance disappears completely, depression arises".

There is an interesting distinction that is helpful to explore between Christianity, which requires allegiance to prescribed beliefs. and Judaism, which simply demands observance of ritual behaviours. This, suggests professor of religions, Steven Kepnes, sets the mind free to discover truths through an open process of discovery. Religious liturgy is a set of highly prescribed routines that Kepnes suggests holds a position between the earthly and holy.

He sets out the way that liturgy is itself a type of "liminal" activity that sits between fantasy and reality.

This means that history, in the Jewish tradition, never needs to tell the story of events that are lost to the past. Rather, they remain "eternally present". For example, Passover Hagaddah involves: "Every single member of this community is bound to regard the Exodus from Egypt as if he himself had been one of those to go out". As such:

"...it is through liturgy that the Jewish people make their way back to their past and are able to represent their past as present". [21]

This understanding of the routines of liturgy reflects the ability to transform the scientific notions of time as moving forward in a linear fashion. Instead through liturgical routines, time is "bent into a circle in which past moments of revelation are relived and the future redemption is ... experienced".

German philosopher Walter Benjamin also challenged the notion of inevitable linear progression or the "maturing of objective conditions," instead allowing us to see that another world is possible if we interrupt this journey. Indeed, as we can see from the liturgical example, memories of past tyrannies and defeats weigh heavily on the minds of the living and can influence the present. [22]

Historian Bruce Lincoln suggests that being human involves us constantly creating ourselves through our actions and as such, there is a case for our routines to be something with the potential to be revolutionary given the way they help us negotiate change and to determine who we will be, and to create a future that is unlike our past. As Robespierre, the key figure of the French Revolution, put it:

"It is not enough to have overturned the throne; our concern is to erect upon it remains holy Equality and the sacred Rights of man".

Historian Christopher Dawson writes that the actors of the French Revolution "were not satisfied with political reforms or republican institutions. They dreamt of a spiritual republic based on moral foundations". Lacking such a moral foundation, the *ancien regime* was cast as illegitimate; the Jacobins considered that legitimate authority derived from eternal reason and virtue alone. [23]

On being human

The notion of habit comes with some very contrasting belief systems. One is aligned with a Descartesian, rationalist, modernist worldview, often represented through the values, currency, and actions of digital. From this perspective, routines are something done to us – they are shaped by marketers and policy makers by whom we are encouraged to adopt routines which affirm our own authentic needs and desires.

A deeply contrasting perspective is the way in which we can see the routines as something that connects us to a much bigger world view. Theologian and activist Walter Wink suggested that it is this wider sense, and in particular the relationship with the vertical dimension that allows us to understand today's complex social realities, such as the storming the Capitol or Brexit. His book, The Powers, sets out how spiritual, or mythical, beliefs are real for many people and failing to respect the reality of this, we lack an understanding of what drives much behaviour.[24]

With this examination of the way we are reappraising habit, we can start to see how, despite centuries of modernist thinking, humans often have a deeply mythical relationship with reality. This may not always be explicit, but we can discern it from the way in which certain acts are considered sacred, how we have a desire to be connected to something beyond the immediate world we inhabit.

13: The Promise

Rhoda Byrne's book "The Secret," sold more than 19 million copies in more than 40 languages. It offers a self-help philosophy based on the "law of attraction," which states that whatever you encounter in life is a direct result of your thoughts. If you think about your bills, you will get more bills, but if you think about getting money instead, then you will be suitably rewarded. [1]

According to "The Secret" your thoughts and feelings have magnetic qualities which "vibrate" and resonate with the "universe," thereby attracting the very things that share those frequencies, to their thinker. The ideology at the heart of what has been called the 'woo-sphere' is that intuition is the one and only thing we need to be using to determine what's true. [7]

A similar perspective, termed Conspirituality was identified by psychologists Charlotte Ward and David

[7] The woo-sphere is a term coined by Katya Weiss-Andersson, a holistic wellness practitioner whose podcast examines New Age beliefs.

Voas. They suggest there is a growing politico-spiritual philosophy based on two key convictions, the first of which is traditional to conspiracy theory, the second one rooted in the New Age (a wide ranging belief system that includes reincarnation, astrology, psychics and the presence of spiritual energy in physical objects): 1) a secret group secretly controls, or is trying to control, the political and social order, and 2) humanity is experiencing a 'paradigm shift' in consciousness. [2]

It is possible to track the way that ideologies and practices between New Age spirituality, the far-right and conspiracy theories have converged in a way that is creating resistance in large segments of the population to a variety of issues that many scientists agree on – such as the need for COVID vaccination. How should we consider and deal with the notion that the only thing that really matters is our own personal perspective?

We shall explore how, as conspiracy theories have developed around climate change and COVID, accompanied by claims of the role of technology, we can see more clearly how our beliefs about ourselves and the world around us are being renegotiated.

The perils of relativism

Writer and activist Richard Seymour suggests that postmodernism has become the "universal scapegoat" of our era. [3] Postmodernism rejects the notion of fact and instead is sceptical towards the notion that we can ever have certainty or stable meanings for the way we understand the world. Matthew D'Ancona argues postmodern intellectuals encourage a toxic relativism by treating "everything" as a "social construct," which means that "fake news" is able to thrive. Some commentators such as Christopher Hitchens and David Aaronovitch have blamed postmodern relativism for the left's seeming softness towards authoritarians and Islamic fundamentalism, as was obvious in their opposition to the invasion of Iraq in 2003.

This is also the tone of a paper by psychologist Stephen Lewandsky who acknowledges that scepticism about the foundations of knowledge and the limits of our tools for measurement has always been an intricate part of the modern scientific enterprise for centuries. [4] But since the 1960s the notion that much knowledge is socially constructed has significantly gained ground, with the job of the social sciences being to understand this constructive process. Lewandsky points out that a corollary of constructivism is relativism, because "in constructivism, the classical notion of truth is replaced by the notion of viability. This notion implies that there may exist alternative constructions, none of which can ever claim truth for itself".

This certainly feels consistent with a changing narrative around perception: a move from a world-to-mind model to a mind-to-world model. If we cannot be sure that we see colour in the same way as each other and indeed that there is no such thing as 'colour information' that is independent of our perceptual systems, then it is only a short step from rejection of predictable laws. On this basis Bruno Latour famously challenged "...the sovereign right of anyone wearing a lab coat to disqualify all other access routes" to truth. [5]

Lewandsky considered that this "radical scepticism" has found its way from the ivory towers of science to everyday life. Conspiracy theorists, allegedly putting "question marks over nearly everything," exemplify this democratized form of scepticism and radical doubt. This has meant we have moved from an era of "systemic lies" to a "shock and chaos" regime of disinformation. While systemic lies are careful efforts to persuade the public of a particular falsehood, such as the existence of WMD in Iraq or the absence of climate change, shock and chaos has little regard for any agreed 'fact' and instead we operate in a storm of unpredictable, often inconsistent, messages.[6]

Purveyors of shock and chaos disinformation select a relativist defence when challenged. For example, Kellyanne Conway declared that she was using "alternative facts" when challenged on the Trump administration assertions that Donald Trump's inauguration crowd was the biggest ever (which it was not).

In the U.K., right-wing commentator Katie Hopkins stated that

"Fact is an antiquated expression . . . There is no such thing as fact anymore". The phrase "ontological gerrymandering" describes attempts to escape accountability by summoning an extreme constructivist and relativist notion of truth". [7]

Consistent with Matthew D'Ancona, Lewandsky considered this shift, from tacit realism to "epistemic insouciance," to be the primary driver of current concern with "fake news".

The underdog effect

In some senses the very illegitimacy of a position offers certain powers. Art historian James Elkin suggests that alchemists, those involved in the ancient practice of attempting to transform materials, revelled in the ruins of their discipline:

"If things looked bad, and they were expelled from court, or called quacks or "puffers," then that meant their art must have some miraculous secret. Because it seemed empty, it must be full. Because it was despised, it must be magnificent". [8]

This notion is examined by professor in history of religions, Egil Asprem, who sets out the way in which New Age thinking is offered sustenance by its very illegitimacy. He considers that New Age is part of a long historical tradition of the 'cultic milieu' a set of belief systems that incorporates esoteric thought, occult rituals, and pseudoscientific theories. The unorthodox and oppositional nature of these beliefs mean they are often considered 'rejected knowledge'. [9]

The area has a huge range of "deviant belief systems" alongside flexible communication channels which means that the content is rapidly shared. The lack of an overarching institutionalized orthodoxy means people can quickly move through a wide range of different beliefs within this, readily bridging what may seemingly appear to be distinct and different. The key thing they have in common is an opposition to "Establishment" beliefs rather than any coherent set of positively shared beliefs.

Given this, is not difficult to see how conspiracy theory provides a common language, bringing these beliefs together as there is an embrace of stigmatized, or "rejected knowledge," in which "claims to truth that the claimant regards as verified despite the marginalization of those claims by the institutions that conventionally distinguish between knowledge and error". [10]

Political scientist Michael Barkun suggests there are several types of stigmatized knowledge, but that "suppressed knowledge" takes primacy in terms of influence. This is because believers consider that when their own ideas about knowledge clash with those of 'the Establishment' then the forces of orthodoxy will challenge, disparage, and delegitimize from a position of self-interest.

Given this, conspiracy thinking is an inevitable feature of stigmatized knowledge.

The cultic milieu makes claims concerning health, social, cultural, political, and economic topics with positions that are in opposition to authorized knowledge. As such, conspiracy provides a ready explanation of the way these claims are marginalised.

We can see the power of suppressed knowledge in the way that political correctness and 'wokeness' are positioned as orthodoxy, the language of the 'Liberal Elite'. As such any views which conflict with this assert that this powerful group with vested interests can collude to stigmatise and marginalise what they may consider to be legitimate perspectives.

This can explain, in part at least, the success of political movements and 'start-up parties'. [11] These are modelled on tech companies and characterized by rapid growth and high scalability, dominating the European political landscape since the financial crisis in 2008. For example, the Five Star Movement in Italy won the most seats in parliament less than four years from its launch. The far-right German AfD, became the official opposition four years from its own founding. The Brexit Party, which won the greatest number of votes in the May 2019 UK European Parliament after just four *months* of its launch.

The divine wars

The battle ground between belief systems of what is accepted and what is rejected, between 'fact' and social construction can be placed into what American sociologist Mark Juergensmeyer calls a “cosmic war”. This reflects modern day metaphysical battles between the forces of Good and Evil that drive religious imagination and compel violent action. [12]

If we see these debates as a spiritual confrontation between Good and Evil, it means that all ordinary claims of political and earthly authority are surpassed. It is in this context we can make sense of the battle for meaning. This battle is fundamentally a question of epistemology: the relation between thought and things, or mind and world.

On one side we have the myth of perfection of being able to observe the world – our own imperfections mean it is always tantalizingly out of our grip. On the other side is the way in which our own individual perspective is hallowed, sacred, territory. Both perspectives are not only supported through stories of events, and characters but also through perspectives that claim to have some epistemological authority.

Supreme fiction

How do we find a pathway through these divinity wars? The perspectives – on the one side the sacred nature for the freedom of my individual perspective and on the other the way in which there exists a hard to argue reality.

Chuck Stacey who had previously said he was "adamant" about not wearing a mask filmed himself in hospital saying:

"I believed this was just the flu, that it was all going to go away, that it was political... If wearing a mask can reduce your chances of getting this, even by 5%, just wear a mask. Do it for your children, for your loved ones. Do it for yourself". [13]

How do we find the line between what seems a hard, objective reality versus our own perspective of what we believe? Philosopher Simon Critchley has explored this in a political context where he considers there is a double miracle at work:[14]

"On the one hand, politics requires a willing suspension of disbelief. It requires that the many believe in the fictions told to them by the few who govern them. That is, government requires make-believe, whether the belief is in the divine right of kings or the quasi-divinity of the people that is somehow meant to find expression through the magic of representative government, the organ of the party, the radiant sun-like will of the glorious leader, or whatever. Government rests on fictions".

As he sets out political representation, which is the central pillar of liberal democracy, sets up a fiction that a particularity can speak for a generality when the latter is not actually present. But nevertheless, legitimacy of the few rests on the fiction of believing that they represent the many:

"It would appear that popular sovereignty is a fiction that cannot bear too close an examination or too

literal an application. It is a fiction that is extremely useful in giving a patina of legitimacy to representative government where what is essentially at stake is popular consent to a governing aristocracy, oligarchy, political class, or, in the case of the United States, a plutocracy. Popular sovereignty is a lie".

He cites how Rousseau suggests for this to work it must be bound to religion. By this we mean shared beliefs, civic values, and political rituals such as pledges of commitment, national anthems, respecting the war dead, the inviolability of the flag, and so on. As Critchley points out, for Rousseau, the fiction of politics cannot be sustained without the fiction of civil theology.

One of the most obvious examples of such a civil religion is that of the Founding Fathers in the United States. Obama managed to reconnect liberal rule bound orthodoxy with a highly motivating civil religion based on the notion of faith in change and progress.

The contingency of belief

Critchley goes on to cite the poet Wallace Stevens who considers that the critical task of poetry is to show that the world is what you make of it – in a sense that it is a fiction of our choosing. But that we are also conscious of its contingency. It may not be like we assume it is.

This is a challenge to Descartes and modern philosophy, which suggests knowledge is only possible if there is a correspondence between thoughts or mental representations and things in themselves. On the other side is Kant, who takes the view that what is true, is that which appears to the self. And that which appears might indeed refer to a thing in itself, but we can never be in a position to know this for sure. On Kant's picture, our access to a world that is indeed real for us, but that world is:

"always already shot through with conceptual content, it is articulated as such through the categories of the understanding and is dependent upon the spontaneity of the subject". [15]

But neither position is entirely right - the world that we inhabit is neither a bubble of subjective dreams, nor of an entirely subject-independent realm. We can explore this by adopting the position of the Romantics, an artistic and intellectual movement that originated in Europe around the end of the 18th century.

Romantics believed that the world might be transformed in and through art and as such our experience of the real is reliant on the work of the artistic imagination. But at the same time, the artist must not move too far away from the real, because then the isolated work of the imagination would result in fantasy or fancy. The artistic imagination must adhere to reality, whereas fancy works without any reference to reality.

Stevens puts it as, 'The real is only the base. But it is the base'.[16] An anti-realist relies only on their imagination and places great emphasis on this as we saw with, for example, The Secret. On the other side is the notion that our world is entirely subject-independent and explainable by the natural sciences. Taking this position would mean we then lack the intellectual, aesthetic, and moral values that give colour and texture to the world we inhabit. In other words, we are necessarily concerned with reality but:

"a poeticized, imaginatively transformed reality is both preferable to an inhuman, contracted and oppressive sense of reality and gives a truer picture of the relation humans entertain with the world". [17]

We can see the way in which the 'divine wars' are being played out in a way that we call conspiracy theories. Theorist Benjamin Bratton examines the way in which lockdown campaigners on both the left and the right of the political spectrum challenge the epidemiological reality of living with COVID:

"Each attacks the ability of society to sense, model, and act back upon itself in terms of biological assemblage according to the best available information. At their extremes, both valorize political performativity over scientific empiricism, both eschew the very notion of objectivity, and both are crippled by self-paralyzing magical thinking". [18]

In other words, we may have a vision of reality that is shaped by the political, social, and cultural landscape we desire but, as Benjamin Bratton points out, the virus does its thing. The real will have its revenge.

We inevitably need a nuanced relationship with reality as Mary Midgely suggests when she talks about using an Atlas:[19]

"When trying to square subjective experience and the laws of matter then the point is that we are not looking for the relation between two places on the same map. We are trying to understand the relation between two maps of different kinds... We have to see the different maps as answering different kinds of question, questions which arise from different angles in different contexts".

The challenge we have is that it is not always recognised that these different maps can be legitimately used to describe the world in different ways. A plurality is still perfectly rational. As Midgely says:

"We have to see the different maps as answering different kinds of question, questions which arise from different angles in different contexts".

On being human

As humans we hold certain things sacred, beliefs that some things are just non-negotiable. In our collective past, the sacred would have been more readily associated with religion. But since Descartes the sacred has arguably coalesced around science, as exemplified around the aspiration to divine perfection of Bayes and Fisher. But today we can see the way that it is the individual that is becoming 'sacrosanct'.

Indeed, philosopher Byung-Chul Han might track the lineage of anti-mask / anti-vaxx protestors to US video artist Jenny Holzer's slogan: "Protect me from what I want". [20] He considers that we have moved from 'Disciplinary power', subjecting people to orders and prohibitions, to the more efficient technique of power that ensures that people subordinate themselves to the system of rule voluntarily. The efficiency of this technique, according to Han, is due to it not working through prohibition but through pleasure and fulfilment the pursuit of which is our sacred right. He considers the subordinated subject is not aware of its position, instead believes themselves to be free. As Han puts it: "Restricting freedom quickly provokes resistance. Exploiting freedom does not".

On this basis, wearing a mask to protect against COVID can be seen by those that take an "anti-mask" stance, as not only a private decision but a very public example of the stance that holds individual liberty as sacred. But as Bratton pointed out during the peak of COVID:

"Waves of Boomers, myself included, grew up in a world in which the bad establishment was (supposedly) hierarchical and rationalist and, therefore, individualism and autonomy and spontaneous irrationality were (supposedly) a position of resistance, but we all find ourselves awake in a world where that opposition appears severely bent if not wholly inverted. Today our hospitals and morgues are full because of the horizontal, spontaneous, individualist irrationality of the status quo".

SECTION 4: LIMINAL LIVING

As humans we find the prospect of zombies threatening, they occupy a space which is neither human nor machine. They are physically identical to a normal human being, but completely lack an inner life. Zombies look and behave like the conscious beings that we know and love, but there is no internal subject experience.

In a way this is the ultimate liminal space, occupying an in-between zone that makes us feel very uncomfortable. But in another way, the combination of COVID, climate change and digital disruption has led us to question what we held to be certain, that in fact the 'in-between-ness' is a defining feature of being human. We are neither entirely individual nor entirely shaped by our physical and social context, but nor are we entirely 'subjects,' as we inhabit very definite objects, our bodies. We have a sense of ourselves as inhabiting a life limited by death but at the same time having a sense of the influence of not only our ancestors but also what comes after us.

All these point to a new reckoning of beliefs about ourselves, indicating that we are less definitive and easily categorised than we may have previously considered. While that comes with a loss for our security that comes with that notion of certainty, at the same time it opens up possibilities for different ways of living and organising ourselves.

14: Not Me but We

The middle of a pandemic seemed a time at which we should keep distance from one another, there is a need to not contact others, in case of spreading COVID. And yet there was a competing sense of need for coming together for collective expression. In the UK, one example was the 'The Clap for Carers' ritual that started on Thursday March 26th at 8pm and continued in many places for 10 weeks. By clapping from windows and doorsteps, many neighbourhoods connected with each other to express gratitude for carers and key workers. [1]

These events were dwarfed by Black Lives Matter, a political and social movement protesting police brutality but also all racially motivated violence against black people. The movement began in July 2013, after the acquittal of police officer George Zimmerman in shooting of African-American teen Trayvon Martin, 17 months earlier in February 2012.

The movement gained further momentum during the global George Floyd protests in 2020 following his murder by Minneapolis police officer Derek Chauvin.

We have also seen the way in which many people come together, sometimes with violent results, to protest some of the ways in which public safety measures during COVID had been imposed, as well as demonstrations by people opposed to COVID vaccination. The UK far-right politician Nigel Farage's Brexit Party was renamed "Reform UK" with its focus on opposing coronavirus restrictions in the UK. This is against the backdrop of a recent report from the United Nations Security Council warning that right-wing groups in the US were seeking to exploit the pandemic to "radicalize, recruit, and inspire plots and attacks".[2]

All these very different examples show the way in which the times we live in are helping us to see more clearly the way that emotion is often associated with collective action, and the way that when people come together, then emotions are created and shared in an apparently contagious way. Through this, a new sense of what emotion is, how it works and what it is for is starting to emerge, offering a new sense of what it means to be human.

Emotion and behaviour

Turning first to the history of the huge topic of emotion, we find that psychologists such as Sigmund Freud, Konrad Lorenz and Clarke L. Hull historically looked at emotion in terms of innate drives: our emotional states are related to the history of the species itself or to the learned and past history of us as individuals. We might have certain instincts that mean we react in particular ways or emotion might be a function of 'conditioning' through our life experiences. In either case, both focus on the way the past determines the emotional response that then shapes a behaviour. This 'classic' view of emotions implies that our emotions are 'built in' templates that 'fire' off – so 'anger', for example, is a built-in defence mechanism of our animal 'fight-flight-freeze' pathways.

From this perspective, emotions have developed to play a key role in directing us towards appropriate responses. Indeed, there is an assumed notion of a universality of expression of emotions which is referenced in Darwin's book 'The Expression of the Emotions in Man and Animals'. [3] This perspective was popularized by the psychologist Paul Ekman, placing emotion very much within the individual - an 'inside out' model as it were, an individual, contextless act. [4]

This is the model on which the facial recognition technology is based, with a huge industry predicated on the capability of AI to scrutinise our faces and recognise emotions that we ourselves may not even be aware of. However, this has been accompanied by a great deal of controversy.

There are detailed accounts of this elsewhere such as Kate Crawford's excellent Atlas of AI in which she cites

Lisa Feldman Barrett on the way that automated detection of facial expressions does not necessarily reflect an internal mental state: “Companies can say whatever they want, but the data are clear. They can detect a scowl, but that’s not the same thing as detecting anger”. [5]

Ugly feelings

One of the dangers of looking at emotion without understanding the context is that it is then easy to gas-light those who have difficult feelings. In her book Ugly Feelings, Sianne Ngai sets how our unpleasant feelings are often dismissed as a purely subjective affect: "it's all in your head" or "you're the one with the problem”. [6]

For Ngai, ugly feelings operate at the boundary between internal feeling and objective reality, between affective consciousness and material political conditions. She sees this as offering diagnostic power, but their liminal nature means they can too readily be reductively converted from actual:

"polemical engagement[s] with the objective world into [reflections] of a subjective characteristic. In other words, your feeling may not be in your head but instead are diagnostic of material conditions and social inequalities”.

This is often discussed in relation to issues of Race and gender. Envy, a classic ‘ugly feeling’, can be actual recognition of social and economic inequalities—and yet our culture's tendency is to stereotypically dismiss envy as a merely "feminine" affect or racial overstatement and hence, in this prejudicial logic, merely trivial. But, in fact, resentment may well be perfectly legitimate, and we saw that play out with the Black Lives Matter movement.

Constructivist theories of emotion

Later theories of emotion do take context much more into account, with a 'constructivist' perspective; this suggests that humans have a more active role interpreting and making sense of emotions. An example is the James-Lange theory of emotion, in which emotions are bodily sensations, which are then interpreted by the mind. [7] Rather than emotion being 'done to us' we instead use situational and cultural cues to provide us with explanations of what type of emotion we are feeling. Therefore, if we take a positive face and put it in a negative situation, people will experience the face as more negative. [8]

This opens the door for challenges to a strictly psychological notion of emotion. If we take a more constructivist approach, then we can see our reaction and behaviour is negotiated between the person and the situation and whatever the opportunities,

[8] This is nicely illustrated by the Kuleshov Effect, a film editing effect invented by Soviet filmmaker, Lev Kuleshov. Here the audience derives more meaning from the interaction of two back-to-back shots one with the actor's face and another of various other shots relating to the context the actor is in. This means that viewers bring their own emotional reactions to the sequence of images, but most importantly attribute those reactions to the actor, investing the otherwise inscrutable face with their own associations and feelings.

constraints, and affordances are of that moment. The implication of this for our reading of emotion is quite radical.

First as leading psychologist Lisa Feldman-Barrett points out, this would indicate that the expressions that we have been told reflect certain emotional states are simply stereotypes and that in fact people express emotions in a vast array of different ways. [8]

But more importantly, we do not construct our emotional concepts individually but are reliant upon our culture. Feldman-Barret illustrates this by pointing out that Russian has two distinct concepts for 'anger'; German has three and Mandarin has five:

"Your personal experience, therefore, is actively constructed by your actions. You tweak the world, and the world tweaks you back. You are, in a very real sense, an architect of your environment as well as your experience. Your movements, and other people's movements in turn, influence your own incoming sensory input. These incoming sensations, like any experience, can rewire your brain. So you're not only an architect of your experience, you're also an electrician".

Barret is challenging the traditional 'inside-out' model of emotion and suggesting that our emotions are in fact a function both of our internal states but also of the external facets of the world we live in.

Barret was by no means the first to approach emotion with external factors in mind. Sociologist Emile Durkheim long ago suggested an 'outside-in' model. He proposed that 'great movements' of feeling, 'do not originate in any one of the particular individual consciousnesses'. On this basis, the individual is not the origin of feeling; instead, it is what binds the social body together. [9]

Princess Diana's death could be considered a good example of this 'outside-in' model – a collective crowd sense of emotion overwhelms us, so we become personally invested. This would infer that the sense of grief of the crowd got internalised by individuals. Lisa Feldman-Barret takes a more nuanced approach with a view of emotion which is both 'outside-in' and 'inside-out'.

We can see the way that these 'outside-in' and 'inside-out' dynamics are reflected in the work of Rimé and David Garcia who analysed a set of data collected from over sixty thousand Twitter users after the Paris terrorist attacks of November 2015. [10] They found that in the months after the attack, Twitter users who had greater participation in social sharing, subsequently expressed higher rates of prosocial behaviour and positive affect in their social-media activity on Twitter. It seems that by engaging in collective emotions through social media, users were able to synchronize their thoughts and emotions, facilitating feelings of social belonging and shared beliefs.

In another example, people living in impoverished conditions in Rio De Janeiro's Complexo do Alemão Favela mobilized digital technologies both for protection as well as emotional support. This allowed them to witness police violence, direct people to sites of protest, and to disrupt discourses that portrayed favela residents as criminals. The technologies not only combatted aggressive social control, but residents also used the same technology to connect the community, forging "digital relationships of care" within the favela. [11]

Emotions as social and cultural practices

Cultural theorist Sara Ahmed also considers our experience of emotion is not a binary choice between either inner or outer source. But she goes further when she suggests that emotions are not something either the crowd or the individual can 'have'. In fact, they should not be regarded as psychological states, but as social and cultural practices. [12]

She suggests they are the means we collectively define the 'surfaces and boundaries' that allow the 'individual' and the 'social' to be defined as such. Her notion of 'affective economies' suggests that emotions circulate, involving relations of difference.

This means that emotions are due to contact with objects, they are *about* something. Indeed, she points out that emotions do not reside in the inner or in the outer, but in the circulation of the objects of emotion. They are the orientations we have towards objects, bodies, and signs, thus both separating as well as connecting us to others.

For example, Ahmed explains that hate does not reside within an individual but is circulated: as such it draws other bodies together and in doing so makes them members of a group united by their hatred of other groups.

It is common and indeed seems intuitively correct that we think of groups such white supremacists and other far-right parties such as Germany's AfD as innately hateful. Yet the explicit narratives espoused by these groups are less about hate – on the contrary the heart is often used in their logos. What can this mean?

Sara Ahmed wrote that "It is out of love that the group seeks to defend the nation against others". Indeed, Donald Trump's video message to his supporters who stormed the Capitol on January 6, 2021 ended with the sentence: "Go home. We love you. You're special". This group deserving of our love included members of the Proud Boys, Oath Keepers, Boogaloo, QAnon and Three Percenters—all white supremacist groups that have been consistently linked to racist death threats and violence.

Far-right groups perpetuate the sentiment of being the "good ones"—they love their country, their people, and their traditions.

On this logic, racism becomes a just and reasonable cause as:

"the racial others become the obstacle that allows the white subject to sustain a fantasy that without them, the good life would be attainable, or their love would be returned with reward and value". [13]

This leads to the justification of strict border controls and increased deportations, all based on the conceptualization of a white nation. Anti-democratic, populist politics are assumed to be irrational, stirring up hatred. But to understand emotion in this way runs the risk of assuming far-right groups are irrational people whose narratives are dripping in emotive evocations. In fact, they are doing exactly what Ahmed sets out, defining the orientation we have towards objects, bodies, and signs, and on this basis separating as well as connecting us to others.

Political anthropologists Julia Leser & Florian Spissinger suggest that far-right politicians distance themselves from hatred and fear, as these classify their projects as illegitimate from the outset. Indeed, their research suggests that hate was something that members and supporters of the AfD refrained from expressing explicitly. [14]

Instead, there is a more subtle way in which far-right groups express themselves as politically legitimate by the use of practices that enable their opposition to groups such as migrants and other vulnerable groups in the population, to be attributed positively.

Journalist Kenan Malik suggests it is through the creation of 'identities' that worldviews then get shaped, feeding hatred:

"The politics of identity is..at root the politics of the reactionary right. The original politics of identity was that of racial difference, the insistence that one's racial identity determines one's moral and social place in the world" [15]

Professor of religion Egil Asprem points to the creation of "affect networks," via social media channels such as 4chan, 8chan, and Reddit where anonymous contributors define and signal in-group membership and belonging through shared posts which perpetuate ridicule, distrust, and disgust of reified outgroup competitors ("SJWs" [social justice warriors], "cuckservatives," "normies"). The goal, as Asprem points out, is to create a web of associations, manufacturing distrust through the networking of negative affect, especially contempt and disgust. [16]

In the same way that social psychologist Serge Moscovitchi references "the thinking society" to describe the social nature of thought, so affective networking is a relational property shared between individuals as well as in relations between persons, things, signs, and situations. [17] The affective network itself has emergent properties that help us to unpick how and why people behave in certain ways rather than others, have certain emotions and not others.

White nationalist mythologies

To illustrate the way this is working Andreas Malm has written about the 'mythical core' of fascism, and how it can speak to the gut feelings of broad swathes of people, inspiring them to believe in the supporting the nation by eradicating its enemies. This is reflected in the English Defence League with its associated offshoots across Europe, wielding symbols from the Crusades, vowing to 'defend our land from 1,400 years of jihad'. [18]

He sets out the way this narrative led the Hungarian government to erect a four-metre-high steel fence topped with barbed wire along its borders with Serbia and Croatia, closing the route migrants had used to travel in search of asylum. Viktor Orbán incited people with collective memories of the way the Hungarian nation had been unrecognised and under-appreciated as the forward defence base when the Ottoman Empire pushed into Europe, keeping the rest of the continent safe but never been thanked for this'. They are now, the narrative flows, taking it upon itself to defend Europe from a Muslim invasion.

In this way, the contemporary European far right discovered the power of the myth of their nation's collective memory and their identity with it offering a heightened meaning to their lives.

Spiritual element

Through the mystical appeals to the notion of nation and whiteness of the far-right we can see echoes of Durkheim, who coined the term "collective effervescence" to set out his understanding of religion and society. [19] He suggests that emotionally arousing collective acts provide something bigger and more powerful and the symbols that are associated with them become the basis of shared identity, imbued with "sacred" power. [20]

This surely helps us to understand the way in which spiritual, or cultic, beliefs are readily adopted by the far-right. Brenton Tarrant, the Australian who massacred 51 worshippers at two Christchurch mosques in March 2019 adopted the Black Sun symbol on the cover of his manifesto. The terrorist who killed Jo Cox MP kept runes in a string bag. [21] The Black Sun is a representation of the sun in ancient Norse paganism. According to the historian of fascism, Roger Griffin, it is "now the ideology…of the mythical white 'Aryan' race fighting the alleged ethnic and ideological enemies of its 'purity' all over the world". [22]

Many aspects of neo-Nazi and white supremacist cultures engage in cultic, esoteric practices that often promise radically alternate spiritual enlightenment. One of the ways this is explored and expressed is through music and in particular black metal music and its offshoot, national socialist black metal (NSBM).

Indeed, historian Nicholas Goodrick-Clarke, suggests that black metal and its "fascination with the occult, evil, Nazism and Hitler" were a plausible motivation for the 1999 massacre, on Hitler's birthday, of 12 students and a teacher at Columbine High School in Colorado.[23]

Of course, not all black metal fans are fascists or Satanists, and many are simply drawn to the genre's ability to shock and entertain, with others attracted by their interest in ancient religion. However, NSBM is aimed to specifically demarcate its politics and religiosity much more clearly than other forms of black metal music by the mixing of extreme-right racism with paganism.[24]

The sociologist of religion Edward A. Tiryakian pointed out the way that charisma and collective effervescence feed into each other. [25] In a social situation of collective effervescence, certain people take on the role of "interpreter" of the strong collective sentiments that are sensed but only dimly understood by each individual in the group. Music has a key role in these settings, providing a narrative that reinforces mythic identities in an accessible manner.

We can also see the way conspiracy theories offer a means by which people are can become engaged in collective acts that offer a portal into something bigger and more powerful. Research has found that the conspiracy theory that the US government was using the pandemic to restrict citizens' freedoms had been key in encouraging calls for a civil war. It is perhaps no co-incidence that COVID saw the rise in the US of the "boogaloo' movement," a loose online network of gun-owning activists that has been linked to violent clashes across the US. [26]

On being human

It is within a crisis that we often see the best and the worst in each other. We have seen the way that COVID has brought people together in a positive way but at the same time has created polarisation and distrust. Through this we can see how we need to think about a basic human characteristic – emotion - in a far more nuanced way that has historically been the case, bringing the work of cultural theorists such as Ahmed and Ngai centre stage.

To illustrate this, if we conceptualise an issue as emotion such as "hatred" then we fail to see the structural vilification of marginalised groups such as migrants and Muslims and the way that ideas of white victimhood are encouraged. [27] We cannot easily separate out emotion from our group identities, moral values, and political ideologies—they are intertwined in shaping our thoughts and behaviours.

A key lesson we have learnt about being human is that a sense of common fate and shared social identities produce better results than working alone. People cooperate more when they are in a meaningful group than when merely part of a set of individuals. This can be powerful in both positive and negative ways.

But these very same mechanisms can be used to promulgate mythical nationalist narratives that then shape new ways of relating involving alienation and distrust. We inhabit a space where individual and cultural ways of understanding ourselves are both true.

Understanding that we sit in-between these zones seems important to help us unpick one of the most fundamental characteristics of being human.

15: Living in the End Times

We live at a time in which we regularly receive alarming news about the climate: huge summer fires, torrential flooding and damaged crops are just some of the obvious and direct manifestations. The Intergovernmental Panel on Climate Changes (IPCC)'s 2021 Report set out the way that within the next two decades, temperatures are likely to rise by more than 1.5C above pre-industrial levels; this will bring widespread devastation and extreme weather. The report sets out:

"The scale of recent changes across the climate system as a whole and the present state of many aspects of the climate system are unprecedented over many centuries to many thousands of years". [1]

Only a course of radical action over the next decade will reduce the chances of crossing thresholds that will in all likelihood commit us to a trajectory of "Hothouse Earth". The United Nations have indicated we have 11 years to avert such a climate catastrophe, and the UK parliament approved a motion to declare an environment and climate emergency. [2]

An emergency equates the climate challenge in terms that are used during a time of war, with some comparing the climate crisis as “our Third World War”. Some have started to observe the way in which this political state of emergency aligns with theological concepts, and in particular millenarianism. [3]

This is the belief in a coming fundamental transformation of society, after which all things will be radically altered, often after a major cataclysm. While millenniumism is a key feature of Christian belief, that of being a ‘final judgement’ and while most do not consider this to be literal, some groups, such as Jehovah’s Witnesses, do await just such an event.

Climate and societal change

This is not the first time in history that humans have collectively worried about their fate at the hands of the climate. Periods in history of climate change have been marked by radical changes in society with profound socioeconomic, as well as political and theological shifts. Historian Philip Jenkins, book ‘Climate, catastrophe, and faith’ sets the scene. [4]

The years between 1310 and 1325 was an era of climatic change, a period of global cooling that came to be known as the Little Ice Age. Societies around the world experienced paranoia and conspiracy-theorising with resulting persecutions of minorities and dissidents, and a huge scale of purges and expulsions. The changes set in place many of the now familiar geographies of the main religions' faiths.

Around 1560, the Little Ice Age entered a new, especially cold era, with social strains threatening the political order. There was huge unrest often involving witch-hunts, which reached their peak in Europe. This time also saw spectacular religious transformation within Christianity, with the fast-growing Calvinist movement representing a revolutionary tide that threatened many ancient religious ways.

The third era, from 1675 to the end of the century, was one of the coldest periods of the Little Ice Age. At this time, Europeans lived in a world of sea travel and distant colonial ownership, and settlements in foreign lands offered the prospect of religious liberty, heralding a new more relaxed phase of religious openness and spiritual experimentation.

Then in 1739–1742, mechanisms of the state were better-developed, alongside increasingly sophisticated media and communication. This facilitated the circulation of ideas and beliefs with popular fears channelled into radical new forms of revivalist religion. New denominations and sects emerged within existing faiths, with many becoming significant.

Jenkins has clearly set out the way that over the centuries, human beliefs have been reshaped by sudden climate shifts. As the world now faces a new, unprecedented crisis, there is again the possibility of sudden changes in the way we think of ourselves and our place in the world.

In a sense this is inevitable – if we feel as if we are living in 'End Times' then this is a profoundly unsettling experience. Examining this allows us to explore the way we understand ourselves more clearly, including the way in which we operate as crowds, often associated with millenniumism, but also how the notions of hope and collective action shape our understanding of being human.

The history of Millenarian movements

Millenarian movements are often associated with violent attempts at taking power. This perspective was popularised by historian Norman Cohn, whose book *Pursuit of the Millennium* aimed to find a coherent explanation of Christian millenarian uprisings between the eleventh to the sixteenth century. [5]

He considered that the strand that links these quite different events was a universal belief-system that placed the responsibility for the redemption of humanity outside of itself, and typically into the hands of the divine.

Cohn regarded a number of factors as defining millenniumism, namely:

a) collective: it is to be enjoyed by the faithful as a group, not simply individually;
b) terrestrial: it is to be manifested on this earth and not in some after-life
c) imminent: it is to come both soon and rapidly;
d) total: it utterly transforms life on earth, so that the new environment will not simply be an improvement but a state of perfection;
e) miraculous: it is accomplished by, or with the assistance of, supernatural agencies.

Cohn's preconditions for millenniumism could be seen as just as relevant for political change today as they were for European peasants living in the sixteenth century. This implies that secular claims for social change are variations of a fanatical set of demands, that we must seek transformative salvation in the shape of divine intervention from the miserable existence we have created for ourselves.

The notion that millenniumism is predicated on the need for violent radical divine intervention means that the claims themselves are readily discredited – in just the same way that labelling a set of beliefs 'conspiracy theories' immediately undermines the points being made or position that is held. As such, Cohn's work has played a key role in the demonization of millenarianism and, by virtue of this, the current strand of eco-millenarism. Environmental activists have long been accused of invoking biblical apocalypse to shift political thinking from publications such as Rachel Carson's Silent Spring through to today's Extinction Rebellion, the theme of End Times is rarely far away.[6]

The notion that millenniumism is inevitably a violent rupture is one that is dominant in our imagination but just how fair is this and does the current climate crisis allow us to see more clearly the mechanisms shaping this but also alternatives for the way we approach living at this point in history?

Millenniumism and protest

Dissent and challenge are often, but not always, associated with protest, with large numbers of people taking part in organised marches, a familiar part of dissent. There have been such protests relating to the climate, globally bringing millions to the streets demanding action on the part of governments. In this environment it is easy to align in our minds' eye these crowds with millenniumism, with the prospect of violence and disorder.

But just how fair is this? To examine this, we look at how historical theories of the crowd have often typically accounted for their impassioned nature by aligning emotionality with a loss of identity and sense. If being part of a crowd involved the loss of personal identity then this meant the loss of behaviour control, leading to emotion dominating over rationality. On this basis, crowds came to represent irrationality. We will then examine more recent thinking about crowds which offers us some directions forward and new ways to navigate the sense of End Times we live in.

Fear of the crowd

Gustave Le Bon is the name most commonly associated with the origins of crowd psychology that supported the view of crowds as irrational and out of control. His book, published in 1895, 'The Crowd: A Study of the Popular Mind' was a huge success at the time but also continues to shape the way we think about this topic today. [7] He wrote that the "unconscious action of crowds substituting itself for the conscious activity of individuals is one of the principal characteristics of the present age".

More recently however it has become clear that Le Bon's views were shaped by the turbulent times he lived in, that of class conflict and popular militancy following the 1871 Paris revolution. It was all too easy to draw a parallel between the presence of crowds and the apparent collapse of social order. Critiques of crowds themselves were often just as much about the fear of the rise of socialism and distrust of democratic politics.

Within this political environment, Le Bon's particular flavour of crowd psychology positioned rational action as the sole property of the individual, and the crowd as that of collective irrationality.

It is not hard to see how this could be seen as a means to delegitimise popular struggle, undermining both the motivation and legitimacy of collectivist movements. As academic Fergus Neville succinctly puts it:

"By a priori pathologizing alternative visions of society as irrational, any challenge to the hierarchical social and political status quo was rendered mindless, and the rejection of identities in traditional (unequal) systems was treated as a lack of identity per se". [8]

If crowds are pathologized as irrational then *de facto* this decontextualizes them, with no attention given to the reasons that led people to assemble, or indeed to the role that security forces can have in driving conflict. Indeed, Neville writes that historical evidence often suggests crowd violence is frequently initiated by these security forces who are often responsible for killing many more people than the crowd.

Pathologizing of dissent

Returning to the topic of millenarianism, critical theorist Alberto Toscano writes about the pathologizing of particular forms of dissents, arguing that the term Millenarianism, has been weaponized and is typically used as a means of demonizing a wide range of social threats. [9]

Aligning the term with fanaticism means that slavery, civil rights, and feminist activists have all faced the accusation of being millenarian fanatics. [9]

Just as with crowds, the fanatic is seen as a person with impassioned beliefs that eventually bypass rationality. People such as Nelson Mandela or Emily Pankhurst were once branded fanatics and terrorists, with their activities considered to be attacks on the reasonableness of the political order. Similarly, climate activists are often considered fanatics with their millenarian zeal bypassing legitimate democratic channels. [10]

There has always been a way in which crowds have been a place where the current political order is threatened. Barbara Ehrenreich sets out the way that medieval carnivals were not only rumbunctious affairs of people dancing in unison, but they also mocked the authorities with 'rituals of inversion". [10] There may for example, be a king of fools or dancers costumed as priests and nuns. There is a rich history of subordinate groups temporarily taking the roles of their social superiors. During Saturnalia, a Roman pagan festival, masters waited on their slaves; carnival therefore allowed peasants to imitate kings.

---

[9] Millenarianism, in Toscano's positive appraisal, signifies a politics of 'getting ahead of oneself'.

[10] Eco-millenarian belief offered by organisations such as Extinction Rebellion offer a view of the world that is in sharp contrast with the dominant notion of historical progress.

We can perhaps see something similar with conspiracy theories – we tend to talk about conspiracy theories in quite sober terms, commenting on the way they promulgate often dangerous ideas such as discouraging people to get vaccinated. However, we are also seeing the way in which conspiracy theories are often 'carnivalesque' in character, appropriating the very same 'rituals of inversion' that we saw in the carnivals of medieval Europe.

Ehrenreich suggests that the rude mockery of carnival crowds highlights their political ambiguity. On the one hand it might serve as a fundamental challenge to the status quo but could also be seen as a simple safety valve for discontent. The maypole, around which so many traditional French and English festivities were based, was often a signal of defiance and a call to action. In England, football could provide an excuse for assembling and a cover for challenges to authority, in each case, social clashes 'coincided' with carnival.

It is this tension that is the basis for centuries of repression of carnival, being replaced instead with what she calls 'spectacles', festivities organised by authorities in which the masses are no longer active participants but merely spectators. Nevertheless, carnival style activities keep bubbling up: whether rock rebellion of the 60's, sporting events (as we saw in the UK engagement of their relative success in Euro2020)[11] and raves. [12]

A more constructive take on crowds

Crowds have been seen by some commentators, less as threatening and irrational, and more as a means to navigate the world, to share our thoughts and feeling, finding ways to make change happen and create a better future. Sociologist Emile Durkheim proffered a positive view of crowds, describing that they provide a way for members of a society to come together and synchronize their thoughts and behaviours using shared slogans, signs, and movements. [13] Emotions of the participants are stimulated, leading to what he called 'collective effervescence' a sense of 'emotional communion', offering participants a means to develop a sense of belonging and shared beliefs.

Psychologist Martin Seligman also offers us a useful lens to explore some of the psychological mechanisms here. He suggests that animals (he uses this term broadly to include humans) become more effective if they do not live simply in the present but rather constantly model what might be ahead and seek information to explore this, evaluating alternatives and then deciding on the best course of action. The advantages this confers has been hugely impactful for shaping humans' collective perceptual, cognitive, affective, and motivational systems. [14]

We have incredibly evolved brains that are constantly 'foraging the world' for value and information, using past experience as evidence, while repeatedly forming and evaluating future options. We can then determine the best course of action from among the possibilities considering what we like and value.

What does this mean for how we understand crowds? Quite a bit it seems with Seligman going on to speculate that a key function of human consciousness is to allow for prospection of the future. But not only in the sense of *individual* prospection but also *shared* prospection. The benefits of collective activity can only come if the group share knowledge, plan alongside each other, jointly carry out plans, monitor collective progress and adjust accordingly. Each of these takes individuals away from a complete focus on their own situation and requires for shared prospection over a period of time.

Seligman considers consciousness is essential for this ability in humans, an ability that might explain how physically vulnerable humans became such a potent force in the world. Shared social consciousness through discourse means people are able to think and plan together, calculating what to expect, or how they might feel, or what they can locate under a variety of contingencies.

Crowds thinking together

To develop this further and more directly to crowds, we turn to Stephen Reicher who sets out some of the key social psychological mechanisms that help to understand crowd behaviour. [15] First, he argues that identity is not lost within the crowd, but rather there is a *cognitive transformation* from personal to social level identification. It is through this that crowd members act meaningfully, reflecting the norms of their salient shared (social) identity.

In addition to the cognitive shift, other work focusses on the relational and emotional transformations within crowds. Crowds result in a *relational transformation* so that social relations improve as we become part of the collective self. There is a wide range of evidence to suggest that ingroup membership facilitates trust, cooperation, a decrease in stress, comfort in close physical proximity, and helping behaviours. This also in turn leads to an *emotional transformation* with crowd members feeling empowered to shape their world realising shared goals creating intense positive affect.

When participants see others in a crowd as sharing their social identity (e.g., communicated through ingroup symbols, behaviours, or emotions), then social between-crowd members have a sense of connectedness and a feeling of being valued by others.

In contrast to 'everyday' life, which may be characterised with doubt and insecurity, the crowd participants can find relief from personal uncertainty as their perspective is reflected by fellow group members.

Making it happen

We have seen the way that millenniumism and crowds, while not the same thing are nevertheless related to each other and have historical parallels in the way they are thought about. Both have a long history of being considered to be violent and irrational. But as professor of theology Stefan Scrimshire asks, does it have to be that way? [16] We first visit those who consider it does, in the shape of political philosopher, Carl Schmitt and then examine alternative thinking that challenges this notion.[11]

The need for change to be accompanied by often violent schism is best represented by Carl Schmitt, who suggests that millenarian thinking reflects the dominant Western liberal order's failure to tackle the problem of climate change. Climate change deliberation simply takes too long and reveals irreconcilable differences of polarised 'rational' positions. [17]

As philosopher Simon Critchley asks, in the battle between the "right" of citizens to travel, own polluting cars and the rights of citizens to have a habitable

---

[11] In Political Theology Scmitt famously asserts that "All significant concepts in the modern theory of the state are secularized theological concepts".

future, who wins and on what basis? He asks if rational science is any help to neutrally arbitrate whose 'world' has a future? [18] Schmitt suggests we need a millenarian vision, a call to arms based on the understanding that the ending of the world is potentially always at hand. Politics for Schmitt is the means of protecting human beings from themselves, something that justifies the forms of dictatorship and state authoritarianism.

This links to the notion of original sin, the idea that humans are defective and need to be saved from themselves. This, claims Schmitt, is not a defunct vestige from the religious past but remains alive and well, providing authoritarians with the rationale that human beings require the governance of the state, God, law, and the police. Politics on this basis is the means for protecting human beings from themselves, from their inclinations towards violence.

The rules-based state is then the success of this theological vision, seen most obviously in the respect of Americans for the Founding Fathers, which Critchley considers a civil religion functioning to sustain the myth of Manifest Destiny. [12]

---

[12] This is the belief widely held in the 19th-century United States that American settlers were entitled to conquer and control the entire North American continent.

But for Schmitt having the rules-based politics of liberalism, means the death of the political as it hands over the decision to an endless structure of discussion and compromise:

"the essence of liberalism is negotiation, a cautious half measure, in the hope that the definitive dispute, the decisive bloody battle, can be transformed into a parliamentary debate and permit the decision to be suspended forever in an everlasting discussion".

He argues that humans can overcome the notion of original sin and find union with others. Indeed, this is necessary as the Achilles heel of deliberative democracy, is "scarcity of time". It is only a state of emergency that creates the moment when the 'sovereign' (whoever that might be in the political system) can then breach normal law to make a decision. We see this thinking regularly in association with terrorist incidents - the link between emergency and declaring a state of *exception* becomes easily endorsed. The rule of law is suspended out of perceived necessity by the sovereign, and indeed it is this that is in danger of now becoming the normal state of affairs in the contemporary state. [19]

While this may seem a little far-fetched in the context of climate change, eco-millenniumism activists do often reflect this strain of exceptionalism with one of the earliest activists James Lovelock suggesting that ordinary humans may be "too stupid to prevent climate catastrophe".[20]

Given the current degree that climate change affects ordinary lives, then an ideology that emphasises original sin and the need for an external force to save us from ourselves, even if it means suspending liberties, does not seem implausible. Indeed, the authoritarian right wing is increasingly offering solutions to the climate crisis with edicts relating to border security, immigration, and the widespread curtailment of human rights for certain parts of the population that precisely rest on the notion that normal rule of law needs to be suspended.

Apocalyptic hope

Turning now to an alternative vision to Millenniumism, Scrimshire cites Jewish philosopher Jacob Taubes who famously suggested that "The greatest threat to our planet is the belief that somebody else will save it". [21] Taubes made a distinction between Schmitt's "counter-revolutionary" apocalypse 'from above' with his own understanding of apocalypse 'from below'. The apocalypse from below does not seek to hold back the forces of anarchy, instead it "welcomes the chaos" of an apocalyptic transformation of the world.

Taubes believed in the radical potential for apocalyptic hope, the vision of the world made new, to be a material, historical hope. And change can happen 'from below'. The suffragette's movement of 1910–1914, which led eventually to female suffrage, was characterized by marches and symbolic protests (such as participants chaining themselves to railings). The Paris protests of May 1968 started with a university protest which led to widespread occupations, wildcat strikes, and huge demonstrations which almost toppled the government of de Gaulle. Among the results, were not only material rewards and worker control in matters of job regulation, but also "an upsurge in worker interest in the construction of an alternative society".

More recently, US presidential nominee Barak Obama ran what is often described as a 'grassroots campaign' involving a dedicated group of volunteers interacting directly with people. The Obama For America campaign trained 10,000 organizers, gathered an email list of 30-million, had 3 million donors, and claimed 2 million active participants. It was the first time that a 'bottom-up', grassroots campaign was built at such a huge scale in such a short period of time. [22]

The belief was 'a dedicated group of volunteers with clear understanding of candidate's vision, interacting directly with people, work better than any digital army'. Technology did not replace 'People to People' connect but it helped to scale, get the message delivered instantly and also proved to be a powerful tool for fundraising.

Another example is the state of Taiwan which has put online collaboration at the centre of their democratic processes. [23] Anyone can begin an e-petition on the platform. Once a case has 5,000 signatures, the relevant ministries must respond in public. In addition to lowering the barriers to democracy, it is considered that this approach facilitates a process of mutual understanding leading to more participation.

On being human

Living at this time of social unrest combined with existential anxiety about our continued ability to live on this planet means it is all too easy to elide anxiety about change to the status quo with fear of crowds, labelling them dangerous, violent, and irrational places.

A long theological tradition of original sin sits deep within Judea Christian thinking, which leads people to be sympathetic to the notion of needing to be saved from themselves. As such this leaves a door open to authoritarian powers proposing exceptional measures to avoid descending into a violent Third World War.

There is abundant evidence of the way in which climate changes throughout history have wrought change on population and this is likely to be no different. But a careful unpicking of the notion of end time does not need to be associated with the type of Millennialism as espoused by Schmitt among others but there is the possibility of a bottom-up approach of people self-organising and making change happen.

This debate surely shifts our thinking about humans in a way that emphasises how we can, in fact, work well together, are open to the ideas of others and are able to collectively work to navigate the shared community in which we live.

16: The everyday alchemist

One of the surprising appearances in COVID was been the development of an anti-lockdown, anti-vaccine social movement that comprised a "cacophonous menagerie— libertarians, anti-vaccine celebrities such as Robert Kennedy Jr., Steve Bannon troops, actual Nazis, New Age yoga instructors, anarchists, 'health freedom' advocates, conspiracy theorists in the mould of David Icke and Piers Corbyn". [1]

Sociologist Benjamin Bratton describes this combination as a refusal of 'secular biopolitics'. In other words, he suggests that this diverse grouping is invested in a particular subjective way of looking at the world (the nation, the individual, personal freedom, mystical intuition, etc.) and as such they refuse to concede to the reality of the situation in which we all found ourselves. In other words, we may see ourselves as sentient beings with a way that we look at the world and a lens we apply to and make sense of it, but we cannot avoid the blunt reality that we are objects. The virus simply does not care how we see ourselves in relation to it.

He considers it futile to allow a privatized subjectivity to take priority over the "cold reality of the planet and its indifferent biochemistries". Regardless of our intentions, personal perspectives, and subjective intent we remain a contagion vector just the same. He goes on to suggest that the pandemic and climate change have similarities as they are phenomenon that are only known to us by statistical models that could not have been gleaned without huge amounts of data collection (sensing as he calls it), calculation indexing and modelling of the 'real'.

The COVID pandemic necessarily made us all into epidemiologists where we understand the world through data and humans as simple units of analysis. In a sense, as epidemiologists we do not need to be virologists, we do not need to know the properties and compositions of the virus – but we need to know its dispositional properties – how does it spread, what is the impact and what do I need to do?

In this chapter we explore the way that COVID has thrown a spotlight on the uneasy relationship in the way we see ourselves both as subjects and objects, a duality that has been an uncomfortable quandary since Descartes set out his thesis in the seventeenth century. We suggest how a new accommodation of this is in progress, challenging centuries of beliefs concerning the way we think of ourselves.

Alchemy

We start our journey in the unlikely place of alchemy, a body of knowledge and practice that dominated in the 16th and early 17th centuries. Historian James Elkins explains that the practice of alchemy was not one of matter according to science (in terms of its atomic or molecular structure), but one of substances that were comprehended by their look and feel, and by determining what happens as they are mixed. As Elkin points out, oils, for example, were not considered hydrocarbons but 'what rose to the surface of a pot of stewing plants or sat dark and fetid at the bottom of a pit of rotting horseflesh'. It was these *dispositional* properties that were the most important to alchemists for almost a millennium. [2]

With the primary focus of alchemy on dispositional properties, the door was left open for a variety of explanations of the nature of matter. George Starkey was a seventeenth century Colonial American alchemist and writer who influenced prominent scientists such as Robert Boyle and Isaac Newton. Writing under the pseudonym Eirenaeus Philalethes, he suggested that "If we say that its nature is spiritual, it would be no more than the truth; if we describe it as corporeal, the expression would be equally correct". We can see the way that explanations of the property of material could be magical in nature: for example, when phosphorus was discovered, it sparked a new interest in the blending of natural and supernatural. As such alchemy was rooted in a vitalist understanding of matter, with the notion that all substances in nature are infused with some kind of 'life' force' that governs their behaviour.

As modern chemistry developed, alchemy lost its status, and in the nineteenth century scientists stripped it of any prestige it had once had. Science then moved from the dispositional properties of alchemists to understanding and measuring the structural similarities which is now at the heart of the scientific culture.

The epistemological unit

This starting point allows us to understand that the way in which we think of things, the units that we use to categorise and understand the world are not necessarily fixed. Alchemists saw matter in a very different way to today's chemists: they were interested in disposition rather than composition, that is the focus for chemists.

Living today, it can be hard to spot this distinction and see just how much we have come to rely on the concept of the modern 'fact' as our core 'epistemological unit' as historian Mary Poovey calls it. [3] The 'fact' structures our understanding of the world in a way that links individual claims about specific observations with generalizations about "larger" or "deeper" principles that are presumed to lie behind the observed phenomena. In contrast to alchemists, we are more interested in the compositional structure of what we see, we assume that this exists and is important. As such, the modern fact is at the heart of an understanding of the world that assumes:

"a syntagmatic relationship between the part and the whole, an ordered universe of natural objects, and a dichotomy between the observing subject and the object that is observed".

We can now see the way in which the 'fact' sets up a distinction between object and subject – with humans as subjects observing the world. This contrasts with alchemists who, with concepts such as vitality shaping their understanding of the material world, were less interested in such a distinction.

More recently (and as noted in Chapter 5), sociologist William Davies has commented on the way we give factual knowledge an apolitical status, granting it a certain authority which is preserved and perpetuated through the institutions such as statistical agencies and universities. [4] The protected status of the facts as a neutral description of the world, independent from political, moral, or theological argument, as such constitutes the basis of political society.

With this in mind, we can perhaps see that what Bratton sets out is the way in which this 'cacophonous menagerie' is leading a challenge to the authority of the 'fact' – that our subjective perspective of the world should in fact have primacy.

How did this come about? One answer to this is offered by writer and thinker Joseph Vogl, who suggests that this loss of authority is due to the increasing logic of financialization. On this basis, our understanding of the world has become "severed from cumbersome ties to logics of reason and justification".[5]

This is due to the way in which financial investment considerations are often less about the underlying properties of something and more to do with the way in which decisions are based on differences between existing expectations and the unexpected. The more improbable or ludicrous, then the greater its informational value.

On this basis the relationship between knowledge and reality (or between the part and the whole) is irrelevant. We no longer need knowledge to be falsifiable, instead the only information that has meaning is performance, what impact it has. The only things of any informational value are movements that might influence demand and subsequent valuation. Of course, this applies to financial items, but the same thing can be applied to wider topics: we need not know what lies under the surface and connections with some kind of underlying fixed reality but instead we simply need to know what a certain piece of information will do in terms of creating a response elsewhere.

This is not all that far from the dispositional characteristics of matter that alchemists relied on in the sixteenth and seventeenth century. It even comes with its own metaphysical understanding, with 'life force' replaced by God-like 'hand of the market'.

Both alchemy and financialization are subtly shaped by their own quasi-theological concepts. The decline of the 'fact' is then accompanied by the rise of what we might call 'alchemical thinking'. This new and dominant epistemology creates a fundamentally different landscape in which information is generated.

We now turn to examining how 'alchemical thinking' can help to explain the rise of conspiracy theories and in particular how conspiracy theories gain their force by effectively being a form of weaponization, of impacting the way we see the world.

Brandishing rhetorical power

It is tempting to think of conspiracy thinking as a means by which those marginalised in society by forces beyond their grasp, seek to make sense by referring to more accessible notions such as individual agency.

But as Anne Merlan sets out in her book, Republic of Lies, we are also seeing conspiracy theories brandished by the powerful against those without power. This would seem to contradict the notion of conspiracy theorising being confined to the powerless and marginalised in society. [6]

Politicians accuse their opponents of being conspiracy theorists, while at the same time appearing to use similar thinking when it suits their political ends. Hillary Clinton blamed a "vast right-wing conspiracy" for women making sexual abuse claims against her husband, the president Bill Clinton. The Bush administration infamously claimed that Iraq had weapons of mass destruction to justify its invasion of the country. US Deputy Secretary of Defence Paul Wolfowitz enthusiastically promoted the idea that Saddam Hussein, not Osama Bin Laden, was the hidden hand responsible for 9/11.

Indeed, Merlan sets out the way that some disinformation purveyors are influenced and fed information by governments that find them useful. American alt-right conspiracy theorists helped in the dissemination of the Macron Leaks, a set of partly real, partly forged documents designed to influence the French elections and put into power the nationalist Marine Le Pen. [7]

There are many examples of conspiracy thinking driving state action: President Richard Nixon kept a well-organized enemies list believing there were Communist-backed plots against him orchestrated by Jews. He used this to justify his own conspiracies: tapping the phones at the DNC headquarters, the Watergate break-in, and bribing the burglary team themselves to stay quiet.

Donald Trump dominated headlines during his precedency with his nods to conspiracy theories used to fan flames of many media headlines. More recently, then British Prime Minister Boris Johnson used a paedophile related conspiracy theory to attack then Opposition Leader, Kier Starmer, widely considered to be an attempt to deflect attention from his own political problems. [8]

Perhaps less of this would withstand scrutiny if the dominant epistemological unit was the fact, but with information driven by the unexpected shaping reactions and outcomes, then it becomes currency. This reflects the much discussed 'dead cat' distraction strategy of Boris Johnson – place a dead cat on the table and that is all we talk about. [9]

Gas-lighting

We can see the way that alchemical thinking is replacing the notion that there is an objective reality that calibrates us all, that we can use as a 'yard-stick' by which to assess the veracity of any statement. This opens the door to powerful possibilities for justifying a wide range of behaviours. Academic Patrick Agbedejobi sees this as a 'post-truth' gas lighting strategy:

"Gaslighters create and harness people's self-doubt, deflect blame onto others or opposition, ruin the accepted reality of others and consolidate such altered reality on the anchor of emotions and sheer partisan loyalty". [10]

To explain, the terms we use derive their power not from some kind of factual power, by referencing a set of shared understanding, a ground truth as it were but instead it is focused on the rhetorical impact. If we take the term "politically correct," for example, we can see the way Donald Trump has used it to explain the Orlando shootings, [11] for NBC's decision in 2015 to sever its ties with him over the speech announcing his candidacy, [12] and for a Scottish university's decision to strip him of an honorary degree. [13] In doing so he weaponized the term, using it for rhetorical effect rather than for any sort of linkage to what might be considered a shared factual reality. Indeed, as digital media scholar Moira Weigel put it:

"Trump did not simply criticise the idea of political correctness – he actually said and did the kind of outrageous things that PC culture supposedly prohibited...Having elevated the powers of PC to mythic status, the draft-dodging billionaire, son of a slumlord, taunted the parents of a fallen soldier and claimed that his cruelty and malice was, in fact, courage". [14]

In a similar way, the term 'woke' has been weaponised by the right and its meaning redefined as representing a liberal elite programme of thought control of our institutions; this new definition suggests a 'woke' person is operating in bad faith, being fake to advance their agenda.

Hence both political correctness and woke have become terms used to suggest there is a deep divide between ordinary people and the 'elite', who the right-wing claim seek to control the speech and thoughts of the public.

Again, this is not a matter of referencing facts, there is little by way of hard evidence to back up this assertion. But no matter, given the alchemical landscape we inhabit, the effect works anyway. 80% of the Americans surveyed in 2018 considered 'political correctness' to be a problem. [15]

Weaving this back to our core point, the unit of the fact is holding us as subjects in a separate sphere from the objects we are considering. But if we are not relating our observations back to any form of ground truth, then the object-subject divide starts to dissolve. What is an object and what is a subject when all can be held in some kind of relativist position?

Entanglements

To unpick this further, we can look at a different way altogether in the form of our relationship with technology. To introduce us to this we turn to philosopher Alva Noe who asks, do you know what time it is? [16] If you do then this is not because of an internal mental skill we have but because we can glance at our wristwatch or, more likely, look at our phone or computer. The repository of information about time is not in our heads but instead derived from machines, objects, which are exterior to us.

However, the question to explore here is whether we can continue to be so binary in the way we think about the subject-object divide now that our interactions with technology seem to be blurring the boundaries? In our daily interaction with digital devices, it seems we no longer deal with objects but with events. For example, we would not think of playing a computer game as engaging with an object but we are instead immersed in the event. And that event is not uniform: instead, the 'permanently connected, programmed and plugged-in environment we inhabit through our interaction...takes shape through a process of continuous modulation'.[17]

Philosopher Bruno Latour reflecting on these increasingly blurry boundaries, coined the term quasi-objects, or hybrids. These are things that do not quite belong to either pole of the nature/society dualism or can't be easily defined as subjects or objects:

"...we find ourselves invaded by frozen embryos, expert systems, digital machines, sensor-equipped robots, hybrid corn, data banks, psychotropic drugs, whales outfitted with radar sounding devices, gene synthesisers, audience analysers and so on...when none of these can be properly on the object side or the subject side, or even in between, something has to be done". [18]

In a not dissimilar vein, returning to COVID, we can see that bacteria and viruses are part of the ecosystems in which we belong. They have also played a role in human evolution.

As philosopher Donna Haraway explains,

"I love the fact that human genomes can be found in only about 10 percent of all the cells that occupy the mundane space I call my body; the other 90 percent of the cells are filled with the genomes of bacteria, fungi, protists, and such, some of which play in a symphony necessary to my being alive at all, and some

of which are hitching a ride and doing the rest of me, of us, no harm". [19]

Haraway suggests this challenges the way in which we have understood the world for centuries in the West. To Haraway, the male-dominated Western belief system needs an Other, which she argues is drawn from the Christian myth of creation. As critic Petra Carlsson Redell puts it:

"To create, to produce and to reproduce in the Christian myth of creation, presupposes dualist relations: the created needs a creator, a design needs an intelligent designer. The world is created, made to exist through a Thou affirming an I". [20]

Again, we can see parallels with our discussion about the 'fact,' setting up a distinction between object and subject with humans as subjects observing the world. But in the technological era in which we now live, Haraway suggests that is not so straightforward:

"It is not clear who makes and who is made in the relation between human and machine".

Who is passive and who is active in the relationship between a human and iPhone, who is in control? Where does the identity of the one end and the identity of the other begin? "Modern machinery," Haraway points out to us "is an irreverent upstart god, mocking the Father's ubiquity and spirituality".

A consistent theme therefore running through the attachment to the subject-object is a theological one: whether the 'life force' that alchemists saw running through matter, the God-like 'hand of the market' in financial movements or here, the view that Judeo-Christian thinking sets up a binary distinction between our-selves and matter that is now being disputed.

Navigating the divisions

In a strange way, perhaps we can consider that conspiracy theories offer us a means to understand how we are collectively renegotiating our relationship both with facts and between subject and object. Conspiracy theories are typically not a definitive set of beliefs with an overarching orthodoxy but instead are often a stance in an argument, a position in a matter of controversy. [21]

The conspiracy theorist is less setting out a coherent belief system that stands alone but, as academic Jovan Byford suggests, is more often arguing against conventional explanations. [22] On this basis, it is an argumentative, rhetorical business often with a shared endeavour and a social activity. It is performed through organisations, movements, and campaigns, or increasingly through jointly produced websites and internet forums where claims and arguments are continuously exchanged, debated, evaluated, and modified. They are a dynamic set of ideas circulating in the public domain, an ideological discourse. In other words, as noted previously, what Sergei Moscovici called 'the thinking society'.[23]

Surely the thinking society is responsible for the way we navigate and negotiate how we choose our divisions and classifications. [24] How we recognise the saliency of certain facts and ignoring certain others. Linking back to alchemists and the desire to turn materials into gold, we know that each atom of the element we call gold contains 79 protons in its nucleus – this is a material fact which has been scientifically discovered and the facts cannot be altered.

Our society has merely decided that having atomic number 79 is what should count as the dividing line in our definition of gold. There are other places at which we could have decided to draw the line but did not. At some stage, the decision was made to take into account atomic number, but to disregard isotope number. [13]

---

[13] Philosopher Keith Donnellan asks us to imagine a Twin Earth situation (after philosopher Philip Putnam's famous thought experiment), involving two cultures with the same language and scientific theory. Importantly for our purposes, they have exactly the same atomic theory. Like us, the Twin Earth people understand that atoms have nuclei containing positively charged protons and neutrally charged neutrons. The number of protons in the nucleus of the atom is called the "atomic number". They also have the concept of an "isotope". Isotopes of a particular element are identified by the combined number of protons and neutrons in the nucleus of the atom. This is known as the "isotope number". Donnellan asks us to imagine that on Twin Earth, as on Earth, it is typically the case that one of the isotopes of a given element makes up the bulk of that element as it naturally occurs. It happens that the Twin Earthians do not specify a natural kind term with an element, but instead with the isotope making up the bulk of that element. On this basis gold, for them, is a specific isotope with a specific isotope number. The much less common isotopes of the element with atomic number 79, which we take to also be gold, they dismiss as not being real gold.

But in a different world, we might consider that what is most important about gold is less the composition and more its beauty, the *look* of it. With that in mind, iron pyrites (or 'fool's gold') looks remarkably like 'real' gold, even though it has a different chemical structure.

But if the requirement for gold is simply what it looks like, and that there is no economic value associated with the gold that has a particular molecular composition, then just as with a wildflower, the only thing that matters is its colour and appearance. We continue to deal with objective facts, but these facts have been used to divide the world up differently.

We chose certain categories, but we could have chosen others. This means that we can in fact be alchemists, we can 'make' gold. This does not depend on physical creation but instead on where we draw boundaries as what gold is depends on how we decide to define it. We can decide that all elements with atomic number 79 are gold, but we can also decide that iron pyrites is gold. The meaning we give things is a human process which rest on a whole bunch of choices, decisions, methods, theories and so on.

On being human

The combination of COVID, financialization and technology allow us to see more clearly the mechanisms that underpin the way our classifications about object and subject are being renegotiated. But also, they highlight the inevitable need to not seek such as harsh division between the two poles.

An illustration of this is from anthropologist, Tim Ingold, who suggests we can see the material around us as 'things' rather than subjects or objects. [25] He draws on philosopher Martin Heidegger who sets out the way that an 'object' stands in contrast to the setting it is in, only showing outer surfaces for our inspection. Ingold prefers the term 'thing' which he describes as a 'going on', a place where several goings on become entangled.

A house is never finished but instead, it requires ongoing effort to manage it in the face of the activities of the human (and non-human) inhabitants. Our most fundamental architectural experiences are verbal rather than nominal and consist less of encounters with objects – the doorframe, window, fireplace and so on – and more of acts of approaching and entering, looking in or out, and the warmth of the hearth. Hence as its inhabitants, subjects, we experience the house less as an object but more as a thing than involves us, just as much as the house. So when, as humans, we are entangled with the physical world which acts as an extension to us the boundaries feel much less obvious than we have considered in the past.

17: This transcendent life

Death is something we tend to look away from as much as possible. There is a strange sense in which we simply do not believe that we will die, while at the very same time knowing full well that it is inevitable. [1] Indeed, the Latin phrase memento mori which means, "Remember that you must die" was whispered by slaves who accompanied Roman generals on victory parades so they could be reminded of their own mortality and prevent them from being taken over by hubris.

COVID has, at the time of writing, killed over two million people worldwide. Indeed, if we consider excess mortality (the number of deaths that exceed statistical models of "expected" deaths for a given year) the death toll is likely to be substantially higher. Although some will not have experienced this directly, it has been difficult to avoid images of overflowing intensive care units and mortuaries, alongside the construction of mass graves.

The way in which we respond to this proximity with death tells us something important about how we understand ourselves as humans. Our response gives us insight into the way we understand consciousness but also the way our notions of death and the afterlife shape the way in which we choose to live.

What is the impact of death on how we live our lives?

To help understand how the proximity and salience of death influences the way we understand ourselves, we can look first at Terror Management Theory. [2] This is the principle that awareness of the inevitability of death gives rise to an existential terror. We seek to avoid, or at least reduce this terror, through a 'buffering system' of beliefs that provide us with answers to core questions about life.

One of these is the notion of self-transcendence: psychologist Paul Wong considers that if we embrace and make the best use of our pain as we become more acquainted with death, then we can not only 'buffer' ourselves from the terror, but also, we have the potential to transform from a self-absorbed existence to a life of fulfilment and self-transcendence. [3]

This means that the individual self is no longer front and centre, but that a balance is found between self-interest and social interest. In the difficult times we inhabit, Wong considers that flourishing is more likely to come from focusing on and addressing our collective needs and making sacrifices for the common good. As Wong suggests, "There is an urgent need for public awareness of the importance of "we" over "me" in times of national crises".

So, what do we mean by self-transcendence? According to the American Psychological Association it is:

"...the state in which an individual is able to look beyond himself or herself and adopt a larger perspective that includes concern for others. Some psychologists maintain that self-transcendence is a central feature of the healthy individual, promoting personal growth and development (first described by Viktor E. Frankl)". [4]

Hence self-transcendence involves going beyond our own limitations and difficulties in life experience so that we relate to something greater. But just what is that 'something greater'?

Transcendence and consciousness

Rene Descartes referenced transcendence when he said we are conscious of occupying a "middle ground" between "supreme being and non-being". We do not have the power to ensure our existence, and so we participate in the temporal order whose law is that of coming-to-be and passing-away. [5] With this fragility at the heart of human existence, the search for transcendence is scarcely a detached intellectual exercise.

This is similar to a more recent philosopher, Eric Voegelin, who suggested that it is consciousness that is situated "in-between" human and divine modes of being, a "site" where transcendence meets human response. On the one hand it is embedded in and conditioned by our biological existence directing our awareness and attention, while on the other hand it is engaging and exploring wider meanings of the human condition that are sensed to be ultimate and timeless.

Voegelin proposed that there was an "ecumenic age" when the search for meaning underwent a fundamental transformation as people started to see the divine order as inconsistent with the limitations of the world as understood in terms of space and time. This was an age when *transcendence* became explicitly understood, identified, and thought about as something separate to the physical world. Prior to that, according to Voegelin, the transcendent was woven into everyday life: it was not seen a separate state.

This introduced the conceptual separation of reality into a "world" and a "beyond," so it was now possible to consider reality to be made up of (1) an "immanent" dimension, of space and time (2) and a "transcendent" dimension, the divine "beyond". The problem of a reality composed of immanent and transcendent dimensions now entered the field of human concern.

The 'discovery' of transcendence revealed consciousness to be something founded in the immanent world but also ultimately responsive to the transcendent ground. It revealed the "in-between" character of consciousness, its character as "the site where immanence and transcendence meet".

Of course, this arose in the context of the rejection of transcendence to understand reality. And for good reason: the assumption that by embracing a particular set of religious principles, that an individual or institution has exclusive access to absolute truth about the human situation is clearly a problematic one.

Of course, the Enlightenment introduced a new faith, that of the complete self-sufficiency of human reason. Originally, confidence in human reason was not considered to be at odds with religious sentiment or conviction. Instead, its target was what is *irrational* in religion, such as reverential acceptance of practices that amounted to a belief in magic, the enthusiastic support of fanciful dogmas, and superstitious belief in miracles and relics.

How consciousness got individual

This allows us to understand the context in which William James' wrote one of his key books, The Varieties of Religious Experience. [6] Karl Davis, writer of the book High Weirdness, considers James' work "the most important book on that menagerie of extraordinary subjective phenomena whose expression and interpretations have so often demanded religious or mystical language". [7]

Davis considers that Varieties continues to influence how we talk, think, and relate to consciousness, perception, and feeling. He sets out how William James established a way of thinking concerning informal, experiential, and individualistic spirituality that has culminated in the popular post-religious identity of "Spiritual But Not Religious". The identity of SBNR can be traced to countercultural spirituality, a rejection of mainstream Christianity and religious institutions generally, and instead turns to practices that offer exalted states of consciousness, typically identified as spiritual, mystical, or religious.

James pushed back against biological determinists who insisted on the psychological phenomena of raptures associated with religious enthusiasm to pathological states of the brain. Instead, James noted that all thought, beliefs, arguments, and empirical perceptions, are states of the brain meaning that "Scientific theories are organically conditioned just as much as religious emotions are".

Davis set out the way James considered we condone certain states of mind over others simply because we enjoy them or because we believe they offer us value. William James' view is very pragmatic: the criterion for beliefs is what they do for us. By this, as Davis points out, he means that establishing the origins of a given trait, belief, or other phenomena, in the brain does not establish its value, as what is important for determining this value is how that belief functions in life itself.

With this, he set the scene for "religious experience" as the central force in spiritual life. He characterized religion as "the feelings, acts, and experiences of individual men in their solitude". This shifted attention away from the collective and historical frameworks of religious institutions, dogma, and community and instead frames individual subjectivity as the centre of modern religious life.

On this basis, Davis argues that James helped to invent the increasingly individualized forms of faith and practice that would explode in the twentieth century. While most of the experience reports that are set out in *Varieties* have to do with revivalism and Christian conversion, he is seen as setting the possibility for everything from bohemian mysticism to the growing identity of "spiritual but not religious".

But perhaps most importantly, James considered mysticism the "root and center" of religious experience, a phenomenon of "inner authority and illumination," mystic flashes take the form of a noetic *insight*—the kind of direct experiential knowing that esotericists call *gnosis*, and that James described as "consciousness of illumination".

By offering an empirical and psychological model of mystical experience, Davis considered James pulled "mysticism" away from its traditional home in Christianity and reframed it as a universal human possibility.

James was primarily an empiricist, albeit a "radical" one. On this basis, he demanded that we dig into the whole range of experience, both the surface and the depth of our felt encounters. He considered that consciousness—which presents us with thoughts and things as well as the relations between them—is the supreme fact.

Davis considers James called for an uncovering of the world as much as we create our experience of it, and that the world is larger, and more cosmic, than we suppose. He offered an analogy for incomplete constructivism when he imagines standing at the back of a moving train, focusing lightly on the vanishing point of the receding track. Within this central field of view is a dynamic but fundamentally stable landscape, increasing its details but without changing its overall consistency.

For James this is the familiar constructed world of representations, concepts, and language. But at the peripheral edges, new objects are also entering the field, offering a trace of the unseen and unknown beyond the margin. He argued that along the fringes of the familiar, there is the possibility of "direct acquaintance," which we can only experience by detuning the fixed layers of the organized centre.

The reverberations in current conspiracy theorising

We can start to perhaps understand why there is often a line drawn from religion (or at least SBNR) and conspiracy theories. Karl Popper considered conspiracy theories to be “the secularization of a religious superstition” and “the very opposite of the true aim of the social sciences”. [8] People such as Popper consider that while conspiracy theories are presented as scientific, they in fact have more sympathy with religious epistemologies: “no matter how much evidence their adherents accumulate, belief in a conspiracy theory ultimately becomes a matter of faith rather than proof”. [9]

Jaron Harambam and Stef Aupersis write that what is criticised are the “forged scientific practices” of conspiracy- theorists and their lack of “respect for truth and evidence” [10]. As such they are not only deemed a menace to society but also subvert the solid foundations of truth in modern societies and it is the work of the scientific institutions to defend their position in knowledge production. Much of the criticism of conspiracy theorists is related to their ideas about science, not only questioning the knowledge of scientific experts, but also the institutional and social position on which their authority is based. [11]

The authority of scientific institutions is challenged as the means to explain how things work and the grounds on which they make such claims. The “knowledge-power nexus,” prominent in the work of Michel Foucault, is often popularized in the cultural milieu of conspiracy thinkers. Importantly for our purposes, what is most critiqued is the materialist nature of the scientific worldview. It is argued that modern science labels phenomena that are inconsistent with its materialistic worldview as illusionary and failing to explanations for phenomena like telepathy, consciousness, and hands-on healing.

Harambam and Aupers emphasize how these "parapsychological" phenomena are discarded, simply because the materialist worldview does not allow for the existence of such occurrences. This reflects the book by Rupert Sheldrake (2013) *The Science Delusion*—which sets out the case for the importance of the nonmaterial world. Those in the conspiracy milieu argue that scientific "facts" are less "discovered" and more "constructed," and this knowledge production is related to political power and economic interests. [12]

The notion that scientific knowledge is embedded in politico-economic power structures is of course not one that is unknown to the social sciences. Bruno Latour famously set out the way that scientific knowledge is inevitably in part the product of particular people, in a particular setting, and in a particular time.

In a sense then Harambam and Aupers consider conspiracy theories do not exist outside science but are right in the middle of its battle between scientific "realists" and "constructivists" circling around notions of objectivity of scientific knowledge alongside the "pollution of science" by external factors.

But although the arguments of conspiracy theorists reverberate with those in the social studies of science, there is a desire to disassociate from conspiracy theories. Bruno Latour—one of the most influential exponents of the "constructivists" in these wars—writes about conspiracy theories as those "mad mixtures of knee-jerk disbelief [that] are an absurd deformation of our own arguments".

Harambam and Aupers conclude that conspiracy theorists face a double form of boundary pressure: they are not only excluded by academics defending the positivistic nature of science *but also* by those coming from the social studies of science. The rise of complementary and alternative medicine offers evidence for an increased distrust toward modern science among the population. The 'boundary work' among social scientists of what is considered legitimate study only validates such critiques and, hence, motivates those that feel repressed by this. [13]

The transcendent in the everyday

With this, we can see the way that conspiracy theories can appear to straddle a line between immanence and transcendence. Another way that we can start to understand the way we walk this line is through our relationship with ancestors. This, according to Ronan Krznaric, is one of the key locations where the modern symbolic boundary between the material and immaterial domains – between matter and spirit – breaks down. [14] In anthropology, ancestor worship lies at the nexus of the study of kinship and the study of religion. Treating ancestors as special or sacred without necessarily worshipping them is a universal human experience. Human corpses are regarded as special or sacred and as such given special treatment such as being sealed, burnt, buried, mummified, or even eaten. The dead are certainly treated with respect even though it does not to matter them.

Of course, chemically and biologically it does not matter what happens to the body, but we do not inhabit that world with a dead relative: instead, we inhabit a world of symbolic human thought. Even if we do not believe in spirits, we still insist on treating her remains respectfully. This is because she was once alive and, on that basis, will always be a person and ancestor. And, as Krznaric points out, “personhood and ancestry transcend science”. Our ancestors are sacred and while they may be corpses the idea that we are part of a lineage is a powerful one, brimming with symbolic energy.

Adding to this, the philosopher Samuel Scheffler argues that, regardless of theological or other metaphysical beliefs, each of us is implicitly invested in the existence of an ‘afterlife’, in the sense of a world that will outlast us. [15] If we knew that the world was going to end the very moment we died, or (as in the storyline for the science fiction film 28 Days Later) that we were the final generation, then in theory this should not affect us. We will be dead after all.

However, Scheffler makes a convincing case that we would find it infinitely harder to find value in the activities that we engage in while we are alive. This is because valuing things involves a historical disposition, as:

"we project ourselves into the future and invest ourselves in that future. Our emotions and our future courses of action both hang in the balance; they both depend on the fate of what we value".

The fact that there will be others succeeding us in the world makes our own individual, time-limited experiences, and values meaningful. This directly contradicts the image of the self-interested, individual, who is focused entirely on their own pleasure.

A reason for this, Scheffler argues, is that we are oriented towards preserving the value that exists today, and as such have a stake in safeguarding that it outlives us. As such, this means we have a commitment to the existence and welfare of future generations. This is not an ordinary moral or contractual one nor does it function via utilitarian calculus, given that there is a potentially infinite number of people whose welfare will be impacted by present choices. But Scheffler argues that just as we derive meaning from having succeeded a previous generation, we also rely ethically and emotionally on the generations to come after us. There is a type of intergenerational reciprocity: we need someone to come after us, just as they need us to factor in their interests. [16]

On being human

It is clear that we give meaning to the parts of life that fall outside the strictly scientific realm. The questions that we keep asking, most agree that science does not have a clear answer for. As historian Hendrik Willem van Loon asked: "Where and what am I, whither bound and for what ends?" [17] To think about values and meaning should not be an alternative to thinking about science: it should be a part of thinking about science. They both occupy the same intellectual space but in different ways.

The modernist notion that the world is entirely understood by science has led to 'scientism,' the way that science is stretched to cover areas that it was never 'designed' for. Indeed, we can see a deep dissatisfaction with mechanistic explanations of reality playing out in conspiracy theorising; here the debate is surely all too often pushed into a realm where people are grappling with big ideas but there are dividing lines around orthodoxy and legitimacy. In fact, we would all surely benefit from a more rounded debate about how we can understand the difficult questions we inevitably ask ourselves about what it means to be human.

Finding new narratives is an exciting challenge that COVID, climate change and technology seems to have reignited. The challenge is now engaging with this, encouraging the often inchoate, stumbling steps and exploring how science both helps to understand and explain but also where the explanatory boundaries may lie.

Our proximity to death that COVID created means we can see the way that we inhabit a world where people are looking for understanding and explanations that are not readily supplied by science alone. Our nature of being, our place in the world, our connection with our ancestors but also with those that come after us shapes the way we live in this world, the things that occupy us.

SECTION 5: WHERE NOW?

As we come to the end of this book, we explore the way in which being human involves us time travelling between the past, present and future. COVID highlighted our profound historical societal inequalities and as such there is perhaps little surprise that there were widespread social justice protests. It is becoming clearer that what is recalled from the past and what is forgotten are less functions of our inefficient brains but are political acts, inextricably tied to social and cultural influences.

In the same way, what and how we imagine the future can be limited, hemmed in by discourses that 'there is no alternative' when in fact other worlds are desperately being sought out, as a dystopian world shaped by climate disaster beckons. There is a need for radical thinking, to recognise that as humans we can find new and different paths and that we have a moral obligation to think about if we are to retain our humanity.

18: Whose memory is it anyway?

On Sunday June 7, 2020, a man climbed up onto a plinth in Bristol, UK to place a noose around the neck of a statue of Edward Colston, a seventeenth-century transatlantic slave trader. The watching crowd then pulled down the near double-life-size bronze and dumped it into the harbour. With this, a community decided what and how to remember the past. [1] [1]

Monuments are not just objects but representations of the past, imbued with meaning. They not only point out to us what is considered worthy of remembering, but also shape a narrative about who we are and how we orient ourselves in the world. As such, monuments set the past in one place, subtly encouraging us not to forget.

We could say that digital technology offers much the same role in the way that children might never quite

[1] Erecting a statue means that the individual or event that is marked is inevitably remembered in a positive way, deemed worthy of remembering.

leave their childhood behind, given so much has been documented online by the parents. [2] At the same time, there is a shakiness to this – with one press of the keyboard it could all be deleted, forever. But barring this, our pasts follow us, meaning that we do not have to keep them alive but similarly not allowing us to lose them. The problem is that some forgetting is healthy, meaning we can reimagine ourselves without our past selves being vivid in our memories, preventing us from moving on. Cultural theorist Mark Fisher bemoaned that "loss is itself lost," with the process of not forgetting effectively being conservatising, keeping us individually and societally, in aspic. [3]

COVID shone a spotlight on the way our memory is woven into historical social injustice, with marginalised groups suffering most due to their exposed position in the economy. Living in cramped housing, earning a living as 'essential workers' meant many were not afforded the protection of others, unable to isolate themselves from exposure to COVID.

We could see afresh the longstanding inequalities in society, putting the spotlight very firmly on the way historic social injustice continues to resonate today. The rise of digital technology throughout our everyday lives has surely sensitized us to the way that we are not allowed to shake off the past, allowing us to rethink and restructure the way we organise ourselves, with the hope of eradicating violent and racist structures and divisions.

Our memory, so central to this, is being increasingly scrutinised. How do we recall the past and whose past has primacy? To what extent do we share memory and how do we reconcile our different perspectives of the past? How and why do these come to inform the present? As these questions come to the fore, we can look afresh at the different ways we understand and use memories and as such we need to unpack and crystalize how we understand the act of remembering.

How to explain this? Traditional notions of memory

How do we understand memory, this phenomenon that seems to be important for beliefs about ourselves? Anderson and Bower's Associative Network Theory (ANT) of memory perhaps best represents how memory is often characterised, [4] proposing that it is structurally organised as a network of nodes linked together. This class of memory theory (and there are many theories like this) represents memory as information processing, operating in a way that encodes cues and associations albeit some are stronger than others. These are then accessed when certain cues are present in the environment, tapping into this 'memory bank'. This suggests our memory operates as a passive recipient of the information around us. The more we receive certain signals (such as through advertising or indeed monuments) then the more we are likely to memorise them.

Memory as a constructive process

Sharply contrasting this, is a school of thought that memory is to be understood less as a means of accurate storage and recall mechanism for the past, and more as a means of a positive, future-oriented characteristic of being human. This is nothing new as, in fact, Frederic Bartlett was one of the founders of this perspective, introducing it in his classic work, 'Remembering', published in the 1930's. [5] In a series of experiments Bartlett recruited participants to take part in an experiment involving people from his hometown of Cambridge, in the UK. He asked them to reproduce a Native American folk story that he shared with them called War of the Ghosts. By looking at different time intervals between sharing the story and asking for the recollection, he found their recall was transformed by the participants to look more like an English story.

The process of memories gradually assimilated into the references we already hold can be seen more recently in the democracy protests in Egypt. Here, graffiti images were created in Cairo, depicting an event in which a veiled female protestor was beaten and stripped, revealing her blue bra. Graffiti artists represented the event in different ways, over time resulting in a simplified image of a blue bra which was sufficient to symbolize the event and solidarity with the values of the revolution, feminism and resistance to oppression. [6] This illustrates the way meaning and memory are intertwined so that we take and embed them into the current day in a very live way. The notion that memory is the equivalent of collecting files from the vaults which may or may not be accurate has been firmly contested.

The relationship between memory and culture

Bartlett's account of memory challenges the ANT notion that we simply input and output memories; instead, we construct them through integrating different traces to build coherent meaning. This means we are always a constant work in progress, reconstructing memories to cater for new information. Bartlett saw this as a positive characteristic, offering us flexibility in a world of inevitable change. This is because of the way that we can then make new connections across different parts of our experience and through this, create a dynamism and flexibility in our responses to different challenges.

However, Bartlett's reproduction experiments arguably themselves became subject to the same 'culturally conventionalising' with the rise of cognitive psychology. Here the metaphor of mind as a computer rose in prominence, which led to the terms that Bartlett used subtly changing: 'meaning' became 'information' and 'construction' became 'processing', 'schema' is also redefined as a set of 'program instructions' for selecting, storing, recovering, and combining information.

On this basis, we can see the direction of travel was to strip out active 'reconstruction' and instead return to the notion of a fixed standard of what memory should be. As part of this process, memory researcher Elizabeth Loftus rose in fame with her theory of false memory syndrome.

False memory syndrome

Perhaps the most famous example of false memory is Loftus' Lost in the Mall experiment. [7] In this study, booklets are shared with participants containing four short stories about their childhood events. Participants were asked to remember as much as possible about each of the four events. Unknown to them, one of the narratives was false; this described getting lost in a shopping mall at around the age of 5, then being rescued by an elderly person and reunited with family. Nevertheless, about 25% of the participants reported remembering the false event. When at the end of the study they were told that one of the 4 events was false, just 5 out of the 24 participants failed to identify the 'lost in the mall' event as the false event and instead picked one of the true events to be false.

Loftus considers this study proof of false memory creation, being formed as a result of a suggested event (being lost in a mall) and then being incorporated into already existing memories of going to a mall. Using this body of knowledge, Loftus has acted as an expert witness in perhaps as many as 300 trials and was involved in the 2022 trial of Ghislaine Maxwell who was on trial for of child sex trafficking and other offences in connection with the financier and convicted sex offender Jeffrey Epstein. [8]

The appearance of Loftus at such a high-profile trial put the subject of false memory firmly on the agenda, acting on behalf of the defence suggesting that some of the alleged victims were potentially remembering things that were false. However, Heather Flowe, a professor of forensic psychology at the University of Birmingham, firmly sets out how there is no evidence to suggest that women might develop false memories of rape. [9]

Flowe is among a number of psychologists who consider that scientists have been overstating the unreliability of memory that false memory implies. While in the laboratory is it not difficult for people to get details mixed up, especially if they are asked misleading questions, it is much harder to implant detailed memories of events that never took place. Even in the mall study, those who falsely remembered getting lost said they did not have a clear memory of the event.

Flowe pointed out "There's a lot of misogyny in this field. Nobody says, 'well, the man, being self-serving, might have reimagined this whole non-consensual rape as consensual because it would certainly behove him to do so'."

Whose memory and why?

False memory is a salutary tale of needing to ensure we understand that remembering is at the intersection between the individual, the social and the context. [10] What we remember, and therefore what is considered true and false is contested ground, inevitably shaped by the underlying power dynamics of any situation. An illustration of this comes from recent studies suggesting the reason eyewitness recall is often unreliable is not because witnesses' memories are somehow false, but because they may be placed under undue pressure by police and lawyers to deliver a confident legal identification. With this in mind, we can see how processes of remembering are a negotiation, a construction and at times, a manipulation, of what is assumed to have occurred in the past.

Power-asymmetries not only affect the interpersonal, but also can operate at a cultural level with dominant nations and cultures holding the power to shape what is globally considered important to remember, as well as to model a representation of the nation and ideology that is considered acceptable, so certain memories become more prevalent and accepted as 'truth'.

The language around remembering that distinguishes between 'true' and 'false', ignores the power-relations shaping which memories are considered more legitimate than others. The inaccuracy may be less a flaw of an individual's memories, but rather the lack of power to get one's memories heard and accepted. As such, we need to ask who is doing the remembering and to what end? Who is the audience, of this act of remembering, and what is their role in this? And what are the implications of following one version of remembering over another?

When memory is involved then asking these questions allows a more explicit acknowledgment of the way power shapes memory. One example of this is nostalgia, which has a great deal of opportunity for a potent influence on what we remember and the way in which this shapes the present and how we think of the future.

Nostalgia as a reawakening

Nostalgia is a topic that writer and musician Grafton Tanner covered brilliantly in his book, 'The Hours have Lost their Clock'. [11] He sets out the often-wistful way which we recall the past: it is widely used in popular culture with TV series such as 'Stranger Things' and films such as 'Liquorice Pizza' depicting a lost world from the 1980's. Perhaps this reflects the time we are living in as uncertain. The combination of technology, COVID and climate change means that for many, the future has a distinctly dystopian feeling. The past, in contrast, seems a so much more stable and attractive place.

One of the most notable social scientists to write about nostalgia is Zygmunt Bauman, who devised the term 'retrotopia' reflecting a societal hope of 'returns' to re-establish an imaginary past. [12] While the far-right seeks a 'return to the nation-state', so the left looks for a 'return to equality'.

Of course, these histories are imaginary, both demonstrating a conservative desire with the implication that the future seems beyond our power to change.

As a reaction to this we can take elements from the past and put them to use in the present — and, as a result, work towards a more habitable future. Mark Fisher considered that "The past has to be continually re-narrated, and the political point of reactionary narratives is to suppress the potentials which still await, ready to be re-awakened, in older moments".[13]

Tanner points out that on this basis, nostalgia, that feeling of warmth and sense of loss for a past can be a re-awakened to remind us of the potentials that were promised by the way we lived in the past."Throughout the last century nostalgia was cast as the antithesis of radicalism," Alastair Bonnett writes in Left in the Past: Radicalism and the Politics of Nostalgia. [14] "Until recently one could say almost anything about nostalgia, as long as it was damning, and few would object". There is a power from invoking the nostalgia of a past that feels more stable and prosperous than the world we inhabit currently.

This power is described by Relative Deprivation Theory that predicts that when an individual or group compares itself to other salient individuals or groups, and finds itself lacking, discriminated against, or disadvantaged, this leads to angry frustration. [15]

Indeed, revolutions are most likely to occur when a prolonged period of economic and social development is followed by a brief period of economic and social decline. [16]

The comparisons we make are not just in the present but also because of comparisons between the past and the present (as well as the future) – giving ample opportunity to assess fairness relative to others and the potential for frustration. Indeed, much of this has been traded on by the right-wing of politics with, for example, UKIP's Brexit campaign promising British people to 'take back control', using a representation of UK's past – the Great British Empire – to set out the case that a future apart from the rest of Europe was desirable. The use of memory in the Brexit campaign included comparisons between the EU and past Empires.

Returning to events in Bristol, there were two contrasting memories at play. First, the British Home Secretary at the time, Priti Patel, described the events as "sheer vandalism" and a "distraction" from the Black Lives Matter cause but perhaps it is worth pointing out that Colston was a Member of Parliament for the Conservative Party, possibly explaining the deeper psychology underpinning Patel's outrage and that of the wider Tory establishment. [17]

On the other side, vandalism has a long political history and therefore memories within Bristol, not least given it is the home city of Banksy, the world's most famous graffiti artist. Two vastly different narratives of the past being brought into play, competing for which history we use to understand the present.

The non-linear nature of time

Tanner cites philosopher Michel Serres suggests that time is like a crumpled handkerchief. If you take a new folded handkerchief and spread it out, then you can see in it certain fixed distances and proximities. But if you take the same handkerchief and crumple it, then two distant points are then close. And if you then tear it, two points that were close can become very distant. He uses this as a metaphor for time which he suggests does not flow but instead 'percolates'. [18] This means that old ideas, theories, and arguments do not vanish but instead, percolate and reappear at apparently unrelated moments to combine with newer arguments and narratives.[19]

This can explain the persistence and reappearance of ideologies that we might have expected to have been left in the past, such as far-right racist ideologies which are currently seeing a resurgence in many countries. For Serres this reflects the way that time does not flow forward to an endpoint but instead is continuously being folded, torn, or bent.

Tanner brings in feminist academic Alison Kafer who suggests this contrasts with a standard, linear conception of time that defines what she calls 'compulsory nostalgia'. This is the "cultural expectation" that we must covet a "before" version of ourselves to be "permitted to exist as part of a desired present or a desirable future". [20]

Instead, she challenges us, as this reflects the questions disabled people are frequently asked: such as "Wouldn't you rather be better?" This assumes that disabled people want a nondisabled version of themselves, trapping them in "curative time," which is where they wait to be cured and restored to their 'former selves'. Refuting this, Kafer makes a case for "crip time" which changes our orientation to time in a way that "bends the clock to meet disabled bodies and minds".

Crip time, says Kafer, "imagin[es] different futures and temporalities [that] might help us see, and do, the present differently". In this way we are then rethinking time to challenge the notion of failure in the present by recognising "the crip pasts behind us or the crip presents surrounding us," as "these very pasts and presents are what make articulating a critical crip futurity so essential".

Crip time, Kafer points out, is also queer time: bent, odd, not "straight time," which flows in a linear direction through past, present, and future. Straight time is "foundational in the production of normalcy". People are supposed to follow certain paths, meet certain goals in a specific order, and clearly demarcate past from present from future. You go to school, get a job, marry, bear and raise children, retire, and die. Queer cultures, on the other hand, have long lived according to "strange temporalities," as Jack

Halberstam has argued. His book, 'In a Queer Time and Place' argues that "queer uses of time and space develop... in opposition to the institutions of family, heterosexuality, and reproduction". Queerness is "an outcome of strange temporalities, imaginative life schedules, and eccentric economic practices". [21]

On this basis, it is transformed by time-bending experiences as varied as coming out, gender transitions, and generation-characterizing events such as the AIDS epidemic. In this way, queerness is represented by its difference from the conventional imperatives of time.

On being human

What we remember is not something that is linear and pre-determined but is instead an organic, complex, and political act. People in the present remember a version of the past which has significant implications for the way they orient themselves to the future.

An integral part of remembering is a political act that carries with it a set of assumptions concerning what we consider to be valuable. Statues that have been standing for decades, and in some cases over a century, are now being contested. This is not news to many segments of the population for whom these statues have particularly difficult and traumatic associations. But the degree to which this has captured a wider discourse surely reflects the way in which we are collectively reckoning with our relationship with the past.

We can see the way in which memories are a source of power and change but also a source of harm. We may not want to forget the harm that has been done by those whom the statues commemorate but at the same time we may wish to forget the power they once had as remembering it allows it to live on.

Understanding how the delete button operates on a hard drive of photos perhaps allows us to recognise that we are collectively able to manage our memories. What we remember collectively shapes who we are, how we see ourselves, our identities. But in the same breath, we can see this applies equally to how we forget and the way we think of time itself.

19: Utopian worlds

Could any of us imagine what it might feel like to have 6 billion people fighting on our side in a fictional war? Having a vivid experience of this in our imagination would surely have real meaning, even if it did not change anything in the real-world value. This is the type of scale that gamers are capable of imagining, ready to work together on extreme scales, toward epic goals, just for the joy of it.

In the universe simulation game Spore, developed by Will Wright and produced by Maxis Software, players are encouraged to think of themselves as capable of changing the world. Wright believes that enhancing our capacity for imagination is critical at this point in human history as it is a matter of survival. The name of the game, Spore draws on the biological definition of 'a reproductive structure that is adapted for dispersal and surviving for extended periods of time in unfavourable conditions'. This is surely a suitable metaphor for our current environment, which is increasingly inhospitable given an unstable climate, extreme weather, and increasingly depleted of natural resources. On this basis, we perhaps need to become like spores ourselves.[1]

It seems we need to bring our imagination to the centre stage despite it often seeming like something that is peripheral to the main task of living, the stuff of daydreams and idle moments or of the writer creating stories. The challenge, however, is that without imagination then surely nothing changes. It is through acts of imagination that people place their trust in a vision of the future, in a world of possibilities that are different from our everyday realities. Indeed, imagination is a deeply political activity with some such as Margaret Thatcher encouraging us to limit our imaginative horizons with the now infamous phrase 'There is no Alternative', which in turn spawned the catchy repost of TAPAS, 'There are Plenty of Alternative Systems'! [2]

Much of our world is based on the notion that what we have experienced in the past determines our future. The widespread integration of Machine Learning into our lives is predicated on the notion that what was true in the past will be true in the future. There are many ways in which we can feel constrained by this but of course, without imagination we cannot break from the here and now and make an alternative imagined future possible.

Sudden fissures in our lives can mean we imagine a different future, shaken out of the routines we are in. Life changes such as death of a close family member, divorce, or a change in financial circumstances can suddenly make us see our lives and futures with a quite different lens. Or it can be that we are simply bored and daydream. Indeed, one study suggests we spend up to 47% of our waking lives letting our minds wander. [3]

What is imagination?

But just what is imagination? [4] At one level we can consider it to be about 'having a mental image'; this notion, often attributed to Descartes, suggests that imagination is essentially a representation of the world that we are able to 'see in the mind's eye', such as the shape of a triangle. This was contrasted to reason which enables us to consider ideas that are not visible, such as a "chiliagon," a polygon with 1,000 sides, which is visually indistinguishable from a circle.

Because of the limitations of our visual representations, Descartes considered that reason is superior. While this notion seems a little blunt, this is in fact the way many psychologists today still think of imagination, primarily as visual representations of the world. By contrast, Giambattista Vico, a contemporary of Descartes, considered imagination to be an 'embodied experience', which offers a significant shift in the way we think about imagination. Instead of imagination being purely visual representations, it means we are also able to grant meaning to things. For example, Vico suggested that myths act as attempts to make sense of alarming events such as thunderstorms, with our imagination suggesting they are the anger of gods. With this, imagination is a creative act, helping to make the environment meaningful rather than being purely representational.

But what and how we imagine, as psychologists Tania Zittoun & Alex Gillespie suggest, is not a purely individual activity, but shaped by the culture we live in. Margaret Thatcher set a very particular cultural agenda that narrowed the possibilities of our imagination. While Descartes saw imagination as an individual act, Vico offered the alternative explanation of imagination being linked to the way meaning is created socially and culturally.

These wider sources do not replace individual imagination but guide and enrich them: humans invented myths of thunder reflecting the anger of the gods, which were shared both orally and through the arts. Other people then internalised the notion of gods causing thunder, and as such imagination is an interplay between both individuals and culture. In other words, a sociocultural process.

Psychologist Frederic Bartlett was saying the very same when he showed the way that what people imagine they see in clouds is heavily influenced by our culture. Culture is no side note in the story of imagination but is instead a core component. [5]

Link with sociocultural psychology

If we align ourselves with the notion that imagination is an interplay between ourselves and the culture we live in, then Zittoun & Gillespie suggest this leads us to the work of Russian psychologist Lev Vygotsky who lived and worked in the former USSR in the early 20th Century. His research interests revolved around the historic and cultural shaping of human mind and consciousness for which he considered imagination had a key role to play.

Not unlike Vico, Vygotsky regarded imagination as the process through which we are able to make our perception of reality complete. In almost direct contrast to Descartes, he considered imagination played the role of filling the gaps left by our (mainly visual) senses. On this basis then "the essential feature of imagination is that consciousness departs from reality," in other words, we are not trapped by a mental replication of the world. Furthermore, Vygotsky considered it provided a creative and a deeply cultural form of thinking. [6]

While imagination can help us remove ourselves from the demands of our immediate lives, Vygotsky also saw imagination as connected to social reality. First, our imaginations are nurtured by the way we experience the social and cultural world; the richer our experience, the more sophisticated is our imagination. Second, imagination is a key means by which we get to know the world: books, pictures and stories allow us to construct a knowledge and understanding of places we have never visited, or of events we have not ourselves experienced. This offers a huge richness of experience provided by the experiences of others.

Third, imagination is not a separate mechanism, independent of our lives but is an intimate part of our real, world-related existence; if we are moved by a book, we engage emotions that echo with our experiences in the world, and vice-versa. As such strengthening our imagination muscles has real implications for the way we live and experience life. Finally, imagination allows for the act of creation in the world: it not only allows us to rethink the way we live but this is of course a prelude to how we act. It is the combination of these elements that led Vygotsky to write:

"...imagination, as the basis of all creative activity, is an important component of absolutely all aspects of cultural life, enabling artistic, scientific, and technical creation alike. In this sense, absolutely everything around us that was created by the hand of man, the entire world of human culture, as distinct from the world of nature, all this is the product of human imagination and of creation based on this imagination".

Imagined futures and remembered pasts

The culture we live in is not of course limited to the here and now but also has an historical element. [7] As set out in Chapter 18, the past is always something that is reconstructed, necessarily then involving at least a degree of imagining. As individuals and as a society we can only ever remember a version of what happened in the past, not an exact replica of it. On this basis remembering is part of this same sociocultural process with imagination and memory interlinked:

"...imagination is vital in reactivating memory, and memory is vital in stimulating imagination" [8]

In doing so, as anthropologist Benedict Anderson notes, we make sense of the present as 'remembering communities', engaging in numerous 'temporal transactions' and imaginative reconstructions in order to produce a nationally relevant collective story. [9]

It can be argued that imagination, as with memory, serves functions beyond concerns with accuracy or truthfulness. There is inevitably a huge diversity of accounts of the past which means that memories cannot be seen simply as fully accurate or truthful accounts but instead are also the function of imaginative reconstructions in "terms of what is being recollected and its significance for ongoing identification with self and others". [10]

On this basis, imagination is a key means by which we can find a coherent narrative for our personal and cultural histories, aligning the past, present and future, offering us a sense of coherence, stability and collective belonging.

Imagination and science

While it is easy to understand how social, cultural, and personal events have contested imagined pasts, one area that we might consider whether we find imagination is the world of science. It is tempting to think of this as an area where we are necessarily required to park our imagination, as science develops through a clear process that values objectivity. Imagination, by contrast, seems the exact opposite of this, filling in for the bits of reality our brains have not captured.

However, philosopher of science Mary Midgely sets out a compelling argument in her book 'Science and Poetry' for the way imagination is an essential component of science. [11] She suggests that new ideas, the life blood of science, are new imaginative visions. Not just in the sense that they involve changes in our larger world-pictures, but in the way in which we conceive life. She suggests that these changes are so vast that they affect the whole shape of our thinking.

The Renaissance offered an imaginative vision — namely that of the world as a machine. The invention of machines such as clocks had given our human imagination something powerful to think about. Machine-imagery changes our worldview profoundly because, unlike a notion of the world pre-renaissance, machines are, by definition, under human control. In addition, they can be fully understood as they can be taken to pieces and then put back together again.

In just the same way, if the world was a machine, then humans can be in control, taking it to pieces and reassembling but in a way that is better.

This imaginative vision made modern science look possible. And, as Midgely sagely points out:

> *"It had to look possible before anybody could actually start doing it".*

That detailed thought relies on non-detailed visions runs throughout her book. Some may criticise the vagueness of these visions, but they are necessarily so. When the Greek atomists discussed the way atoms had their own specific movements, they had no idea what these movements might be or how anybody could trace them and did not have the evidence to supply examples. All they had was the vague medium of imagery, or as Midgely puts it:

"What they were supplying was much more like a Turner sketch than it was like a photograph, and it was not in the least like an engineer's diagram".

At this imaginative stage, vagueness is not a problem, but instead offers the basis from which detailed thinking can arise. Theories do not gain their influence by offering precise facts about the world. These typically come a long time afterwards. Instead, they are ways of looking at the facts, allowing us to see the world differently.

Theories are not persuasive because of facts or their precision but because there is some other quality in their vision that answers to a wider need: that of imaginative appeal as well as an intellectual desire for understanding. In this way, Midgely puts little if anything outside the purview of imagination – it sits at the very heart of the way in which we conceptualise ourselves and the world.

How our collective imagination can be influenced by framing

Given our imagination is a sociocultural process, it is not simply a neutral, individual activity:

"We imagine the future as it is told to us by our leaders. We imagine the wonders and terrors promised by campaigns. We demonize the other and rally to restore humanity".[12]

In other words, there is a political, social, cultural, historical system that shapes our imaginations so what we remember is vulnerable to being shaped by power dynamics, as they provide a sense of authority and believability to certain versions of memory. Our institutions are therefore part of shaping these memory processes as certain versions of the past are legitimized over others, thereby determining how the past and future is understood. [15]

Referring to Thatcher, we can see the interconnection between memory, identity, public marking of events and the manner we choose to remember history. For example, historian Berthold Molden writes that:

"after 1989, it has become all but outrageous to argue, in mainstream media and discourse, outside the paradigm of market liberalism, as alternatives

(communism, socialism) have been proclaimed historical errors that failed to survive the evolutionary competition of ideas". [13]

Shaping what is acceptable to imagine

One of the key mechanisms that shapes 'what is acceptable' is that of framing, which refers to "the process by which people develop a particular conceptualization of an issue or reorient their thinking about an issue". This involves selecting some key aspects of the perceived reality and making them more salient in the process of communication. Of course, we often have our a-priori "frames in thought" which are influenced by "frames in communication". The impact of communication on thought is typically called a *framing effect.* [14]

We are often of course aware of framing – for example, we can see the way in which politicians have sought to frame themselves as regular people, with possibly the wealthiest politician in the UK parliament in 2022 at least, Rishi Sunac, borrowing a supermarket worker's humble Kia to fill up with petrol (rather than his own less modest set of family cars). [15] The frames we can spot are of course less influential than those that are mostly "invisible" to the public and, thus, difficult to comprehend for many. [16]

Of course, framing is unavoidable, every word is defined in relation to the sentence it sits within. Every issue, including that of climate change, can be viewed from a variety of different angles so if those doing the communicating are able to knowingly and skilfully use framing, they can better convey their argument. News media have a key role to play in setting of the agenda, which is surely why we see media being pursued by the ultra-wealthy. [17]

The topic of climate change is susceptible to the impact of framing because of the high number of factors associated with the issue - questions pertaining to the science and future climate forecasts, impacts, public policy, and related trade-offs, to name a few. One such issue is the degree to which the steps to be taken to mitigate the impact of climate change is the responsibility of the individual members of the public versus businesses or governments.

This is a very live political debate with people such as climatologist Michael Mann suggesting that attention has disproportionately and unreasonably been placed on individuals to act, rather than on governments and brands. As the Netflix series Broken suggests, the framing is increasingly that the onus is on the consumer to take the necessary action for their own and societal good, something that can be hard to spot.

This is not to say that individual behaviour change is not an important issue to remedy: researcher Michał Czepkiewicz, considers that the concept of carbon footprints has real value for illuminating the vast inequality that exists between low- and high-carbon lifestyles. But rather than this being a discussion that takes place very publicly, this is a debate taking place with an informed minority of people who are cognisant of these frames, rather than a wider population who are less aware.[18]

In a similar vein, a paper by sustainability researcher William Lamb suggests there are subtle discourses, or frames, that accept the existence of climate change, but justify inaction or inadequate efforts. [19] The paper points to an underlying logic used to discourage climate action, revolving around four key questions: (1) Is it our responsibility to take actions? (2) Are transformative changes necessary? (3) Is it desirable to mitigate climate change, given the costs? (4) Is it still possible to mitigate climate change? While each of these build on reasonable concerns and fears, they can readily become arguments for delay when they 'misrepresent rather than clarify, raise adversity rather than consensus or imply that taking action is an impossible challenge'. As such we can see how this can reduce our imagination for what types of solutions are possible.

We can see that humans are suggestible beings, a finding that was viewed by early psychologists such as William McDougal as an indicator of our vulnerability to manipulation. Suggestible minds, in this prism, are too influenced by what other people say. [20]

However, this capacity for suggestibility is also something to be celebrated as it is what makes learning, emotions, socialization, and social cohesion possible. We take our cues from another, and yet it is only through such socialization that something like an 'individual' capable of rationally checking the evidence supporting the propositions she/he entertains, can ever emerge.

Philosopher Neil Levy sets out the way in which humans live in a 'cumulative culture' in which our collective, shared knowledge has a type of a 'ratchet effect'. [21] This means we are not all having to learn anew each time, instead our collective knowledge becomes a shared platform on which others can build. For example, we do not need to learn about vaccines anew each time, we have a collective understanding of what they are and how they work. When a vaccine becomes available for a new condition, then we can consider this application rather than having to be educated about vaccines from scratch.

It is this shared mechanism that means humans can achieve far more than any individual or indeed any generation can achieve. Levy sets out the way that the evolution of cultural knowledge means that we can collectively detect signal in noise when the degree of noise is greater than the capability of our individual cognition to analyse. By this we mean that when the relationship between an action and the effects are slow to become apparent and are probabilistic, then we find it difficult to tease out the relationships.

In some ways, we need to stay close to the way in which others are framing an issue, as we need to be able to learn and understand if we are to succeed, both collectively and individually. But, of course, that framing comes with risks if we fail to spot them or do not imagine other ways in which the same information could be framed.

Other worlds have always been possible

It is all too easy to accept the framing that is offered to us and stay trapped within it, limiting our curiosity. [22] The writer Baudelaire criticised professional artists who merely wanted to 'copy nature'. 'These doctrinaires', he writes, 'are completely satisfied by Nature', while someone with imagination has to instead declare: 'I consider it useless and tedious to represent what exists, because nothing that exists satisfies me'. One might say the same of a scientist, it is this restlessness and curiosity, the dissatisfaction with received wisdom (or framing) that drives curiosity.

Baudelaire suggested that there is nothing more formidable than a fertile imagination for "disposing of an immense armoury of observed facts". As such, imagination 'supplements' nature and 'embraces also the critical spirit' with those that give up on imagination then become 'timid and servile', who simply, 'conform to a purely conventional set of rules – rules entirely arbitrary, not derived from the human soul, but simply imposed by routine'. [23]

Imagination for Baudelaire is about being faithful to ourselves, rather than slaves to routine, allowing us to break out of convention, and embrace a vision of poetic excitement about the world and ourselves within it. Baudelaire says 'imagination has a positive relationship with the infinite' so we can 'escape' from routine and live with intensity as it is this that contests existing reality.

In a not entirely dissimilar vein, anthropologists David Graeber and David Wengrow suggest that civilizations through human history have all enjoyed a mix of three key freedoms: the freedom to go somewhere else and be welcomed thanks to duties of hospitality; the freedom to disobey orders and the freedom to imagine a different social arrangement. Their wide-ranging book "The Dawn of Everything," sets out how throughout the long history of people on earth, those civilisations that have enjoyed these freedoms were able to lead complex, introspective, and above all, imaginative lives. [24] They consider that the most important of these freedoms is the third one – the freedom to imagine something else. The attack on our collective imagination (whether framing of climate science or Thatcher's TINA) means that we can occupy a certain fatalism about the inevitability of our collective direction.

Freedom to imagine something else is the purview of Teppo Eskelinen's work, given he is an expert on utopias and social movements. He observes a general decrease in collective utopian struggles, [25] citing many studies that indicate a growing individualization of political dreams and aspirations. While people still have hopes and expectations concerning broader societal changes, Eskelinen suggests that the perceived lack of real alternatives to liberal democracies and capitalism means people place their more tangible hopes on themselves as individuals rather than on wider societal transformations. He suggests that the notion of self-invention is a form of 'utopianism' that is fundamentally different from how it is understood in collective struggles.

In collective endeavours self-invention means personal development to drive social change, a process in which we become revolutionary subjects. But in the dominant individualised realm we typically inhabit today, self-invention is personal change for becoming a better, stronger, and healthier person, without any resonance for wider socio-structural transformations. Influence on welfare within this individualised framework is doing sports, dieting, yoga, and mindfulness. He suggests that striving for political change simply means personal consumption choices and radical statements in social media.

So collective and individualized utopias have fundamentally different background rationalities: the rationality of collective utopia is a new type of political and economic system, while in contrast the rationality of private utopia is the political economy of the 'competition state'. This makes the subject of a collective utopia as structural change, with the subject of private utopia as structural status quo.

Eskelinen suggests the main point of utopianism is to open up the social imagination. This is about creating an understanding of the current society we live in, helping to understand current fears and anxieties and grasping hopes and desires rather than creating fixed visions of a future society or social blueprints.

Take the red pill?

Sometimes it seems as if we live in a constructed world where it can be hard to tell if what we are seeing is the result of frames of other people's agendas or something of our own making. How we unpack this is always a challenge. This was the dilemma of the Matrix movie, in which Neo (Keanu Reeves) is told that his world is, in fact, a simulation within a larger reality. The choice he has to make is to either take a blue pill and keep on living obliviously in the Matrix or take a red pill and wake up into the "base" reality. Neo took take the red pill – and goes on to save both the external and simulated worlds.

But, as Chalmers wrote, in an article commissioned by the makers of The Matrix, finding that you have lived your entire life inside a simulation does not necessarily invalidate the 'reality' of that life. [26] If you have never seen a non-simulated tree, all this means is that everything you know about "trees" can be rephrased as being about "simulated trees". In many ways this is no different to discovering that what you have been calling "trees" are, technically, "accretions of subatomic particles" or "collapsed quantum waveforms" or "temporarily captured energy".

This argument has taken on a new resonance with Facebook changing its name to Meta, to reflect the immersive environments it is developing. In a sense, nothing changes from what we have been discussing: what we can imagine, regardless of the environment we are in, is always going to be a tension between how reality is presented to us and our ability to challenge it.

Taking a somewhat different position, Nathan Jurgenson argues that "online" and "offline," like "body" and "mind," aren't like two positions on a light switch — a perspective he calls digital dualism. Instead, all our lives are made of both information and material; it is technological and human, virtual and real. [27]

Surely, we do not occupy a separate existence to the tools that we use and that surround us. The notion that technology has led us to live in a simulacrum where facts have become disconnected from reality seems far-fetched. But we can see the way in which political power might seek to use the resources at hand to shape our imaginative agenda whether a physical newspaper or a virtual world we might inhabit.

And that framing will increasingly be mediated via digital channels as we become ever more used to consuming and communicating in that dimension. But it is the same question of who is shaping what frames for what reason that is no different from the question that we have always needed to ask ourselves.

On being human

What we can imagine, regardless of the environment we are in, is always going to be a tension between how the world is presented to us and our ability to be curious and consider different possibilities.

As humans we have the capacity for individual responses rather than being mindlessly shaped by wider forces, and with that we have the capacity to create new collective thinking and drive change. Technology and gaming have potential for both homogenising and constraining our thinking but also a means to stretch our imagination of new ways of being and living both individually and collectively.

There are of course dangers here – our very strength, that of suspending our disbelief and being suggestible, is also a human weakness. We can be tempted to think of possibilities that become untethered from reality or led astray by bad actors. But the alternative, to not imagine the unimaginable, to assume that the future is fixed and inevitable, surely means that we simply acquiesce to someone else's vision of what the future looks like rather than taking responsibility for shaping and articulating our own.

20: Radical thinking

It can seem as if we are in a thinking crisis. Nicholas Cage famously considered that 'Google is making us stupid' and leading us to not think. [1] The conversation around technology often seems to be one where our needs are anticipated and what we are likely to do is predicted in advance. The notion that we may think so we can determine our behaviour or indeed our needs, seems to have little sway at times.

Counter to this, COVID has surely made us realise just how much we do think about things – when our normal habit and routines are disrupted then even the most straightforward act of greeting someone has a degree of complexity about it.

Likewise with climate change – what should we be doing, how can we do it, what makes sense and what is a waste of time? All these are things make us realise that engaging with life does require us to think carefully, engaging with the issues and then refining depending on what happens.

Suddenly it seems thinking is something we all need to get more serious about.

The Libet experiments

Yet there is a widespread notion that the act of thinking to shape our decision making is illusory, with evidence often cited in the form of a series of experiments from 1980's by Benjamin Libet. [2] These are often cited as evidence that conscious thought follows behaviour (and not the other way round).

In these experiments, Libet attached participants to an EEG and then asked them, at random, to lift a finger or move their wrist. He also asked them to watch the second hand of a clock and then state its precise position when they decided to move. Libet then measured the electrical activity in the part of the brain identified as being involved in the planning of movements. He found activity in the motor area could be identified approximately four hundred milliseconds prior to participants stating their decision to lift a finger or move their wrist. It seemed as if the participants' conscious awareness lagged the neuronal activity that was associated with the move.

At first glance, measurement of this neuronal activity in advance of the participants' stated awareness seems like a pretty convincing argument that we have, at least, some behaviour that is caused by processes outside our awareness. This is again consistent with the notion of Jonathan Haidt that our thoughts are merely 'riders' on the elephant of our brains, offering little more than post hoc rationalisation of the actions of the elephant. [3] Libet himself was a little cautious in his interpretation of these results, considering that although awareness may be a little late to the game, we still nevertheless have freedom to overturn actions that are driven by processes outside awareness.

However, psychologist Magda Osman points out a fundamental flaw with the way Libet's findings are interpreted. [4] Libet's experimental protocol means you just have to decide when to lift your finger but keeping an internal accurate sense of when you decided to lift the finger is incredibly hard. If anything, therefore, his experiment is a demonstration of very deliberate thinking rather than unconscious processing.

Of course, our brains offer the material means through which thinking and consciousness more generally is sustained. But we cannot make the leap that we can then assume we have no agency.

As Julian Baggini writes, if I shout to another person, 'Duck!' and they ducked then you may be able to trace a line of cause and effect which describes sound waves entering the ear, translating into brain signals, which then lead to their muscles moving in such a way that they then duck. But we can only make sense of what happened if we accept that the meaning of 'duck' played a key role in the causal chain. If I had shouted 'Swing!' they would have reacted differently. Their behaviour is only understood if we ascribe importance to the meaning of 'swing'. On this basis, a purely physical description of what happened would not offer a complete account of why they did what they did.

Even if Libet type experiments were empirically and theoretically unchallenged, then perhaps it is of little consequence. If my neuronal activity is going to decide 300 milliseconds before a decision that involves future consequences such as whether to buy a house, then perhaps I might be concerned. But an experiment that shows that 'thoughts have no causal efficacy in this instance' cannot show that 'thoughts have no causal efficacy in any instance'. That is like claiming that because a person's religious belief does not affect their choice of food preferences, it does not affect their place of work or TV viewing. The evidence so far does not extend to situations in which the action has any serious consequence. Libet's finding does not undermine, in any meaningful way, the notion of our ability to think and as such our agency in life.

In famous experiment by psychologist John Bargh, participants who were asked to read passages that included words associated with old age subsequently walked more slowly than subjects who weren't. None of the people involved were aware that they had changed how they moved. [5] But our thoughts do not typically feature very strongly in how we walk unless we are purposefully acting or adapting for some reason. So typically, if you ask someone why they walked more slowly than usual to some stairs, they simply do not know. But if you asked them why they walked to the stairs then you will typically get a perfectly considered answer.

People will act purposefully, and no known experiment has shown that people's beliefs have anything to do with these sorts of actions. [6]

The arrogance of the position

The position that thoughts do not matter seems to be a somewhat arrogant position taken by people who spend a lot of their time thinking. Perhaps they mean that this applies to other people as surely the process of writing a book on the subject requires a train of purposeful thought that gets translated into action.

We have an idea, we read books, we write, we talk to others, we change our minds and so on. Someone committed to the notion that we are mere puppets to the strings of our neuronal activity would suggest that this is the result of a myriad of complex stimuli in the environment which are sparking our neurons and driving certain behaviours. Ultimately, it is impossible to empirically disprove this model, just as we cannot empirically refute that aliens are controlling all our actions. We need to turn to our critical thinking to help resolve this.

We are more than neurons

Philosopher Mary Midgley argues that writing cannot be the result of neuronal activity alone, as the time order is wrong:

"The thought is the source of the behaviour not the outcome". [7]

This, she suggests, is readily apparent if you ask about my train of thought. It is hard to think of another credible way of accounting for my activity. There are no answers to be found from an EEG scan of my brain activity. If you ask why I referenced John Bargh earlier and I give you the answer 'dishwasher' then my EEG will not help you understand my reasoning.

Most of our actions would simply never take the form they do unless they were the outcome of conscious thought and effort: they are actions that had no other kind of cause to occur. What we cannot claim, of course, is that all our actions are determined by our conscious efforts alone. There is a huge range of things that shape our behaviour, many of which we are aware of, others we are not. But if my writing is challenged then people would not expect me to respond that I was non-conscious and at the mercy of my neuronal activity when I wrote it. They will want to understand what influenced my selections, what made me not cite another writer, have I not considered this reference and so on.

For all the research showing how we are manipulated by non-conscious processes, a great deal of what we do is clearly based on our thoughts. No plausible account of the mind can mean we conclude that thoughts have no role in directing our behaviour.

Spawning a legion of nudge

But the notion that our behaviour is shaped by factors that do not involve thinking is highly popular, reflected by the popularity of 'nudge,' the idea from behavioural economists that small, barely noticeable, changes to the environment can result in significant changes in behaviour. People such as Cass Sunstein, Richard Thaler and Daniel Kahneman have promoted this body of knowledge, with 'Nudge Units' now commonplace for governments across the world hoping for low-cost ways to change people's behaviour en-masse.

Magda Osman has pointed out that much is made of the power of nudging because large field studies, involving millions of people and conducted by government-funded organisations reporting that they work. [8] The logic is that while the effects of the nudges may be small, when scaled to a population, one to two percentage points may translate into a great deal of change in behaviour. However, it is important to note that this is similar to the size of effects that are found in psychological experiments using a placebo.[9] The effect sizes are also similar to statistical noise (random irregularity in data) in scientific studies.

Long-term studies into nudges also show that the effects are not only small, but they don't last [10] and typically only work on those already motivated. Added to this, nudges can fail – and indeed can even backfire.[11] A nudge removing bottled water to reduce plastic waste directly increased sugary drink consumption, resulting in a similar number of discarded bottles as before. [12] The failure rate of nudging is also still unknown, [13] as typically only studies of successful nudges are submitted to scientific journals for publication.[14] While there will be value in some instances, the evidence base suggests their use needs careful consideration. [15]

How thinking is needed to drive participation

It is worth expanding this issue a little to discuss the danger of failing to encourage people to engage in an issue, in other words to apply some critical thinking. This is illustrated by the actions taken to counter the lack of transplantable organs in the United Kingdom. To tackle this problem a nudge was designed that entailed moving from a default opt-in system (where the donor specifically has to register their choice to have their organs used after their death) to one which is opt-out (where the donor is assumed to be willing to donate their organs unless they have registered to specify they do not want this to be the case). On this basis, people do not need to think, a change to the 'decision architecture' meant they were simply directed in a different direction.

However, most organ donation systems, (both opt-in and opt-out), include a clause that allows the final decision to donate to be made by family members.

This means that, in effect, family members can veto the decision made by their deceased relative. Families vetoing the decision is one of the main reasons for the gap between supply and demand of organs. [16]

There is a great deal of evidence that if the deceased relative had made their decision known to other family members in advance, then the family is more likely to honour their deceased relative's wishes. This is different from a presumed consent system (i.e., default opt-out) where although the absence of an objection is recorded as consent, people are less convinced of the underlying preference to donate. Which then leads to family members not giving their consent for the donation to be undertaken. And this was just what happened – without clear engagement by the donor with their family, thinking things through, there was a huge drop in consent versus the planned scenario of near universal donation.

There is a clear case for promoting an active choice system that provides a clearer underlying preference and indeed in experimental work this is exactly what Osman and colleagues found. When we move from peculiar laboratory set-ups such as the Libet experiment into real world settings we can see more clearly the importance of engagement and thinking about our behaviours.

Thinking in the world

The story of Hannah Arendt is a good way to explore the importance of thinking, allowing us to think a little more clearly how we necessarily need to do this to navigate the world. As an eighteen-year-old she was taught by Martin Heidegger at the University of Marburg. Heidegger could be considered to be an advocate of 'thinking as pure activity', in many ways the way in which 'philosophy' – was and still is considered to consist of.

However, as writer and philosopher Shai Tubali sets out, Arendt become concerned this led to Heidegger's self-immersion, a remoteness from the actual world. [17] We shall follow the points she makes in some detail as it offers us an important lesson of the value of thinking.

Heidegger's involvement with the Nazis, particularly his appointment as the Rector of the University of Freiburg in 1933 seemed to prove this point. By doing philosophy, we are not automatically having a moral engagement with the world.

On this basis, introspection was equivalent to isolation: there is only one interesting object, the inner self. As the Nazi Party increased its power in German elections at that time, her tolerance of philosophers who seemed to be indifferent to the political situation was wearing thin. The point at which things radically changed for Arendt was in 1933 when the Reichstag was burned down, leading to a series of arrests and ever greater discrimination of Jews. She had been considering emigration for months but felt she needed to take a more active stance. She offered her home as a place to stay for people fleeing Germany. This was the starting point of her thesis for not simply thinking but also acting.

Upon escaping to Paris, she involved herself in anti-war as well as pro-Jewish campaigning. She started to think less in individual terms and see herself more collectively, as a world-citizen, writing that “when one is attacked as a Jew, one must defend oneself as a Jew”. Clearly moving from the style of thinking that places the individual at the centre of life, she started to articulate the way we understand ourselves historically, within a ‘we’ consciousness. Any one person is an intricate part of common structures, shaped by the conditions of our birth, neighbourhood, and the group we are part of. The human condition, Arendt concluded, lay in general structures, or in other words, in the political realm.

On this basis Arendt considered that any substantive change in the human situation can take place only in the political realm. A movement, which does not enter the political arena, and does not translate its beliefs into tangible goals that drive changes will simply be abstract and ineffective. To act in the world, we must get politically involved.

Arendt’s thinking became deeply interwoven with the world, with the flux of the changes of the time. This active thinking is not only a highly engaged form of thought that we can use to act in the real world but is already a form of action, as through thinking in this manner, we are aware we are a responsible participant in the world. Thinking shifts from a form of retreat and silent introspection to a commitment to think responsibly. When we move from being bystanders, we can understand that it is only through engagement that we are able to properly judge.

On this basis thinking becomes a means by which people bring new awareness to their actions and as such is a powerful tool of engagement. But for Hannah Arendt, political thinking is not limited to what we might usually consider as politics – with elected members making decisions on behalf of voters. For Arendt, politics is about public mass exchange, dialogue, and interaction. It is only in this way that people can judge, and act.

She considered that the way Ancient Greece had entwined philosophy and politics was right, and that philosophy, as pure thinking detached from the world, had gone astray. At this point in history we can again see, as Arendt did in Nazi Germany, the danger of how this detached attitude means we can be uninvolved and irresponsible, unaware of our critical role in the world. Arendt wanted to liberate thinking from the hands of professional thinkers and encourage us all to develop our capacity to actively think.

The Man Who Stopped Thinking

There are, Arendt warned, dangers in wait for those who have not developed the ability to actively think. Her famously controversial example of this was the Adolf Eichmann, whose war crimes trial in Jerusalem in 1961 she covered in a series of news reports.

Arendt had been investigating and developing an understanding of the evil of totalitarianism. Eichmann had been key in organising the Holocaust and as such she had the opportunity to look close-up at this example of evil and try to locate the forces that led to terrors of that totalitarian regime. While she was expecting an inhuman monster, she was surprised not to find it, instead, concluding there was an absence, a lack of thought, that was in fact the enabler of his evil.

Watching Eichmann for this time, Arendt realised that her notion that there was a demonic evil inherent in human beings was wrong. Instead, she considered that people like Eichmann had effectively turned off their thinking abilities with little or no capacity to think or to act independently. He renounced responsibility, and when testifying that he had only obeyed another's will, he was effectively saying that he was not a real person. On this basis Arendt made the case for the importance of thinking to enable good judgement, that people have a moral obligation to profoundly engage in thinking to be able to make judgements.

Arendt shows us how the tendency not to think can lead to a weakening of our humanness and our ability to properly participate in the world. As such thinking is something that we all necessarily need to do, it does not belong only to intellectuals but also it is not and cannot be something that we somehow rationalise away as a mechanism that is unconnected with our behaviour.

On being human

We have seen throughout this book that the notion that humans do not think and that we are simply passively reacting to the forces of our environment is one that many have as central to their model of being human. This notion is cemented by discourses concerning the way that our non-conscious minds can be harnessed to 'nudge' us to adopt certain behaviours or by the way that scientific findings such as the Libet experiments are interpreted to support the notion that thinking is a mere post rationalisation for our neuronal activities.

We return to the notion that 'Whoever is searching for the human being first must find the lantern". What does it mean to study the human-being? What are we becoming and what else could we be?

Diogenes railed against his non-thinking fellow Romans suggesting that, "Even with a lamp in broad daylight I cannot find a real human being". In fact, he was a precursor to Hannah Arendt making the same point that a human being is not just something we automatically are, it is also something we must try to be.

Thinking is critical to our humanity but not simply thinking in abstract: we desperately need thinking that is about the way we participate in the world, as embedded beings in an uncertain world.

EPILOGUE

What are we to conclude from the essays in this book? As set out, this book is not aiming for a grand 'theory of everything', rather to provoke, inspire and speculate about some of the directions we may be heading in that can allow us to make sense of this point in history in which we find ourselves. Nevertheless, it is clear that some themes recur throughout the book.

We can surely suggest that we are in the midst of revolutionary times. Not in the way we might necessarily expect from the way this term is often deployed, people in the streets overthrowing the government but we can see the way in which Modernity is being severely challenged. The notion of the individual actor being the means by which we both act and make sense of the world, of the awkward issue of consciousness as something that sits within us and is separate from the material world, that sense that we are too modern for spirituality to influence our acts, that there are facts and truth we can all find to agree on. These are all being ruthlessly tested albeit this is not the stuff of people storming barricades but of often vigorous debate taking place in ways that we might label misinformation, disinformation, fake news and conspiracy theories.

As humans we hold certain things sacred. At some points in our history, and still today, these might be physical places that are considered critical to our way of being, our lives and history. At other times it might be the scientific method, the drive for a positivist understanding of the world that means we can assuredly progress. Others may hold dear the notion of a being that transcends our material existence, that transcends our day to day. This might be a religious or spiritual force, or it might be our brains uploaded into the digital realm. Throughout these essays there is a sense in which for many, these and other beliefs are sacred, they can be seen as non-negotiable and not to be transgressed.

This is what can make debate often so polarised and vicious – as wrapped up in these beliefs is a struggle between power and the powerless, legitimacy and illegitimacy, official versus unofficial, the orthodox versus the unorthodox. Any account of human belief is inevitably wrapped up with a question of who controls, or at least attempts to control, the narrative. We have seen the way in which some beliefs are ridiculed and marginalised while others, which might seem at times past their sell by date, lumber on as the all too easy go-to-explanation of the world. This is certainly not the first time in our history that we have come to explore and question fundamental beliefs about ourselves. Cave paintings are surely an example of the very same thing.

The question that is hard to answer is whether we are living at a time of similar degree of change to those humans may have experienced in the past. At the very least we are seeing a sea-change in the beliefs that ushered in the Enlightenment and Modernity. We are moving to a place where what we believe about ourselves is a version that is more pluralistic, collective, and even transcendent than we had expected. We can see ourselves more clearly as embedded in a complex world with other beings, no longer holding quite the position of primacy we thought we were entitled to.

But at the same time, above all this, we can see more clearly how we are creatures that are a constant work in progress. We are purposeful and yet indeterminate, which can feel uncomfortable as there are no certainties. But if we can see life in which we believe of ourselves as being in a state of constant negotiation, reframing, rethinking, of sitting between the past and the future with different possibilities allowed by that, then we might seize the opportunities that this presents us. If our beliefs of who we are more 'Liquid' than we thought, then this opens many more possibilities to manage the challenges that are facing humans at this point in our history.

And throughout the essays is a theme of the willingness, creativity, intelligence, and spontaneity of people to seize the initiative, undertake acts of altruism, to challenge narratives and offer an alternative explanation or set of beliefs.

Far from people being irrational, selfish, or stupid, we can see the myriad of ways that this is challenged and with that a chaotic yet invocational challenge is taking place. It is not always coherent, not always eloquent but it represents that way in which people are not content for others to be the ones who own beliefs about them, and that we have a sense in which we want a stake in an account of who we are and our place in the world.

And surely that, if nothing else, is a source of sustenance and hope.

NOTES AND REFERENCES

Epilogue

[1] Turner, V., & Turner, V. W. (1970). The forest of symbols: Aspects of Ndembu ritual (Vol. 101). Cornell University Press.
[2] I found this blog post by Lorraine Daston quite inspirational at the time it was published at the start of COVID and the points it made still hold true: https://critinq.wordpress.com/2020/04/10/ground-zero-empiricism/
[3] Buytendijk, F. J. J. (1941). De rangorde der organismen in de biologie. Tijdschrift voor Philosophie, 3(1), 3-42.

Chapter 1: When things come apart

[1] https://plato.stanford.edu/entries/berlin/#HistIdea
[5] Lewin K (1951) Field Theory in Social Science: Selected Theoretical Papers (ed. Cartwright D). New York: Harper & Row
[6] Zygmunt Bauman (2007) Liquid Times: Living in an Age of Uncertainty
[7] This is a quote from Hannah Arendt's 1958 book, The Human Condition
[8] Mumford, L. (1956). The transformations of man. Routledge.
[9] https://critinq.wordpress.com/2020/04/10/ground-zero-empiricism/
[10] Harari, Y. N. (2014). Sapiens: A brief history of humankind. Random House.
[11] https://sociable.co/technology/tech-arms-race-corporations-governments-hack-human-beings/
[12] https://www.who.int/health-topics/infodemic
[13] https://www.theguardian.com/news/2018/mar/17/cambridge-analytica-facebook-influence-us-election
[14] Roozenbeek, J., van der Linden, S. Fake news game confers psychological resistance against online misinformation. Palgrave Communications, 5(1), 1-10.
[15] https://www.nytimes.com/2012/02/19/magazine/shopping-habits.html
[16] https://medium.com/@colin.fraser/target-didnt-figure-out-a-teen-girl-was-pregnant-before-her-father-did-a6be13b973a5
[17] https://www.theguardian.com/news/2018/mar/17/cambridge-analytica-facebook-influence-us-election
[18] https://www.ft.com/content/aa235c45-76fb-46fd-83da-0bdf0946de2d

[19] https://www.newstatesman.com/long-reads/2020/10/how-cambridge-analytica-scandal-unravelled
[20] Tim Hwang (2020) Subprime Attention Crisis: Advertising and the Time Bomb at the Heart of the Internet, published by FSG Originals
[21] https://www.edge.org/conversation/jaron_lanier-the-myth-of-ai
[22] This is from: https://www.bbc.co.uk/bitesize/articles/zwcgn9q
[23] Adams G, Dzokoto VA. Genital-Shrinking Panic in Ghana: A Cultural Psychological Analysis. Culture & Psychology. 2007;13(1):83-104. doi:10.1177/1354067X07073651
[24] https://www.theguardian.com/lifeandstyle/1999/jul/06/healthandwellbeing.health
[25] https://www.theguardian.com/commentisfree/2020/dec/19/if-women-are-hesitant-about-the-vaccine-its-because-the-health-industry-hasnt-earned-their-trust
[26] https://gwtoday.gwu.edu/online-parenting-communities-pulled-closer-extreme-groups
[27] https://www.theinsight.org/p/so-what-about-that-self-coup?s=r
[28] https://tinyletter.com/reallifemag/letters/resuming
[29] van Der Linden, S., Roozenbeek, J., & Compton, J. (2020). Inoculating against fake news about COVID-19. Frontiers in psychology, 11, 2928.
[30]https://www.theguardian.com/commentisfree/2017/jan/08/blaming-fake-news-not-the-answer-democracy-crisis
[31] Benkler, Yochai and Tilton, Casey and Etling, Bruce and Roberts, Hal and Clark, Justin and Faris, Robert and Kaiser, Jonas and Kaiser, Jonas and Schmitt, Carolyn, Mail-In Voter Fraud: Anatomy of a Disinformation Campaign (October 2, 2020). Berkman Center Research Publication No. 2020-6, Available at SSRN: https://ssrn.com/abstract=3703701 or http://dx.doi.org/10.2139/ssrn.3703701
[1] O'neil, C. (2016). Weapons of math destruction: How big data increases inequality and threatens democracy. Broadway Books.
[2] https://twitter.com/AINowInstitute/status/1052330194437050370
[3] For example see MacKenzie, D., & Wajcman, J. (1999). The social shaping of technology. Open university press.
[4] https://www.khoslaventures.com/fireside-chat-with-google-co-founders-larry-page-and-sergey-brin
[5] Seth Stephens-Davidowitz (2017) Everybody Lies: Big Data, New Data, and What the Internet Can Tell Us about Who We Really Are. Published Day Street Books
[6] Greenwald, A. G., Banaji, M. R., Rudman, L. A., Farnham, S. D., Nosek, B. A., & Mellott, D. S. (2002). A unified theory of implicit attitudes, stereotypes, self-esteem, and self-concept. Psychological Review, 109(1), 3–25. https://doi.org/10.1037/0033-295X.109.1.3
[7] https://www.technologyreview.com/view/525741/how-your-tweets-reveal-your-home-location/

[8] de Montjoye, YA., Hidalgo, C., Verleysen, M. et al. Unique in the Crowd: The privacy bounds of human mobility. Sci Rep 3, 1376 (2013). https://doi.org/10.1038/srep01376
[9] Fazio, R. and Olson, M., 2003. Implicit Measures in Social Cognition Research: Their Meaning and Use. Annual Review of Psychology, 54(1), pp.297-327.
[10] Gawronski, B., Hofmann, W., & Wilbur, C. J. (2006). Are "implicit" attitudes unconscious? Consciousness and cognition, 15(3), 485-499.
[11] Louise Barrett (2015) Beyond the Brain: How Body and Environment Shape Animal and Human Minds. Princeton University Press
[12] This draws on the writing of Margaret Boden (2016) AI: Its nature and future. Published by OUP
[13] Alison Adam (1998) Artificial Knowing: Gender and the Thinking Machine. Published by Routledge
[14] For more detail see Levesque, H., Davis, E., & Morgenstern, L. (2012, May). The winograd schema challenge. In Thirteenth international conference on the principles of knowledge representation and reasoning.
[15] Wang, Y., & Kosinski, M. (2018). Deep neural networks are more accurate than humans at detecting sexual orientation from facial images. Journal of personality and social psychology, 114(2), 246.
[16] See here for more detail: https://medium.com/@blaisea/do-algorithms-reveal-sexual-orientation-or-just-expose-our-stereotypes-d998fafdf477
[17] Young, E., 2012. The use of the »Brainwashing« Theory by the Anti-cult Movement in the United States of America, pre-1996. Zeitschrift für junge Religionswissenschaft, (7).
[18] Highly recommended reading: Mary Midgeley (2006) Science and Poetry Published by Routledge
[19] John Dewey (1910) How we think
[20] AI Now Report (2018) See: https://ainowinstitute.org/AI_Now_2018_Report.pdf

Chapter 4: Reading minds

[1] Manzi, F., Peretti, G., Di Dio, C., Cangelosi, A., Itakura, S., Kanda, T., Ishiguro, H., Massaro, D., & Marchetti, A. (2020). A Robot Is Not Worth Another: Exploring Children's Mental State Attribution to Different Humanoid Robots. Frontiers in psychology, 11, 2011. https://doi.org/10.3389/fpsyg.2020.02011
[2] https://nobaproject.com/modules/theory-of-mind
[3] http://www.incompleteideas.net/IncIdeas/BitterLesson.html
[4] Manzi, F., Peretti, G., Di Dio, C., Cangelosi, A., Itakura, S., Kanda, T., ... & Marchetti, A. (2020). A robot is not worth another: exploring children's mental state attribution to different humanoid robots. Frontiers in Psychology, 2011.
[5] https://www.softbank.jp/robot/special/pepper/
[6] https://www.theguardian.com/technology/2018/jul/06/artificial-intelligence-ai-humans-bots-tech-companies

[7] https://logicmag.io/failure/the-automation-charade/
[8] https://www.politico.eu/article/facebook-content-moderation-automation/
[9] Cuzzolin, F., Morelli, A., Cirstea, B., & Sahakian, B. J. (2020). Knowing me, knowing you: theory of mind in AI. Psychological medicine, 50(7), 1057-1061.
[10] https://www.vice.com/en/article/wnbwbm/driving-is-social-autonomous-cars-arent-argues-computer-scientist
[11] Sleek, S., Michel, A., & Mikulak, A. (2016). Self-driving cars need social skills. Retrieved May, 10, 2016.
[12] This book influenced my thinking of the social nature of psychology: Fernbach, P., & Sloman, S. (2017). The knowledge illusion. Penguin Random House Audio Publishing Group.
[13] A great book by a hugely important philosopher: Midgley, M. (2015). Are you an illusion? Routledge.
[14] Prevost, M., Brodeur, M., Onishi, K. H., Lepage, M., & Gold, I. (2015). Judging strangers' trustworthiness is associated with theory of mind skills. Frontiers in Psychiatry, 6, 52.
[15] Knack, S., & Keefer, P. (1997). Does social capital have an economic payoff? A cross-country investigation. The Quarterly journal of economics, 112(4), 1251-1288.
[16] Holm, E. A. (2019). In defense of the black box. Science, 364(6435), 26-27.
[17] O'neil, C. (2016). Weapons of math destruction: How big data increases inequality and threatens democracy. Broadway Books.
[18] https://www.theguardian.com/education/2020/aug/13/almost-40-of-english-students-have-a-level-results-downgraded
[19] https://twitter.com/HUCKmagazine/status/1294985562106015750
[20] https://blogs.lse.ac.uk/impactofsocialsciences/2020/08/26/fk-the-algorithm-what-the-world-can-learn-from-the-uks-a-level-grading-fiasco/
[21] https://www.phenomenalworld.org/interviews/historicizing-the-self-evident/
[22] An excellent book: Crawford, M. B. (2015). The world beyond your head: On becoming an individual in an age of distraction. Farrar, Straus and Giroux.
[23] Zeynep Tufekci is an excellent commentator and public intellectual: https://zeynep.substack.com/p/a-counter-argument-against-public
[24] Saul, J. M. (2012). Lying, misleading, and what is said: An exploration in philosophy of language and in ethics. Oxford University Press.

Chapter 5: Life in the multiverse of truths

[1] I recommend reading anything by William Davies but this book is particularly good: Davies, W. (2018). Nervous states: How feeling took over the world. Random House.

[2] Gitelman, L. (Ed.). (2013). Raw data is an oxymoron. MIT press.
[3] See: https://www.theguardian.com/commentisfree/2020/apr/28/theres-no-such-thing-just-following-the-science-coronavirus-advice-political
[4] https://www.ft.com/content/3be49734-29cb-11e6-83e4-abc22d5d108c
[5] Angela Saini should be required reading for all: Saini, A. (2019). Superior: the return of race science. Beacon Press.
[6] Saini, A. (2017). Inferior: How Science Got Women Wrong. Beacon Press.
[7] 'Just 1 in 4 people trust Government to present statistics honestly', Independent, 27 February 2017.
[8] Herbst, S. (1995). Numbered voices: How opinion polling has shaped American politics. University of Chicago Press.
[9] Salganik, M. J. (2019). Bit by bit: Social research in the digital age. Princeton University Press.
[10] William Davies, Nervous States, How Feeling Took Over the World, New York, Random House, 2018.
[11] Simon, H. A. (1990). Bounded rationality. In Utility and probability (pp. 15-18). Palgrave Macmillan, London.
[12] Kahneman, D. (2003). Maps of bounded rationality: Psychology for behavioral economics. American economic review, 93(5), 1449-1475.
[13] For an example see: https://www.bain.com/insights/infobesity-the-enemy-of-good-decisions/
[14] See: https://blogs.lse.ac.uk/impactofsocialsciences/2021/01/13/to-communicate-scientific-research-we-need-to-confront-motivated-ignorance/
[15] Williams, D. (2021). Motivated ignorance, rationality, and democratic politics. Synthese, 198(8), 7807-7827.
[16] Sunstein, C. R., & Vermeule, A. (2008). Conspiracy theories.
[17] https://www.newscientist.com/term/conspiracy-theories/#ixzz6lgrulSTx
[18] Ariely, D., & Jones, S. (2012). The (honest) truth about dishonesty (pp. 30367-0). New York: Harper Collins Publishers.
[19] This article was very influential in my thinking for this chapter and book generally: https://onezero.medium.com/how-to-destroy-surveillance-capitalism-8135e6744d59
[20] For an example of this thinking see Pariser, E. (2011). The filter bubble: What the Internet is hiding from you. Penguin UK.
[21] https://www.psychologytoday.com/gb/blog/social-dilemmas/201508/the-surprising-power-conspiracy-theories
[22] Dentith, M. R. (2016). When inferring to a conspiracy might be the best explanation. Social Epistemology, 30(5-6), 572-591.
[23] See this superb article with links to papers: https://aeon.co/essays/are-humans-really-blind-to-the-gorilla-on-the-basketball-court
[24] See this book for examples of how different perspectives are often overlooked: Connell, R. (2020). Southern theory: The global dynamics of knowledge in social science. Routledge.

[25] Finkel, E. J., Bail, C. A., Cikara, M., Ditto, P. H., Iyengar, S., Klar, S., ... & Druckman, J. N. (2020). Political sectarianism in America. Science, 370(6516), 533-536.
[26] See: https://www.theguardian.com/us-news/2021/jan/18/texas-woman-capitol-attack-donald-trump
[27] Bjerg, O., & Presskorn-Thygesen, T. (2017). Conspiracy theory: Truth claim or language game?. Theory, Culture & Society, 34(1), 137-159.
[28] Grant, A. (2021). Think again: The power of knowing what you don't know. Penguin.
[29] Viswanath, K., Synowiec, C., & Agha, S. (2019). Responsive feedback: towards a new paradigm to enhance intervention effectiveness. Gates Open Research, 3.

Chapter 6: On changing

[1] See https://www.theguardian.com/society/2022/feb/21/england-second-pandemic-mental-health-issues-nhs-covid
[2] Keats, John (1899). The Complete Poetical Works and Letters of John Keats, Cambridge Edition. Houghton, Mifflin and Company. p. 277
[3] This paper has shaped by references to 'rear-view psychology': Seligman, M. E., Railton, P., Baumeister, R. F., & Sripada, C. (2013). Navigating into the future or driven by the past. Perspectives on psychological science, 8(2), 119-141.
[4] This is a definite 'must-read': Susan Wolf (2012) Meaning in Life and Why It Matters
[5] Thomas Nagle (1998) The View From Nowhere
[6] Scripter, L. (2018). Ordinary Meaningful Lives. International Philosophical Quarterly, 58(1), 79-91. doi: 10.5840/ipq2018215102
[7] Callard, A. (2018). Aspiration: The agency of becoming. Oxford University Press
[8] For a review of this model see here: Sarayreh, B. H., Khudair, H., & Barakat, E. A. (2013). Comparative study: The Kurt Lewin of change management. International Journal of Computer and Information Technology, 2(4), 626-629.
[9] Solnit, R. (2006). A field guide to getting lost. Canongate Books.
[10] Zygmunt Bauman (2007) Liquid Times: Living in an Age of Uncertainty
[11] Hartmut Rosa (2015) Social Acceleration: A New Theory of Modernity (New Directions in Critical Theory)
[12] Pfeffer, J., & Sutton, R. I. (1999). Knowing "what" to do is not enough: Turning knowledge into action. California management review, 42(1), 83-108.
[13] Matthew Crawford (2016) The World Beyond Your Head: How to Flourish in an Age of Distraction
[14] Kahneman, D. (2011). Thinking, fast and slow. Macmillan.
[15] Moscovici, S. (1984). The Phenomenon of Social Representations. In: R. M. Farr, & S. Moscovici (Eds.), Social Representations. Cambridge: Cambridge University.

[16] Wagner, W., Elejabarrieta, F., & Lahnsteiner, I. (1995). How the sperm dominates the ovum. Objectification by metaphor in the social representation of conception. European Journal of Social Psychology, 25, 671-688.
[17] See https://raadbijwoord.com/2020/12/03/debunked-tame-your-inner-trump-or-make-kahneman-angry/
[18] Seligman MEP, Railton P, Baumeister RF, Sripada C. Navigating Into the Future or Driven by the Past. Perspectives on Psychological Science. 2013;8(2):119–41.
[19] See:https://www.fastcompany.com/3026265/always-wear-the-same-suit-obamas-presidential-productivity-secrets
[20] Seligman MEP, Railton P, Baumeister RF, Sripada C. Navigating Into the Future or Driven by the Past. Perspectives on Psychological Science. 2013;8(2):119-141. doi:10.1177/1745691612474317
[21] Magda Osman (2014) Future-Minded: The Psychology of Agency and Control
[22] Justin E. H. Smith (2019) Irrationality
[23] Mahase, E. (2020). Covid-19: Was the decision to delay the UK's lockdown over fears of "behavioural fatigue" based on evidence?.
[24] See: https://www.socialsciencespace.com/wp-content/uploads/Together-Apart-Complete-ms.pdf
[25] https://www.ipsos.com/ipsos-mori/en-uk/britons-increasingly-abiding-covid-19-rules-social-responsibility-and-nhs-primary-drivers
[26] https://www.ipsos.com/ipsos-mori/en-uk/covid-19-trends-majority-britons-remain-concerned-about-risk-covid-19-themselves-and-country
[27] Drury, J., Cocking, C., & Reicher, S. (2009). Everyone for themselves? A comparative study of crowd solidarity among emergency survivors. British Journal of Social Psychology, 48(3), 487-506.

Chapter 7: Breaks in time

[1] I strongly recommend this book for an overview of Walter Benjamin's thinking – it shaped much of the references to him in this book: Lowy, M. (2005). Fire alarm: reading Walter Benjamin's' On the concept of history'. Verso.
[2] Benjamin, Walter. Illuminations, Penguin, Harmondsworth, 1973
[3] Bregman, R. (2020). Humankind: A hopeful history. Bloomsbury Publishing.
[4] Spencer, H. (1882). The principles of sociology (Vol. 2). D. Appleton.
[5] Gray, J. (2016). Straw dogs: Thoughts on humans and other animals. Farrar, Straus and Giroux.
[6] Morris, D. (1994). The naked ape: A zoologist's study of the human animal. Random House.
[7] https://www.forbes.com/sites/rainerzitelmann/2020/03/02/steven-pinker-evolution-has-saddled-our-species-with-many-irrational-and-destructive-psychological-traits/?sh=2a1e7c6a1a6f

[8] See this article that shaped the thinking in this chapter: https://aeon.co/essays/if-history-was-more-like-science-would-it-predict-the-future
[9] Piketty, T. (2013). Capital in the 21st Century. Cambridge, MA: President and Fellows, Harvard College.
[10] https://www.theatlantic.com/magazine/archive/2020/12/can-history-predict-future/616993/
[11] Pinker, S. (2018). Enlightenment now: The case for reason, science, humanism, and progress. Penguin UK.
[12] A great read: Krznaric, R. (2020). The good ancestor: How to think long term in a short-term world. Random House.
[13] https://www.theguardian.com/commentisfree/2019/jan/29/bill-gates-davos-global-poverty-infographic-neoliberal
[14] Gitelman, L. (Ed.). (2013). Raw data is an oxymoron. MIT press.
[15] Saini, A. (2019). Superior: the return of race science. Beacon Press.
[16] Bennett, C. M., Miller, M. B., & Wolford, G. L. (2009). Neural correlates of interspecies perspective taking in the post-mortem Atlantic Salmon: an argument for multiple comparisons correction. Neuroimage, 47(Suppl 1), S125.
[17] Vul, E., Harris, C., Winkielman, P., & Pashler, H. (2009). Voodoo correlations in social neuroscience. Perspectives on psychological Science, 4(3), 274-290.
[18] Popper, K. R. (1963). Science as falsification. Conjectures and refutations, 1(1963), 33-39.
[19] Kuhn, T. S. (1970). The structure of scientific revolutions (Vol. 111). University of Chicago Press: Chicago.

Chapter 8: Subverting times arrow

[1] Fukuyama, F. (1989). The end of history?. The national interest, (16), 3-18.
[2] O'Callaghan-Gordo, C., & Antó, J. M. (2020). COVID-19: The disease of the Anthropocene. Environmental Research, 187, 109683.
[3] Benjamin, W. (1999). The arcades project. Harvard University Press.
[4] Chenoweth, E., Stephan, M. J., & Stephan, M. (2011). Why civil resistance works: The strategic logic of nonviolent conflict. Columbia University Press.
[5] https://www.newyorker.com/magazine/2020/11/23/how-to-stop-a-power-grab
[6] Fitzgerald, F. S. (1991). The Great Gatsby (1925). na.
[7] See: http://www.thegreatdebate.org.uk/DarwinDarwinitis.html
[8] Tallis, R. (2016). Aping mankind. Routledge.
[9] Andreoni, J. (1989). Giving with impure altruism: Applications to charity and Ricardian equivalence. Journal of political Economy, 97(6), 1447-1458.
[10] https://www.psychologytoday.com/us/blog/the-athletes-way/201707/small-acts-generous-behavior-can-make-your-brain-happier

[11] http://news.bbc.co.uk/onthisday/hi/dates/stories/december/31/newsid_2560000/2560075.stm
[12] Midgley, M. (2013). Science and poetry. Routledge.
[13] Graeber, D., & Wengrow, D. (2021). The dawn of everything: A new history of humanity. Penguin UK.
[14] See https://slate.com/culture/2019/11/history-is-written-by-the-victors-quote-origin.html
[15] Hartman, S. (2019). Wayward lives, beautiful experiments: Intimate histories of riotous Black girls, troublesome women, and queer radicals. WW Norton & Company.
[16] I really rate Thomas Frank and recommend this book: Frank, T. (2020). The people, no: A brief history of anti-populism. Metropolitan books.
[17] https://www.foreignaffairs.com/articles/united-states/2017-02-13/how-america-lost-faith-expertise
[18] Postel, C. (2007). The populist vision. Oxford University Press.

Chapter 9: To be a cyborg

[1] See: https://www.vox.com/recode/2020/8/28/21404802/elon-musk-neuralink-brain-machine-interface-research
[2] Huxley, J. (1968). Transhumanism. Journal of Humanistic Psychology, 8(1), 73-76.
[3] Erik Davis' work is superb: Davis, E. (2019). High weirdness: Drugs, esoterica, and visionary experience in the seventies. MIT Press.
[4] Kurzweil, R. (2014). The singularity is near. In Ethics and emerging technologies (pp. 393-406). Palgrave Macmillan, London.
[5] Davis, E. (2019). High weirdness: Drugs, esoterica, and visionary experience in the seventies. MIT Press.
[6] Moravec, H. (1993). Pigs in cyberspace. NASA. Lewis Research Center, Vision 21: Interdisciplinary Science and Engineering in the Era of Cyberspace.
[7] Medin, D. L., & Ortony, A. (1989). Psychological essentialism.
[8] Gutting, G. (2015). What philosophy can do. WW Norton & Company.
[9] Edmonds, D., & Warburton, N. (Eds.). (2015). Big ideas in social science. Sage.
[10] https://www.edge.org/conversation/bruce_hood-essentialism#
[11] Clark, A. (2004). Natural-born cyborgs: Minds, technologies, and the future of human intelligence. Canadian Journal of Sociology, 29(3), 471.
[12] For more on this see here: https://www.thenewatlantis.com/publications/humanism-and-Transhumanism
[13] https://aeon.co/essays/theres-no-philosophy-of-life-without-a-theory-of-human-nature
[14] Crawford, M. B. (2015). The world beyond your head: On becoming an individual in an age of distraction. Farrar, Straus and Giroux.

[15] Hebert Jr, L. J. (2007). Individualism and intellectual liberty in Tocqueville and Descartes. The Journal of Politics, 69(2), 525-537.
[16] For more on this see: https://philosophynow.org/issues/141/Jose_Ortega_y_Gasset_1883-1955
[17] Ingold, T. (2015). The life of lines. Routledge.
[18] This is from Bridle, J. (2018). New dark age: Technology and the end of the future. Verso Books.

Chapter 10: Iceberg minds

[1] https://nautil.us/the-worlds-most-inspirational-iceberg-is-a-fake-3881/
[2] This chapter owes much to this fabulous book: Goff, P. (2019). Galileo's error: Foundations for a new science of consciousness. Vintage.
[3] Chalmers, D. J. (1995). Facing up to the problem of consciousness. Journal of consciousness studies, 2(3), 200-219.
[4] Klein, N. (2020). Care and repair: Left politics in the age of climate change. Dissent, 67(1), 97-108.
[5] This is a truly great and important book: Malm, A. (2021). White skin, black fuel: on the danger of fossil fascism. Verso Books.
[6] https://www.research-live.com/article/features/questioning-the-nature-of-research/id/4005918
[7] Huxley, T. H., 1874, “On the Hypothesis that Animals are Automata, and its History,” The Fortnightly Review 16 (New Series): 555–580. Reprinted in Method and Results: Essays by Thomas H. Huxley, New York: D. Appleton and Company, 1898.
[8] James, W., 1879, “Are We Automata?” Mind, 4: 1–22.
[9] Crick, F. (1996). The astonishing hypothesis: the scientific search for the soul. The Journal of Nervous and Mental Disease, 184(6), 384.
[10] Chater, N. (2018). Mind Is Flat. In Mind Is Flat. Yale University Press.
[11] This section is informed by Boden, M. A. (2016). AI: Its nature and future. Oxford University Press.
[12] Papineau, D. (2002). Thinking about consciousness. Clarendon Press.
[13] Midgley, M. (2015). Are you an illusion? Routledge.
[14] Gutting, G. (2015). What philosophy can do. WW Norton & Company.
[15] Taken from Gutting, G. (2015). What philosophy can do. WW Norton & Company.
[16] Goff, P. (2019). Galileo's error: Foundations for a new science of consciousness. Vintage.
[17] Fernbach, P., & Sloman, S. (2017). The knowledge illusion. Penguin Random House Audio Publishing Group.
[18] Wohlleben, P. (2016). The hidden life of trees: What they feel, how they communicate—Discoveries from a secret world (Vol. 1). Greystone Books.
[19] I found this book fascinating and brilliant: Fudge, E. (2014). Pets. Routledge.

[20] https://www.theguardian.com/technology/2021/apr/21/study-inner-life-ai-robot-thinks-out-loud
[21] Morton, T. (2013). Hyperobjects: Philosophy and Ecology after the End of the World. U of Minnesota Press.

Chapter 11: Denial Wars

[1] See https://morningconsult.com/2021/08/09/climate-change-natural-disasters-ipcc-report-data/
[2] Kahan, D. M. (2015). The politically motivated reasoning paradigm. Emerging Trends in Social & Behavioral Sciences, Forthcoming.
[3] Nyhan, B., & Reifler, J. (2010). When corrections fail: The persistence of political misperceptions. Political Behavior, 32(2), 303-330.
[4] McIntyre, L. (2018). Post-truth. MIt Press. This section was informed by this great read
[5] Haidt, J. (2012). The righteous mind: Why good people are divided by politics and religion. Vintage.
[6] Haidt, J. (2007). The Happiness Hyphotesis: Putting ancient wisdom to the test of modern science (Vol. 1).
[7] Adorno, T. (2002). The stars down to earth. Routledge.
[8] Felin, T., Koenderink, J., & Krueger, J. I. (2017). Rationality, perception, and the all-seeing eye. Psychonomic bulletin & review, 24(4), 1040–1059. https://doi.org/10.3758/s13423-016-1198-z
[9] Stacey, T. (2018). Myth and solidarity in the modern world: Beyond religious and political division. Routledge.
[10] Midgley, M. (2003). The myths we live by. Taylor & Francis.
[11] This section is informed by Silver, N. (2012). The signal and the noise: Why so many predictions fail-but some don't. Penguin.
[12] Laplace, P. S. (1814). Essai philosophique etc.
[13] See https://www.tylervigen.com/spurious-correlations
[14] Chater, N., Oaksford, M., Hahn, U., & Heit, E. (2010). Bayesian models of cognition. Wiley Interdisciplinary Reviews: Cognitive Science, 1, 811–823.
[15] Kahneman, D. (2011). Thinking, fast and slow. Straus: Farrar.
[16] Campolo, A., & Crawford, K. (2020). Enchanted determinism: Power without responsibility in artificial intelligence. Engaging Science, Technology, and Society, 6, 1-19.
[17] Adam, A. (2006). Artificial knowing: Gender and the thinking machine. Routledge.
[18] Yudkowsky, E. (2008). Artificial intelligence as a positive and negative factor in global risk. Global catastrophic risks, 1(303), 184.
[19] Kahneman, D. (2003a). Maps of bounded rationality: Psychology for behavioral economics. American Economics Review, 93, 1449–1475.
[20] Matthew Crawford (2016) The World Beyond Your Head: How to Flourish in an Age of Distraction
[21] Merleau-Ponty, M., & Smith, C. (1962). Phenomenology of perception (Vol. 26). London: Routledge.

[22] Nagel, T. (1974). What is it like to be a bat. Readings in philosophy of psychology, 1, 159-168.
[23] Gigerenzer, G., & Todd, P. M. (1999). Simple heuristics that make us smart. Oxford University Press, USA.
[24] Chabris, C. F., & Simons, D. J. (2010). The invisible gorilla: And other ways our intuitions deceive us. Harmony.
[25] Kahneman D. Thinking, fast and slow. Straus: Farrar; 2011
[26] Levy, N. (2021). Bad beliefs: Why they happen to good people.

Chapter 12: Creatures of habit

[1] See https://www.nbcnews.com/id/wbna44423594
[2] Robinson, T. E., & Berridge, K. C. (1993). The neural basis of drug craving: an incentive-sensitization theory of addiction. Brain research reviews, 18(3), 247-291.
[3] Benartzi, S., & Lehrer, J. (2015). The smarter screen: what your business can learn from the way consumers think online. Hachette UK.
[4] Fogg, B. J. (2002). Persuasive technology: using computers to change what we think and do. Ubiquity, 2002(December), 2.
[5] https://medium.com/@richardnfreed/the-tech-industrys-psychological-war-on-kids-c452870464ce
[6] https://www.wired.com/story/science-says-fitness-trackers-dont-work-wear-one-anyway/
[7] https://www.gartner.com/en/newsroom/press-releases/2016-12-07-gartner-survey-shows-wearable-devices-need-to-be-more-useful
[8] Patel, M. S., Asch, D. A., & Volpp, K. G. (2015). Wearable devices as facilitators, not drivers, of health behavior change. Jama, 313(5), 459-460.
[9] Finkelstein, E. A., Haaland, B. A., Bilger, M., Sahasranaman, A., Sloan, R. A., Nang, E. E. K., & Evenson, K. R. (2016). Effectiveness of activity trackers with and without incentives to increase physical activity (TRIPPA): a randomised controlled trial. The lancet Diabetes & endocrinology, 4(12), 983-995.
[10] Jakicic, J. M., Davis, K. K., Rogers, R. J., King, W. C., Marcus, M. D., Helsel, D., ... & Belle, S. H. (2016). Effect of wearable technology combined with a lifestyle intervention on long-term weight loss: the IDEA randomized clinical trial. Jama, 316(11), 1161-1171.
[11] Fernbach, P., & Sloman, S. (2017). The knowledge illusion. Penguin Random House Audio Publishing Group.
[12] Hobson, N. M., Schroeder, J., Risen, J. L., Xygalatas, D., & Inzlicht, M. (2018). The psychology of rituals: An integrative review and process-based framework. Personality and Social Psychology Review, 22(3), 260-284.
[13] Grosz, E. (2013). Habit today: Ravaisson, Bergson, Deleuze and us. Body & Society, 19(2-3), 217-239.

[14] Highly recommend reading this book: Noë, A. (2009). Out of our heads: Why you are not your brain, and other lessons from the biology of consciousness. Macmillan.
[15] Schilbrack, K. (2004). Thinking Through Rituals. Philosophical Perspectives. New York, NY: Routledge, 10, 9780203644416.
[16] Dewey, J. (1997). How we think. Courier Corporation.
[17] Matthew Crawford (2016) The World Beyond Your Head: How to Flourish in an Age of Distraction
[18] Jennings, T. W. (1982). On ritual knowledge. The Journal of Religion, 62(2), 111-127.
[19] Bell, C. (1992). Ritual theory, ritual practice. Oxford University Press.
[20] An important and highly readable philosopher: Byung-Chul, H. (2020). The Disappearance of Rituals: A Topology of the Present.
[21] Kepnes, S. (2018). Reasoning after revelation: Dialogues in postmodern Jewish philosophy. Routledge.
[22] Benjamin, W. (1999). The arcades project. Harvard University Press
[23] Dawson, C. (2015). The gods of revolution. CUA Press.
[24] Wink, W. (1993). Unmasking the powers: The invisible forces that determine human existence (Vol. 2). Fortress Press.

Chapter 13: The Promise

[1] Byrne, R. (2008). The secret. simon and schuster.
[2] Ward, C., & Voas, D. (2011). The emergence of conspirituality. Journal of Contemporary Religion, 26(1), 103-121.
[3] See https://www.newstatesman.com/politics/2021/06/how-postmodernism-became-universal-scapegoat-era
[4] Lewandowsky, S., Ecker, U. K., Seifert, C. M., Schwarz, N., & Cook, J. (2012). Misinformation and its correction: Continued influence and successful debiasing. Psychological science in the public interest, 13(3), 106-131.
[5] Latour, Bruno. 1987. Science in Action, Cambridge, MA: Harvard University Press
[6] For more on this see McCright, A. M., & Dunlap, R. E. (2017). Combatting misinformation requires recognizing its types and the factors that facilitate its spread and resonance.
[7] Anjum, S., McVittie, C., & McKinlay, A. (2018). It is not quite cricket: Muslim immigrants' accounts of integration into UK society. European journal of social psychology, 48(1), O1-O14
[8] Elkins, J. (2004). What painting is. Routledge.
[9] The work of these authors is important and inspiring: Asprem, E., & Dyrendal, A. (2015). Conspirituality reconsidered: How surprising and how new is the confluence of spirituality and conspiracy theory?. Journal of Contemporary Religion, 30(3), 367-382.
[10] Barkun, M. (2015). Conspiracy theories as stigmatized knowledge. Diogenes, 62(3-4), 114-120.

[11] Gerbaudo, P. (2018). The digital party: Political organisation and online democracy. Pluto Press.
[12] Juergensmeyer, M. (2016). Cosmic war. In Oxford Research Encyclopedia of Religion.
[13]https://www.businessinsider.com/video-coronavirus-patient-hospital-florida-wear-a-mask-2021-1?r=US&IR=T
[14] This is an excellent read and very influential in shaping this chapter: Critchley, S. (2012). The faith of the faithless: Experiments in political theology. Verso Books.
[15] Critchley, S. (1996, January). The Philosophical Significance of a Poem (On Wallace Stevens). In Proceedings of the Aristotelian Society (Vol. 96, pp. 269-291). Aristotelian Society, Wiley.
[16] Stevens, W. (1957). From the" Adagia". Poetry, 40-44.
[17] Critchley, S. (1996, January). The Philosophical Significance of a Poem (On Wallace Stevens). In Proceedings of the Aristotelian Society (Vol. 96, pp. 269-291). Aristotelian Society, Wiley.
[18] A great read: Bratton, B. (2021). The Revenge of the Real: Politics for a Post-Pandemic World. Verso Books.
[19] Midgley, M. (2013). Science and poetry. Routledge.
[20] Han, B. C. (2018). The expulsion of the other: Society, perception and communication today. John Wiley & Sons.

Chapter 14: Not me but we

[1] https://thepsychologist.bps.org.uk/collective-emotions-and-covid-19
[2] https://www.kcl.ac.uk/coronavirus-and-conspiracies-how-the-far-right-is-exploiting-the-pandemic
[3] Darwin, C. (2015). The expression of the emotions in man and animals. In The expression of the emotions in man and animals. University of Chicago press.
[4] Ekman, P., & Friesen, W. V. (1971). Constants across cultures in the face and emotion. Journal of personality and social psychology, 17(2), 124.
[5] Crawford, K. (2021). The atlas of AI. In The Atlas of AI. Yale University Press.
[6] Ngai, S. (2005). Ugly feelings. Harvard University Press.
[7] Cannon, W. B. (1927). The James-Lange theory of emotions: A critical examination and an alternative theory. The American journal of psychology, 39(1/4), 106-124.
[8] https://www.theverge.com/2017/4/10/15245690/how-emotions-are-made-neuroscience-lisa-feldman-barrett
[9] Durkheim, E. (1966). Suicide.(Ed. George Simpson. Trans. John A. Spaulding & George Simpson).
[10] Garcia, D., & Rimé, B. (2019). Collective emotions and social resilience in the digital traces after a terrorist attack. Psychological science, 30(4), 617-628.

[11] Liu, W., & Opotow, S. (2020). On protest, discourse, and the livable life: the role of identity and affect. Current Opinion in Psychology, 35, 132-137.
[12] Ahmed, S. (2013). The cultural politics of emotion. Routledge.
[13] https://futuress.org/magazine/in-the-name-of-love/
[14] Leser, J., & Spissinger, F. (2020). The functionality of affects: Conceptualising far-right populist politics beyond negative emotions. Global Discourse: An interdisciplinary journal of current affairs, 10(2), 325-342.
[15] https://www.theguardian.com/commentisfree/2020/feb/23/beware-politics-of-identity-they-help-legitimise-toxic-far-right
[16] Recommended reading: Asprem, E. (2020). The magical theory of politics: memes, magic, and the enchantment of social forces in the American magic war. Nova Religio: The Journal of Alternative and Emergent Religions, 23(4), 15-42.
[17] Billig, M. (1993). Studying the thinking society: Social representations, rhetoric, and attitudes.
[18] Malm, A. (2021). White skin, black fuel: on the danger of fossil fascism. Verso Books
[19] Durkheim, E., & Swain, J. W. (2008). The elementary forms of the religious life. Courier Corporation.
[20] Asprem, E. The Magical Theory of Politics: Meme Magic, the Cult of Kek, and How to Topple an Egregore. Forthcoming in Nova Religio.
[21] https://www.adl.org/resources/hate-symbol/sonnenrad
[22] Griffin, R. (2019). Mussolini Predicted a Fascist Century: How Wrong Was He?: Third Lecture on Fascism–Amsterdam–22 March 2019. Fascism, 8(1), 1-8.
[23] Goodrick-Clarke, N. (2003). Black sun: Aryan cults, esoteric Nazism, and the politics of identity. nyu Press.
[24] Olson, B. H. (2011). Voice of our blood: National Socialist discourses in black metal. Popular Music History, 6.
[25] Tiryakian, E. A. (1995). Collective effervescence, social change and charisma: Durkheim, Weber and 1989. International Sociology, 10(3), 269-281.
[26]https://theconversation.com/far-right-boogaloo-movement-is-using-hawaiian-shirts-to-hide-its-intentions-142633
[27] https://www.theguardian.com/commentisfree/2022/feb/12/the-global-freedom-movement-is-a-carnival-of-crank-and-conspiracy-and-very-dangerous

Chapter 15: Living in the End Times

[1] Masson-Delmotte, V., Zhai, P., Pirani, A., Connors, S. L., Péan, C., Berger, S., & Zhou, B. (2021). Climate change 2021: the physical science

basis. Contribution of working group I to the sixth assessment report of the intergovernmental panel on climate change, 2.

[2] https://www.bbc.co.uk/news/uk-politics-48126677

[3] This chapter draws on an excellent paper as a framing and referencing throughout: Skrimshire, S. (2019). Activism for end times: Millenarian belief in an age of climate emergency. Political Theology, 20(6), 518-536.

[4] See this book for an excellent review of the topic: Jenkins, P. (2021). Climate, catastrophe, and faith: how changes in climate drive religious upheaval. Oxford University Press.

[5] Cohn, N. (2011). The pursuit of the millennium: Revolutionary millenarians and mystical anarchists of the middle ages. Random house.

[6] Carson, R. (2009). Silent spring. 1962.

[7] Le Bon, G. (1895) The crowd: A study of the popular mind.

[8] Neville, F. G. (2012). The experience of participating in crowds: Shared identity, relatedness and emotionality (Doctoral dissertation, University of St Andrews).

[9] Toscano, A. Fanaticism. London: Verso, 2010

[10] Ehrenreich, B. (2007). Dancing in the streets: A history of collective joy. Macmillan.

[11] https://www.thesun.co.uk/sport/15518009/england-fans-pack-pubs-euro-2020-semi-finals/

[12]https://www.standard.co.uk/news/uk/met-police-illegal-raves-covid-summer-parties-steyning-b943440.html

[13] Durkheim, E., & Swain, J. W. (2008). The elementary forms of the religious life. Courier Corporation.

[14] Seligman, M. E., Railton, P., Baumeister, R. F., & Sripada, C. (2013). Navigating into the future or driven by the past. Perspectives on psychological science, 8(2), 119-141.

[15] Acar, Y. G., & Reicher, S. 13 How crowds transform identities. In the Shadow of Transitional Justice, 183.

[16] Skrimshire, S. (2019). Activism for end times: Millenarian belief in an age of climate emergency. Political Theology, 20(6), 518-536.

[17] Schmitt, C. (2008). The concept of the political: Expanded edition. University of Chicago Press.

[18] Critchley, S. (2012). The faith of the faithless: Experiments in political theology. Verso Books.

[19] Skrimshire, S (2019) Activism for End Times: Millenarian Belief in an Age of Climate
Emergency. Political Theology, 20 (6). pp. 518-536. ISSN 1462-317X

[20] https://www.theguardian.com/science/2010/mar/29/james-lovelock-climate-change

[21] Taubes, J., & Assmann, A. (2004). The political theology of Paul. Stanford University Press.

[22] https://dash.harvard.edu/bitstream/handle/1/27306258/Organizing-Obama-Final.pdf

[23] https://www.economist.com/open-future/2019/03/12/inside-taiwans-new-digital-democracy

Chapter 16: The everyday alchemist

[1] Bratton, B. (2021). The Revenge of the Real: Politics for a Post-Pandemic World. Verso Books.
[2] This is a highly readable and thought provoking book: Elkins, J. (2004). What painting is. Routledge.
[3] Poovey, M. (1998). A history of the modern fact: Problems of knowledge in the sciences of wealth and society. University of Chicago Press.
[4] Davies, W. (2018). Nervous states: How feeling took over the world. Random House.
[5] Vogl, J. (2017). The ascendancy of finance. John Wiley & Sons.
[6] Merlan, A. (2019). Republic of lies: American conspiracy theorists and their surprising rise to power. Random House.
[7] https://en.wikipedia.org/wiki/2017_Macron_e-mail_leaks
[8] https://www.independent.co.uk/news/uk/politics/boris-johnson-labour-jimmy-savile-police-prime-minister-b2011897.html
[9] https://en.wikipedia.org/wiki/Dead_cat_strategy
[10] Agbedejobi, P. (2021). Gaslighting as a post-truth strategy. Academia Letters, 2.
[11] http://thehill.com/blogs/ballot-box/presidential-races/283298-trump-decries-political-correctness-in-post-orlando
[12] http://money.cnn.com/2015/06/29/media/donald-trump-statement-nbc-brian-williams/
[13] http://www.bbc.com/news/uk-scotland-north-east-orkney-shetland-35060868
[14] https://www.theguardian.com/us-news/2016/nov/30/political-correctness-how-the-right-invented-phantom-enemy-donald-trump
[15] https://www.theatlantic.com/ideas/archive/2018/10/large-majorities-dislike-political-correctness/572581/
[16] Noë, A. (2015). Strange tools: Art and human nature. Hill and Wang.
[17] Marenko, B. (2014). Digital Materiality.
[18] Latour, B. (2012). We have never been modern. Harvard university press.
[19] Haraway, D. J. (2013). When species meet (Vol. 3). U of Minnesota Press.
[20] Redell, P. C. (2020). Avantgarde art and radical material theology: a manifesto. Routledge.
[21] This is an excellent paper: Byford, J. (2014). Beyond belief. Rhetoric, ideology and social psychology: Essays in honour of Michael Billig, 83-94.
[22] Byford, Jovan (2014). Beyond belief: the social psychology of conspiracy theories and the study of ideology.

In: Antaki, Charles and Condor, Susan eds. Rhetoric, Ideology and Social Psychology: Essays in Honour of Michael Billig. Explorations in Social Psychology. London: Routledge, pp. 83–94.
[23] Billig, M. (1993). Studying the thinking society: Social representations, rhetoric, and attitudes.
[24] This section (and the footnote) draws on this excellent article: Bryant, R. (1995). Why Alchemists Can Make Gold. Philosophy Now, 14, 15-18.
[25] Ingold, T. (2010). The textility of making. Cambridge Journal of Economics, 34(1), 91-102.

Chapter 17: This transcendent life

[1] Baillie, J. (2013). The expectation of nothingness. Philosophical Studies, 166(1), 185-203.
[2] Pyszczynski, T., Lockett, M., Greenberg, J., & Solomon, S. (2021). Terror Management Theory and the COVID-19 Pandemic. Journal of Humanistic Psychology, 61(2), 173–189.
[3] Wong, P. T., Mayer, C. H., & Arslan, G. (2021). COVID-19 and existential positive psychology (PP2. 0): The new science of self-transcendence. Frontiers in psychology, 12.
[4] American Psychological Association (2020a). Self-Transcendence. APA Dictionary of Psychology. Available online at: https://dictionary.apa.org/self-transcendence
[5] Descartes, Meditations on First Philosophy, Meditation Four, 79
[6] James, W. (1961). The varieties of religious experience: A study in human nature. London: Collier Books.
[7] Davis, E. (2019). High weirdness: Drugs, esoterica, and visionary experience in the seventies. MIT Press
[8] Popper, K. R. (2020). The open society and its enemies. In The Open Society and Its Enemies. Princeton University Press.
[9] Barkun M (2006) A Culture of Conspiracy: Apocalyptic Visions in Contemporary America.
Berkeley, CA: University of California Press.
[10] Showalter, E. (1997). Hystories: Hysterical epidemics and modern culture. Columbia University Press
[11] This section is leans heavily on this excellent paper: Harambam, J., & Aupers, S. (2015). Contesting epistemic authority: Conspiracy theories on the boundaries of science. Public understanding of science, 24(4), 466-480.
[12] Sheldrake, R. (2012). The Science Delusion: Freeing the Spirit of Enquiry (NEW EDITION). Hachette UK.
[13] This section is drawn from Harambam, J., & Aupers, S. (2021). From the unbelievable to the undeniable: Epistemological pluralism, or how conspiracy theorists legitimate their extraordinary truth claims. European Journal of Cultural Studies, 24(4), 990-1008.

[14] Krznaric, R. (2020). The good ancestor: How to think long term in a short-term world. Random House
[15] Scheffler, S. (2018). Why worry about future generations?. Oxford University Press.
[16] See the excellent paper by Will Davies for more on this: Davies, W 2020. Succession Economics: Sustaining prosperity beyond death. CUSP Working Paper No 24. Guildford: Centre for the Understanding of Sustainable Prosperity. Online at: www.cusp.ac.uk/publications.
[17] Van Loon, H. W., Sullivan, R., & Merriman, J. (2013). The Story of Mankind (Updated Edition)(Liveright Classics). WW Norton & Company.

Chapter 18: Whose memory is it anyway?

[1] https://www.aaihs.org/civic-memory-in-a-radical-bristol-edward-colston-and-black-lives-matter/
[2] Eichhorn, K. (2019). The End of Forgetting. In The End of Forgetting. Harvard University Press.
[3] Mark Fisher (2014) Ghosts of My Life Writings on Depression Hauntology and Lost Futures
[4] Anderson, J. R., & Bower, G. H. (1974). A propositional theory of recognition memory. Memory & Cognition, 2(3), 406-412.
[5] Bartlett, F. C. (1932). Remembering: A study in experimental and social psychology. Cambridge University Press.
[6]
https://www.npr.org/sections/pictureshow/2011/12/21/144098384/the-girl-in-the-blue-bra
[7] Loftus, E. F., & Pickrell, J. E. (1995). The formation of false memories. Psychiatric Annals, 25(12), 720–725. https://doi.org/10.3928/0048-5713-19951201-07
[8] https://www.theguardian.com/us-news/2021/dec/18/miss-sweden-and-bugs-bunny-add-up-to-a-bad-day-in-court-for-ghislaine-maxwell
[9] https://www.thecut.com/article/false-memory-syndrome-controversy.html
[10] Obradović, Sandra (2017) Whose memory and why: a commentary on power and the construction of memory. Culture & Psychology, 23 (2). pp. 208-216. ISSN 1354-067X DOI: 10.1177/1354067X17695765
[11] Very much recommend the excellent Tanner, G. (2021). The Hours Have Lost Their Clock: The Politics of Nostalgia. Repeater Books.
[12] Zygmunt Bauman (2017) Retrotopia. Polity Press
[13] Fisher, M., & Colquhoun, M. (2020). Acid Communism (Vol. 13). Pattern Books.
[14] Bonnett, A. (2010). Left in the Past: Radicalism and the Politics of Nostalgia. Bloomsbury Publishing USA.
[15] Power, S. A. (2020). Why a richer world will have more civic discontent: The infinity theory of social movements. Review of General Psychology, 24(2), 118-133.

[16] Davies, J. C. (1962). Toward a theory of revolution. American sociological review, 5-19.
[17] https://news.sky.com/video/priti-patel-toppling-edward-colston-statue-utterly-disgraceful-12002452
[18] Michel Serres, Conversations on Science, Culture, and Time, with Bruno Latour, trans. Roxanne Lapidus (The University of Michigan Press, 1995),. This was sourced in Tanner, G. (2021). The Hours Have Lost Their Clock: The Politics of Nostalgia. Repeater Books.
[18] Zygmunt Bauman (2017) Retrotopia. Polity Press
[19] Robin E. Jensen, Infertility: Tracing the History of a Transformative Term (The Pennsylvania State University Press, 2016),
[20] Alison Kafer, "Time for Disability Studies and a Future for Crips," Feminist, Queer, Crip (Indiana University Press, 2013), 44
[21] Halberstam, J. J., & Halberstam, J. (2005). In a queer time and place: Transgender bodies, subcultural lives (Vol. 3). NYU press.

Chapter 19: Utopian worlds

[1] This example and the chapter is draws on McGonigal, J. (2011). Reality is broken: Why games make us better and how they can change the world. Penguin.
[2] https://www.thealternative.org.uk/dailyalternative/2020/5/30/tina-tacos-commons-bubblng-up
[3] https://www.nytimes.com/2021/04/10/at-home/daydreaming.html
[4] This section is informed by this excellent work: Zittoun, T., Glaveanu, V., & Hawlina, H. (2020). 10 A Sociocultural Perspective on Imagination. The Cambridge Handbook of the Imagination, 143.
[5] For more on this see Wagoner, B. (2017). Frederic Bartlett. In Routledge Handbook of the Philosophy of Memory. Routledge.
[6] Vygotsky, L. S. (1987). The collected works of LS Vygotsky: The fundamentals of defectology (Vol. 2). Springer Science & Business Media.
[7] This section draws on Tileagă, C. (2018). Troubled pasts, collective memory, and collective futures. In Imagining Collective Futures (pp. 153-172). Palgrave Macmillan, Cham.
[8] Pickering, M., & Keightley, E. (2013). Communities of memory and the problem of transmission. European Journal of Cultural Studies, 16(1), 115-131.
[9] Anderson, B. (2006). Imagined communities: Reflections on the origin and spread of nationalism. Verso books.
[10] Brown, S. D., & Reavey, P. (2013). Experience and memory. Research methods for memory studies, 45-59.
[11] Midgley, M. (2013). Science and poetry. Routledge.
[12] Tileagă, C. (2018). Troubled pasts, collective memory, and collective futures. In Imagining Collective Futures (pp. 153-172). Palgrave Macmillan, Cham.

[13] Molden, B. (2016). Resistant pasts versus mnemonic hegemony: On the power relations of collective memory. Memory Studies, 9(2), 125-142.
[14] Stecula, D. A., & Merkley, E. (2019). Framing climate change: economics, ideology, and uncertainty in American news media content from 1988 to 2014. Frontiers in Communication, 6.
[15] https://www.dailymail.co.uk/news/article-10648305/Rishi-borrowed-12-000-Kia-Rio-Sainsburys-worker-photo-op.html
[16] Stecula, D. A., & Merkley, E. (2019). Framing climate change: economics, ideology, and uncertainty in American news media content from 1988 to 2014. Frontiers in Communication, 6.
[17] Lakoff, G. (2010). Why it matters how we frame the environment. Environmental communication, 4(1), 70-81.
[18] https://twitter.com/mczepkiewicz/status/1430636208464359424
[19] Lamb, W. F., Mattioli, G., Levi, S., Roberts, J. T., Capstick, S., Creutzig, F., ... & Steinberger, J. K. (2020). Discourses of climate delay. Global Sustainability, 3.
[20] W. McDougall: An Introduction to Social Psychology. 6th ed. John W. Luce & Co., Boston 1912
[21] Levy, N. (2021). Bad beliefs: Why they happen to good people.
[22] This section draws on the excellent Merrifield, A. (2018). The amateur: The pleasures of doing what you love. Verso Books.
[23] 12Charles Baudelaire, 'The Salon of 1859' in Baudelaire, Art in Paris, 1845– 1862: Reviews of Salons & Other Exhibitions (Phaidon, London, 1965), p. 155.
[24] Graeber, D., & Wengrow, D. (2021). The dawn of everything: A new history of humanity. Penguin UK.
[25] Highly recommend this book: Eskelinen, T. (Ed.). (2020). The revival of political imagination: Utopia as methodology. Bloomsbury Publishing.
[26] Chalmers, D. (2003). The Matrix as metaphysics. Science Fiction and Philosophy: From Time Travel to Superintelligence. http://consc.net/papers/matrix.html
[27] Jurgenson, N. (2011). Digital dualism versus augmented reality. The Society Pages, 24.

Chapter 20: Radical thinking

[1] Carr, N. (2008). Is Google making us stupid? Yearbook of the National Society for the Study of Education, 107(2), 89-94.
[2] Libet, B. (1999). Do we have free will? Journal of consciousness studies, 6(8-9), 47-57.
[3] Haidt, J. (2007). The Happiness Hypothesis: Putting ancient wisdom to the test of modern science (Vol. 1).
[4] Osman, M. (2014). Future-minded: The psychology of agency and control. Macmillan International Higher Education.
[5] Bargh JA, Chen M, Burrows L (1996) Automaticity of social behavior: direct effects of trait construct and

stereotype-activation on action. Journal of Personality and Social Psychology 71: 230–244: https://psycnet.apa.org/doiLanding?doi=10.1037%2F0022-3514.71.2.230

[6] This section is informed by this fabulous book: Baggini, J. (2021). Freedom Regained. In Freedom Regained. University of Chicago Press.

[7] Midgley, M. (2013). Science and poetry. Routledge.

[8] DellaVigna, S., & Linos, E. (2022). RCTs to scale: Comprehensive evidence from two nudge units. Econometrica, 90(1), 81-116.

[9] Boot, W. R., Simons, D. J., Stothart, C., & Stutts, C. (2013). The pervasive problem with placebos in psychology: Why active control groups are not sufficient to rule out placebo effects. Perspectives on Psychological Science, 8(4), 445-454.

[10] Rivers, N., Shenstone-Harris, S., & Young, N. (2017). Using nudges to reduce waste? The case of Toronto's plastic bag levy. Journal of environmental management, 188, 153-162.

[11] Osman, M., McLachlan, S., Fenton, N., Neil, M., Löfstedt, R., & Meder, B. (2020). Learning from behavioural changes that fail. Trends in Cognitive Sciences, 24(12), 969-980.

[12] Berman, E. R., & Johnson, R. K. (2015). The unintended consequences of changes in beverage options and the removal of bottled water on a university campus. American journal of public health, 105(7), 1404-1408.

[13] Hummel, D., & Maedche, A. (2019). How effective is nudging? A quantitative review on the effect sizes and limits of empirical nudging studies. Journal of Behavioral and Experimental Economics, 80, 47-58.

[14] Mertens, S., Herberz, M., Hahnel, U. J., & Brosch, T. (2022). The effectiveness of nudging: A meta-analysis of choice architecture interventions across behavioral domains. Proceedings of the National Academy of Sciences, 119(1).

[15] See this article by Magda Osman for a good overview of the issues (which this section draws on): https://theconversation.com/nudges-four-reasons-to-doubt-popular-technique-to-shape-peoples-behaviour-174359

[16] Lin, Y., Osman, M., Harris, A. J. L., & Read, D. (2018). Underlying wishes and nudged choices. Journal of Experimental Psychology: Applied, 24(4), 459–475. https://doi.org/10.1037/xap0000183

[17] This section is informed by this fabulous essay: Tubali, S. (2018). Hannah Arendt and the Human Duty to Think. Philosophy Now, 125, 14-17.

Printed in Great Britain
by Amazon

39119326R00225